PRAISE FOR *LORDS OF SECRECY*

"Scott Horton's *Lords of Secrecy* is a brilliantly devastating exposé of the shadow government that runs US national security policy. No matter who wins the White House, this secretive clique retains control over America's darkest secrets and will stop at nothing to keep them from the public. Its members' names are largely unknown and its actions unchecked. In an era of an unprecedented war against whistleblowers, and the very existence of a free press, Horton's book provides an essential playbook for battling this undemocratic beast."

—Jeremy Scahill, author of *Blackwater* and *Dirty Wars*

"A government accountable to its citizens is one of the foundations of a democratic society. Horton demonstrates how secrecy corrodes democratic institutions, stifles the freedom of information, and protects the powerful from accountability. *Lords of Secrecy* makes the case that in order to strengthen the rule of law and keep government power in check, we must demand critical debate, civic participation, and above all, transparency."

—George Soros

"This book will resonate widely, a searing indictment of the national security state that undermines the very values it purports to protect. Scott Horton is a consistent, powerful voice against the abuses of power, an apostle for reason and liberty under the law."

—Philippe Sands, professor of law, University of London, and author of *Torture Team: Rumsfeld's Memo and the Betrayal of American Values*

"*Lords of Secrecy* is one of the most important contributions to the vital debate about democracy in the post-Cold War era yet published. Scott Horton diligently peels away layers of hypocritical rhetoric designed to obscure what has been happening. This is a call to arms: American democracy is under threat and the power of increasingly unaccountable agencies must be brought under control."

— **Misha Glenny, author of *McMafia: A Journey through the Global Criminal Underworld***

"In his theoretically sophisticated and eye-opening book, Scott Horton brilliantly traces the many documented follies of the American national security establishment and examines the unjustifiable use of government secrecy. The lethal challenge to the survival of the country's democratic principles has never been more chillingly diagnosed."

— **Stephen Holmes, professor of law, New York University, and author of *The Matador's Cape: America's Reckless Response to Terror***

"From drone wars to Middle East fiascos to the war on whistleblowers, Scott Horton brilliantly blends original reporting with a reasoned defense of democratic ideals going back to ancient Athens. Lucid, learned, judicious, and hard-hitting, *Lords of Secrecy* is an indispensable book for any reader interested in public affairs."

— **David Luban, professor of law and philosophy, Georgetown University**

"Scott Horton has revealed the real secret at the heart of all the exposés about the NSA, torture, the Iraq War, the CIA spying on the Congress — and this is the secret — it's the secrecy. And by understanding the secret of secrecy, Horton discloses just how the mysticism surrounding it has created a momentum that threatens what Hannah Arendt once called 'a crisis of the republic.'"

— **Sidney Blumenthal**

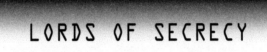

LORDS OF SECRECY

LORDS OF SECRECY

.....

The National Security Elite and
America's Stealth Warfare

SCOTT HORTON

NATION
BOOKS

Published by Nation Books,
A Member of the Perseus Books Group
116 East 16th Street, 8th Floor
New York, NY 10003

Nation Books is a co-publishing venture of the Nation Institute
and the Perseus Books Group.

Books published by Nation Books are available at special discounts
for bulk purchases in the United States by corporations, institutions,
and other organizations. For more information, please contact the
Special Markets Department at the Perseus Books Group,
2300 Chestnut Street, Suite 200, Philadelphia, PA 19103,
or call (800) 255-1514, or e-mail special.markets@perseusbooks.com.

Book design by Cynthia Young

Cataloguing in Publication Data is available from the Library of Congress
ISBN 978-1-56858-745-5 (HC)
ISBN 978-1-56858-488-1 (EB)

First Edition

10 9 8 7 6 5 4 3 2 1

This book is dedicated to the memory of Andrei Dmitrievich Sakharov, a man who passed most of his life confined in a world of secrecy. While scrupulously observing his oath to keep momentous secrets, Sakharov nevertheless deeply appreciated the destructive force of secrecy in human society. He dedicated his life to a dialogue that informed the public about the secrets that responsible citizens need to know. His life and example provide a solution for America's current secrecy crisis.

CONTENTS

I believe that very few secrets are really important. As I see it, the less there are of them, the better it is for world stability.

— Andrei D. Sakharov,
  in an interview with Jean-Pierre Barou,
  Le Figaro, January 1989

PROLOGUE

ON MARCH 11, 2014, California sen. Dianne Feinstein stepped to the well of the Senate to deliver a speech exposing in stark terms a struggle between congressional investigators and their oversight subject: the Central Intelligence Agency. Feinstein was an unlikely critic of the practices of the intelligence community. The wife of investment banker Richard C. Blum, who managed enormous capital investments in corporations serving the American defense and intelligence communities, Feinstein had distinguished herself among Senate Democrats as a staunch CIA defender. In her long service on the Senate Intelligence Committee, which she had chaired since 2009, Feinstein established close personal ties with key senior agency figures—championing the candidacy of former deputy director Stephen Kappes to head the agency after Barack Obama was elected.[1]

Patiently and meticulously, Feinstein unfolded the string of events that led her committee to launch the most exhaustive congressional probe of a single CIA program in the nation's history. "On December 6, 2007, a *New York Times* article revealed the troubling fact that the CIA had destroyed video tapes of some of the CIA's first interrogations using so-called enhanced techniques," she stated.[2]

CIA director Michael Hayden had assured congressional overseers that they had no reason to be concerned: routine written field reports, what Hayden called CIA operational cables, had been retained. These documents, Hayden said, described "the detention conditions" of prisoners held by the CIA before it decided to shut down the program as well as the "day-to-day CIA interrogations." Hayden offered the senators access to these cables to prove to them that the destruction of the tapes was not a serious issue. Moreover, he reminded them that the CIA program was a historical relic: in the fall of 2006 the Bush administration ended the CIA's role as a jailer and sharply curtailed its program of "enhanced interrogation techniques" (EITs)—specifically eliminating techniques that most of the international community, including the United States in the period before and after the Bush presidency, had viewed as torture, such as waterboarding.

Nevertheless, the Senate committee had never looked deeply into this program, and Hayden's decision to offer access to the cables opened the door to a careful study, which was accepted by then-chair Jay Rockefeller. Early in 2007, two Senate staffers spent many months reading the cables. By the time they had finished in early 2009, Feinstein had replaced Rockefeller as committee chair, and Barack Obama had replaced George W. Bush as president. Feinstein received the first staff report. It was "chilling," she said. "The interrogations and the conditions of confinement at the CIA detention sites were far different and far more harsh than the way the CIA had described them to us."[3]

This first exploration of the dark side of CIA prisons and torture led committee members to recognize a serious failure in its oversight responsibilities. The committee resolved with near-unanimity (on a 14–1 vote) to launch a comprehensive investigation of the CIA program involving black sites and torture.

But the CIA was not simply going to acquiesce to a congressional probe into the single darkest and most controversial program in the organization's history. Since it could not openly do battle with its congressional overseers, the agency turned to a series of tactics that it had honed over the difficult decades following the Church Committee inquiries of the mid-1970s.[4] Throughout the subsequent decades, the CIA complained loudly about the burdens of oversight and accountability—while almost always getting its way.

Indeed, the dynamics had changed dramatically after the coordinated terrorist attacks on the World Trade Center and the Pentagon on September 11, 2001. In the ensuing years, the CIA's budget ballooned to more than double its pre-2001 numbers. Moreover, it got the go-ahead to launch programs previously denied or sidetracked, and clearance to encroach on the Pentagon's turf through extensive operations using armed predator drones. Washington, it seemed, had forgotten how to say no to Langley. Still, the operation of the black site and EIT program involves a strikingly different dynamic—because the spring that fed it came not out of Langley but from the office of Vice President Dick Cheney, inside the White House.

Senior figures in the CIA, including the agency's senior career lawyer, John Rizzo, fully appreciated that the black sites and the EITs presented particularly dangerous territory.[5] Exposure of these programs could damage some of the agency's tightest points of collaboration with foreign intelligence services—authoritarian regimes such as Egypt, Jordan, Morocco, Pakistan, Thailand, and Yemen, as well as among new democracies of Eastern Europe, like Lithuania, Poland, and Romania. British intelligence had been deeply involved and feared exposure, considering the domestic political opposition and the rigorous attitude of British courts.[6]

CIA leadership was also focused on the high likelihood that the program, once exposed, would lead to a press for criminal prosecutions under various statutes, including the anti-torture act.[7] It therefore moved preemptively, seeking assurances and an opinion from the Justice Department that would serve as a "get out of jail free" card for agents involved in the program. But when those opinions were disclosed, starting hard on the heels of photographic evidence of abuse at the Abu Ghraib prison in Iraq—much of it eerily similar to techniques discussed in the Justice Department opinions—a political firestorm erupted around the world. The Justice Department was forced to withdraw most of the opinions even before George W. Bush left Washington.

Leon Panetta, arriving at the CIA in 2009, found top management preoccupied with concerns about fallout from this program.

The CIA chose to react to plans for a congressional probe cautiously, with a series of tactical maneuvers and skirmishes. Its strategy was apparent from the beginning: slow the review down while hoping for a change in the political winds that might end it. And from the outset it made use of one essential weapon against its congressional overseers—secrecy. For the agency, secrecy was not just a way of life; it was also a path to power. It wielded secrecy as a shield against embarrassing disclosures and as a sword to silence and threaten adversaries. It was an all-purpose tool.

• • •

The agency's first line of defense was to insist on what at first blush were minor inconveniences: congressional staff could not sit in their offices on Capitol Hill—not even if secured and cleared for the examination of classified materials. Instead, they had to travel to a CIA-leased facility in suburban Virginia to do so. Moreover, the investigators could not use congressional staff computers for these purposes. Materials were to be installed on "a stand-alone computer system" furnished by the CIA but with its own "network drive segregated from CIA networks" and under the control of the Senate. These requests seemed innocuous, and consequently Feinstein and her vice chair, Missouri sen. Kit Bond, agreed to them.[8] Later these measures would provide cover for more devious antics.

Before any materials could be turned over, the CIA insisted on its own review to be certain that the documents were relevant to the committee's request and were not subject to a claim of executive privilege. As it turns out, more than 6 million pages of documents were covered by the Senate request. It would take many months to review them all—and that of course meant a delay of many months before the Senate researchers could do so. The CIA, guided by its lawyers, thus assumed a posture that was common for American corporate lawyers engaged in high-stakes commercial litigation—"discovery warfare."

The adversary's requests for documents could not be denied but could be slowed down, complicated, and subjected to privilege claims. But this was not a billion-dollar battle between corporate giants with comparable legal rights. It was an exercise of democratic process in which the Senate was discharging its constitutional duty of oversight over an organ of the executive branch, the CIA. The agency's right to assert claims of privilege was at best legally doubtful, and its insistence on the need to test the materials for relevance was still thinner gruel. Even if irrelevant, the CIA would have no right to withhold the documents from the investigators. Moreover, the Senate, and not the CIA, was the ultimate judge of relevance for these purposes.

Even more absurd, in order to avoid wasting valuable man-hours of CIA agents on this review process, the CIA proposed bringing in outside contractors—not government employees—to complete it. In order to filter submissions to its congressional overseers, the CIA decided to let another team of persons, who otherwise would not have reviewed these documents, read and evaluate all of them. As they did so, the review team simply dumped the documents (which ultimately would amount to 6.2 million pages) on the committee, without offering them any index, organization, or structure. Delay was clearly the principal operating motivation for the CIA.

Furthermore, the CIA soon turned its skills of spycraft against its congressional overseers. "In May of 2010, the committee staff noted that documents that had been provided for the committee's review were no longer accessible," Feinstein noted in her speech. When confronted about this, the committee's CIA interlocutors responded with a series of lies. First they denied that the documents had been removed, then that it was a problem for personnel servicing the computers. Finally they asserted that the "removal of the documents was ordered by the White House." But the White House denied this and provided further assurance that the CIA would stop accessing the committee's computers and removing documents.

That same year, committee investigators made another curious discovery. As the Senate committee was reviewing the documents, some CIA staffers were doing the same and were preparing an internal memorandum that summarized them, apparently intended as a document to brief Director Panetta. This document was also delivered to the committee and reviewed by its investigators. It would play a critical role after December 2012, when the committee delivered a 6,300-page study with a 480-page executive summary from its report to the White House and CIA for review and comment.

True to its slow-walking strategy, the CIA took more than six months—until June 27, 2013—to respond. When it did so, the earlier confidential response was backed by the curiously coordinated crossfire of an assortment of actors—former CIA directors and senior officials, disgraced former CIA agents whose involvement in the torture program was documented in the report, and media figures, often with close ties to the Bush administration authors of the program. Their message was simple: waterboarding has produced major breakthroughs and disrupted actual terrorist plots, ultimately putting American Special Forces in a position to kill Osama bin Laden in the Abbottabad raid of May 2, 2011. However, the CIA's own records furnished no support for these claims.

This unofficial CIA response was driven heavily by apparent leaks from within the agency, and the hand of Director John O. Brennan was later revealed in the process.[9] While the agency's defenders concentrated their fire on specific facts found and conclusions drawn by the report, it would turn out that the CIA's own internal review had come to most of the same conclusions. This was hardly surprising, since both the committee and the CIA were summarizing the same documents.

Both the internal Panetta report and the Senate committee report scrutinized the documents and evidence and found nothing to support claims that torture, particularly waterboarding, produced anything that materially advanced the search for terrorist leaders or planned strikes; both apparently concluded that these claims were unfounded. That produced intense embarrassment for the CIA and exposed the CIA's criticism of the Senate report as disingenuous—as Feinstein noted, it stood "factually in conflict with its own internal review."

Even more worryingly, while the Senate report was for the moment holding back from policy recommendations and other action, it set the stage for a high-stakes game on accountability for torture, including unexplained homicides involving prisoners.

The CIA had thus far escaped meaningful accountability through a combination of internal reviews and an independent examination of these questions through a special prosecutor appointed by the Bush administration Justice Department. In the end, the special prosecutor, John Durham, focused on a handful of cases involving homicide. He did not exonerate those involved but opted not to file charges on the basis of prosecutorial discretion. Durham had apparently concluded that the prosecution would inevitably involve the disclosure of highly classified information—including the Justice Department's authorization of torture and the CIA's use of it—that would harm the interests of the United States (or, more particularly, the Justice Department and CIA). He therefore dropped the investigation, even though the evidence collected had already proven sufficient in some instances for successful prosecutions in the military justice system.

In the second half of 2013 and the early months of 2014, the feud between the CIA and the Senate oversight committee continued to percolate. The roles played by the White House and President Obama himself were consistently ambiguous. On one hand, Obama assured Feinstein, other key members of Congress, and significant supporters who felt strongly about the issue that he was "absolutely committed to declassifying that report."[10] On the other hand, aides quickly clarified that it meant *only the 480-page executive summary,* and only after the CIA and other agencies had reached a consensus with the White House on redactions from the report.

Obama's key spokesman on the issue continued to be his former counterterrorism adviser, John O. Brennan, a career CIA man whose own involvement with the program was never fully clarified, and whose hostility to the Senate investigation and report could hardly be contained. By March 2013, Brennan had succeeded Panetta as head of the CIA.

As this controversy developed, it became clear that Senate investigators had read the agency's own internal review and therefore knew that the agency's criticisms of the report were specious. This had stung figures at the CIA who were trying to manage the fallout from its torture and black site programs. The CIA never actually contacted the Senate committee and asked how it had come by the Panetta review. Instead, perhaps convinced that the information had been gained improperly (though that is a strange word to apply to an oversight committee's examination of documents prepared by the agency it is overseeing), someone at the agency decided to break into the Senate computers and run searches.

On January 15, 2014, Brennan met with Feinstein and had to acknowledge that the CIA had run searches on the Senate computers. Far from apologizing for this intrusion, Brennan stated that he intended to pursue further forensic investigations "to learn more about activities of the committee's oversight staff."[11]

The Senate committee responded by reminding Brennan that as a matter of constitutional separation of powers, the committee was not subject to investigation by the CIA. It also pressed to know who had authorized the search and what legal basis the CIA believed it had for its actions. The CIA refused to answer the questions.

By January 2014, before Feinstein gave her speech, the controversy had reached a fever pitch. Reports that the CIA had been snooping on the Senate committee and had gained unauthorized access to its computers began to circulate in the Beltway media. Through its surrogates, the CIA struck back. Unidentified agency sources asserted that Senate staffers had "hacked into" CIA computers to gain access to the Panetta report and other documents. The staffers had then illegally transported classified information to their Capitol Hill offices, removing it from the secure site furnished by the agency.

In addition, the Justice Department had become involved. The CIA inspector general, David Buckley, had reviewed the CIA searches conducted on Senate computers and had found enough evidence of wrongdoing to warrant passing the file to the Justice Department for possible prosecution. Perhaps in a tit-for-tat response and certainly with the aim of intimidating his adversaries, the acting CIA general counsel, Robert Eatinger, had made a referral of his own, this time targeting Senate staffers and apparently accusing them of gaining improper access to classified materials and handling them improperly. Secrecy was unsheathed as a sword against an institution suddenly seen as a bitter foe: the US Congress.

Eatinger's appearance as a principal actor in this drama was revealing. He was hardly an objective figure. A key point for the committee investigators was the relationship between CIA operations and the Department of Justice, and particularly the process the CIA had used to secure opinions from Justice authorizing specific interrogation techniques, including waterboarding, that amounted to torture.

As the senior staff attorney in the operations directorate, Eatinger would certainly have played a pivotal role throughout the process leading to the introduction of torture techniques.[12] The Senate investigators concluded that the CIA had seriously misled the Justice Department about the techniques being applied in an effort to secure approvals that would cover even harsher methods than those described, and Eatinger was right at the center of those dealings. Indeed, Eatinger's name appears 1,600 *times* in the report.

Like many agency figures closely connected with the black sites and torture program, Eatinger had skyrocketed through the agency, ultimately becoming senior career lawyer and acting general counsel. No figure in the agency would have had a stronger interest in frustrating the issuance of the report. All those involved with the torture and black sites program risked being tarnished by the report, but few more seriously than the CIA figures who dealt with the Justice Department. Moreover, other risks were looming on the horizon outside the Beltway. As Eatinger struggled to block the Senate report, courts in Europe were readying opinions concluding that the CIA interrogation program made use of criminal acts of torture and that the black site operations amounted to illegal disappearings. The United States was not subject to the jurisdiction of these courts, but its key NATO allies were, and the courts would soon be pressing them to pursue criminal investigations and bring prosecutions relating to the CIA program. Those involved in the program, including Eatinger, thus risked becoming international pariahs, at risk of arrest and prosecution the instant they departed the shelter of the United States.[13]

Feinstein had refused press comment throughout this period, but other sources from the committee or its staff had pushed back with blanket denials of these accusations.

US media relished the controversy and presented it in typical "he said/she said" style. But rarely is each view of a controversy equally valid or correct. Indeed, within the agency suppressing media coverage of the highly classified detention and interrogation program was considered a legitimate objective, which helps to account for the numerous distortions, evasions, and falsehoods generated in Langley with respect to it. But the CIA's campaign against the Senate report was approaching a high-water mark of dishonesty.

As Feinstein ominously noted, these developments had a clear constitutional dimension: "I have grave concerns that the CIA's search may well have violated the separation of powers principle embodied in the United States Constitution, including the speech and debate clause. It may have undermined the constitutional framework essential to effective oversight of intelligence activities or any other government function."[14]

. . .

A fundamental concept underlying the American Constitution is the delicate rapport established between Congress and the various agencies of the executive. The massive government apparatus, including the ballooning intelligence community, is controlled by the executive. Yet the individual agencies, including the CIA—called into existence and defined by acts of Congress—operate using money that Congress gives them, subject to any limitations Congress may apply. The legislative branch exercises specific powers of oversight and inquiry into the work of agencies of the executive, including the right to conduct investigations, to require documents to be produced and employees of the government to appear and testify before it, and to issue reports with its findings and conclusions.

Throughout history executives have used the administration of justice as a tool to intimidate and pressure legislators. To protect legislators against this sort of abuse, the Constitution's speech and debate clause provides a limited form of immunity for members of Congress. The Supreme Court has confirmed that this immunity extends to congressional staffers, such as Senate committee staffers, when they are supporting the work of their employers, and protects them against charges of mishandling classified information.

Feinstein's suggestion that CIA activities had violated the Constitution and several federal statutes was on point. Eatinger's decision to refer allegations against committee staffers to the Justice Department also reflected an amazing lack of understanding of the Constitution and the respective roles of the two institutions. And so did Brennan's public statements. Brennan first pushed back against Feinstein's account, strongly suggesting it would be proven inaccurate: "As far as the allegations of CIA hacking into, you know, Senate computers, nothing could be further from the truth. We wouldn't do that. That's just beyond the scope of reason in terms of what we would do." He also suggested that the Justice Department would be the arbiter of the dispute between the CIA and the Senate: "There are appropriate authorities right now both inside of CIA, as well as outside of CIA, who are looking at what CIA officers, as well as SSCI staff members did. And I defer to them to determine whether or not there was any violation of law."[15]

This formulation was of course nonsense—the CIA had turned to the Justice Department as a dependable ally, not as an independent fact finder. The department was the second government agency likely to be excoriated by the report. Its national security division, to which Eatinger had turned, was little more than the CIA's outside law firm.

But when an internal probe by the CIA's inspector general vindicated Feinstein and found that CIA employees had likely misled the Justice Department, Brennan was compelled to issue an apology to the Senate committee;[16] when he again appeared before the committee, Brennan refused to identify the responsible CIA agents or provide other details.[17] The incident prompted bipartisan calls for Brennan to be fired,[18] but President Obama went before the cameras to express his ongoing confidence in his CIA director.[19]

The CIA, in its frenzied maneuvering to suppress an essential Senate report, had made predictable use of secrecy as its chief weapon—against its own congressional overseers. The agency cast itself as an intrepid force protecting American democracy from its enemies. But in this case, the agency had unambiguously emerged as the enemy of democracy.

One century ago, the brilliant German sociologist Max Weber, looking at the calamity of World War I and the wide-ranging struggle it had spawned between intelligence services and parliament, drew a series of far-reaching conclusions about the effects that secrecy would have on democratic government. Tenacious parliamentary oversight of the operations of intelligence agencies was essential, he concluded, if democracy was to survive. The experiences recounted by Sen. Feinstein provided a rare glimpse into precisely the struggle that Weber predicted.

One commentator quipped, "This is death of the republic stuff."[20] Hyperbole? Maybe not. More precisely it is what Hannah Arendt labeled a "crisis of the republic."[21] At the peak of popular discontent over the Vietnam War, as the *Pentagon Papers* were published and highly classified news about the war effort was regularly splashed across the pages of American newspapers, Arendt focused on the use of secrecy and its close ally, the political lie, to impede public discussion of vital national security issues. However, Arendt had high confidence that the crisis would pass—America's democratic institutions were sound, its press was resilient, and politicians who made bad mistakes regularly saw accountability at the polls.

Forty years later, America faces another crisis of democracy. But now the dynamics have shifted considerably in favor of national security elites. They have carefully calculated the points likely to alarm the public and stir it to action. More effectively than before, they use secrecy not only to cover up their past mistakes but also to wrest from the public decisions about the future that properly belong to the people. Increasingly, Congress seems no match for them.

The Senate committee had emerged from a long period of somnolence to finally ask meaningful questions about a hideous CIA project involving torture and secret prisons. And the lords of secrecy were striking back.

1

BATTLING FOR DEMOCRACY

Though it may be true that, at least in history, values, be they of a nation or of humanity as a whole, do not survive unless we fight for them, neither combat (nor force) can alone suffice to justify them. Rather it must be the other way: the fight must be justified and guided by those values. We must fight for the truth and we must take care not to kill it with the very weapons we use in its defense; it is at this doubled price that we must pay in order that our words assume once more their proper power.

—Albert Camus[1]

IN 2011, already fighting three wars in the Middle East,[2] America decided to open military operations in Moammar Qaddafi's Libya. The move was opposed by the leaders of the professional military, the secretary of defense, and the director of central intelligence. But other leaders of the national security team, led by Secretary of State Hillary Clinton, UN ambassador Susan Rice, and presidential adviser Samantha Power, supported the concept.

The decision to commit American forces was taken suddenly and engendered relatively modest public discussion. President Obama made no dramatic televised speech to the nation from the Oval

Office—departing from a long-standing custom of modern presidents whenever American service personnel were sent into conflict, or even when a single strike was launched against some nation. The House of Representatives held hearings on the Libyan operations, but no legislation or resolution was voted either approving or disapproving the president's decision. The trigger dates for wind-down and withdrawal under the war powers resolution came and went,[3] and that statute—in which Congress granted the president some latitude to take military action abroad in exchange for presidential reports which would trigger a need for congressional approval—was essentially ignored. The president's lawyers in the Justice Department dutifully issued him an opinion: he had the power to commit the American military to the Libyan operation because it was apparently not what the framers meant by "war" nor what Congress meant by "hostilities."

The operation launched against Qaddafi had been approved by the UN Security Council for purposes of protecting the civilian populace from an impending massacre at the hands of their arguably unstable dictator. American, French, and British forces together with other allies were, in theory, engaged in a protective operation. Their military activities, however, soon grew and turned to the offensive: President Obama had determined that the only way to protect the Libyans was to overthrow their government—regime change.

The Libyan operations were broadly popular at first and enjoyed the support of key national security elites. Liberal interventionists like Rice and Power joined with neoconservatives like Charles Krauthammer and William Kristol in advocating the quick use of military force to stop a potential humanitarian disaster (and remove a despised dictator). Critical voices were barely heard, and those questioning the process were mostly constitutional law scholars. Americans generally seemed happy to let President Obama make the call and did not worry about the diminished role of Congress and the public in the decision.[4]

Contrast these facts with the situation forty years earlier. America was sharply divided over the lingering war in Indochina. It overshadowed the 1968 and 1972 presidential elections and influenced many congressional races. Hundreds of thousands of Americans, mostly the young, took to the streets to protest the war effort. Fringe groups bombed draft boards. America faced a sharp cultural divide, and attitudes toward the prosecution of a foreign war seemed to be at the heart of the division. Congress probed and conducted hearings filled with pointed criticism; measures were introduced to defund or cut back aspects of the military effort; legislation sought to wrest control over war making back from the executive.

There are also marked dissimilarities between the two wars: their ideological background, the scope of commitment and time consumed in the effort, the risk to young American service personnel. But focus for a minute on the question of process. In the late 1960s and early 1970s, Americans at all levels were deeply engaged in the issue of war. It mattered to them, and it strongly influenced their conduct as voters and participants in a political system. This was equally true whether they opposed the war as something rash and unethical or supported it as part of a twilight struggle against the forces of global communism. But a decade into a new century, American political consciousness had shifted radically; both the public and its representatives in Congress were paying far less attention to the new war.

As a fourth military front was opened, military efforts in Iraq and Afghanistan continued despite sagging popular support, enabled by a prevailing sense of indifference. The third theater of conflict, a drone war maintained by America's intelligence services in far-flung areas such as northwestern Pakistan, Yemen, and Somalia, was cloaked in mystery, with official Washington denying its very existence. A president overruled his senior military advisers—troubled by the fatigue and exhaustion of their overextended forces—to pursue it. Yet the decision to enter into hostilities in Libya drew a collective shrug from American voters. This contrast shows how issues surrounding the use of force abroad are fading from our nation's democratic agenda.

This is not uniformly the case, however. Twice in the last generation, the nation went to war against Iraq. The first war followed Iraq's invasion and occupation of Kuwait. President George H.W. Bush led America in a large alliance aimed at liberating Kuwait and restoring its government. The Gulf War of 1990–1991, now more frequently called the First Iraq War, had been launched with significant internal deliberation within the executive branch and following extended consultation with Congress. Dramatic televised debates occurred in both houses as the case for and against going to war in the Gulf was fully vetted and votes were taken. Around the country, hundreds of thousands of Americans gathered to express their views about the planned military campaign—almost all of them opposed—while public opinion showed that the population was closely divided on the issue.

There was a measure of friction between the executive and Congress just the same. Congressional leaders had challenged Bush Senior's war plans, insisting that a military expedition to retake Kuwait could not proceed without the approval of Congress.[5] At the same time, rumblings from the advocates of executive prerogative could also be heard. Dick Cheney, then secretary of defense, was outspoken in denying that President Bush needed a green light from anybody.[6] The president, however, did not accept Cheney's advice. On January 8, 1991, he asked Congress for an up-or-down vote on authority to launch Operation Desert Storm—driving Iraq out of Kuwait. The vote in Congress was close; in the end, Bush secured only fifty-two votes in the Senate but was granted the authority he sought. Thus this Gulf War was not to provide a testing ground for these divergent theories. To the contrary, it provided a solid example of going to war the old-fashioned way: with congressional debates, public demonstrations, and televised Oval Office speeches.

The Second Iraq War was in some respects like the first one. A new President Bush was surrounded by many of the same advisers—Colin Powell, Dick Cheney, and Donald Rumsfeld—who supplied much of the same advice about his war-making powers. Although he may have been persuaded that he possessed unilateral war-making powers, in September 2002, the younger Bush sought a vote in Congress to explicitly authorize the Iraq invasion. Extended congressional debate followed, and American streets swelled with the largest demonstrations since the end of the Vietnam War. Finally Congress granted Bush what he sought—with a large majority of the Senate Democrats supporting the measure. Like the First Iraq War, the second proceeded through the familiar stages: presidential advocacy, congressional deliberation, public discussion, and an authorizing vote.

The two Iraq wars thus constitute outliers to the process to be discussed, even as we can trace the seeds of change within them. There are several likely reasons for this, but one stands out. Even the most zealous advocates of unilateral presidential war-making power are reluctant to commit to a long-term ground war likely to produce thousands of American casualties without some measure of democratic process. They will deny that this process is legally necessary, given their imperial reconstruction of the Constitution, but nonetheless they will urge the president to secure it.

Conflicts that involve lower-profile military engagement are managed by largely anonymous national security elites. Some of them stream across the media stage as talking heads. Others remain unknown to the public while influencing the figures in the executive who increasingly make all the decisions. This includes the nation's national security elite—figures who occupy key decision- and policy-making positions in agencies charged with the nation's defense, like the Pentagon, the CIA, the FBI, the Department of Homeland Security, and the NSA, which is emerging from obscurity as a result of scandalous disclosures—as well as dozens of others, particularly in the area of intelligence gathering and analysis.

I call these elites the lords of secrecy for several reasons. They are by and large the sources of secrecy, and they control, through classification powers, what the public is allowed to know. Increasingly they use secrecy to enhance their own power and authority, both in notorious intra-agency rivalries and at the expense of Congress and the public. Secrecy is highly corrosive to any democracy. When facts are declared secret, decisions that need to be made with knowledge of those facts are removed from the democratic process and transferred to the apex of the secrecy system, where only the lords of secrecy can influence them. What is properly public thus becomes the property of a private and secretive group who claim to hold a proxy for the public.

The public may learn of neither the issue that has arisen nor the decisions taken, nor even the lethal steps deployed in their name.

As senator (and former Navy secretary) Jim Webb puts it, "Year by year, skirmish by skirmish, the role of the Congress in determining where the U.S. military would operate, and when the awesome power of our weapon systems would be unleashed, has diminished."[7] And the role of the American populace in this process has faded almost into oblivion.

This book holds no brief for any particular approach toward national security and foreign affairs. Rather, it focuses on the fundamental question of how national security decisions are managed in a democratic state on three levels—the public, Congress, and the executive. The president and his team will always be the implementers of policy, and history has consistently given them the key role as formulators of policy as well. But in questions of war and peace, America has been careful to ensure that the president's power of initiative has been balanced with some form of congressional action. Congressional deliberation has, in turn, historically been moved to a great extent by public opinion—some voices calling for retribution or passionately assessing a threat to the country, others urging caution and warning that the costs associated with a war can rarely be forecast with any certainty nor the outcome known with any great assurance.

How does America go about making decisions on war and peace? Is this process evolving? Is our current process consistent with the vision of those who framed the American Constitution? Does it match our claim to be a democracy? The way a country goes about making vital decisions about its national security is a good sign of whether a country's claims to be democratic are genuine.

Most nations around the world today make some pretense of democracy; it is now widely (outside of theocracies like Saudi Arabia and the Vatican) accepted as the only source of state legitimacy. Yet in most nominal democracies, the people have no say about whether their nation goes to war or makes peace. Are the people able to gather information and do they have a meaningful voice, whether through a formal or informal process? Or is war invariably presented as an unavoidable fait accompli by their leaders? Sometimes nations are attacked or invaded and war is thrust on them. These wars rarely prove controversial. A more difficult case exists with respect to wars of choice, when a nation can elect to start a war or not, often based on differing assessments of nonexistential threat, the costs, and the benefits imagined to flow from a war.

America has changed the way it makes fundamental national security choices over time, influenced by factors such as the modern technology of warfare, which collapses response times and puts a premium on the state's ability to respond rapidly to perceived threats. But perhaps the most powerful factor driving change has been secrecy.

All governments use secrecy, particularly in connection with military and diplomatic dealings. The role of secrecy in America has accelerated steadily, first with the advent of nuclear technology, then with the commencement of the cold war, and finally—and almost inexplicably—after the cold war with a series of nonexistential threats involving modestly armed and organized terrorists. As we will see, secrecy has transformed both the way America wages war around the world and the way it shares information about threats and its own operations with the American people. Today Americans know less about what their national security forces are doing than ever before. And Americans frequently know less than citizens of other nations.

The consequence of this information blackout is that Americans also have less effective say about what their country does and what strategies and objectives it pursues. Decision-making authority has passed from the American people, the ultimate sovereign, and the Congress, the organ of oversight and balance, to the president and his unelected and essentially unaccountable advisers in the national security arena—the lords of secrecy.

• • •

Defining how an informed citizenry makes decisions about the country's security is the central challenge of democracy in our age. And by this measure, American democracy is in trouble. For most of the republic's history, whether to go to war or keep out was a question at the center of the nation's political discourse. But after World War II, things started to change.

The challenge of atomic weapons and the cold war—an ideological struggle with foes who threatened the nation's extinction—changed everything. America adapted by creating the national security state: permanent government structures addressing intelligence gathering, planning, and defense needs on a continuous basis during a time of quasi-peace. With the national security state came a new American elite: the national security expert and a vast bureaucratic apparatus. This apparatus in turn created an immense world of secrets: information so sensitive that only members of the elite have access to it. Secrecy is also used to justify disenfranchising citizens on national security issues: they can't have classified information and therefore they can't participate in critical decisions about war and peace; these matters are reserved for national security elites.

The architects of the national security state in the wake of World War II were concerned about the issues of democratic process that their new system presented. They envisioned legislative oversight as the key mechanism to balance the growing power and authority of the executive. They also viewed this as a springboard for public participation and information. This vision faced some significant institutional challenges—over time the national security apparatus expanded dramatically and the zeal and capacity of Congress to manage it shrank. National security elites were challenged to understand points of public interest and defuse them in a way that dampened public interest in national security issues and checked the press in taking a public voice in them.

This institutional drift can be understood most clearly as the product of the Vietnam era. In the period from 1964 to 1973, America engaged in its most unpopular foreign conflict of the modern age. Hundreds of thousands of Americans joined protest marches as sizable majorities of the American population opposed the war and questioned its wisdom. Discontent over the war fueled an immense counterculture that questioned and even ridiculed American values.

America's national security elites felt vulnerable in the face of this movement, and a series of policies were formulated that served to buffer the national security decision-making process against public backlash. One was to introduce a volunteer army. The draft had been a lightning rod for opposition to the war. Protesters firebombed draft boards and burned draft cards. Inequities were highlighted as those with the means could evade service by obtaining education or family deferments (as did Dick Cheney) or by pulling strings to secure appointment to a "champagne unit" of the national guard as a low-risk service substitute (as did George W. Bush), while the sons of the working class and those from the fringe of society were more often called up. The fact that young men were forced to serve without their consent and faced criminal prosecution and imprisonment if they refused embittered many. Eliminating the draft removed much of the anger that powered opposition to military campaigns waged abroad; it deflated public interest in national security issues generally.

A second policy strategy sought to develop low or even zero-casualty military technologies. This led to a focus on air war, the development of tactical missile technologies like cruise missiles and smart bombs, and robotic weapons systems such as drones. National security elites consider that the risk of physical harm to Americans legitimates and drives public concern and interest in foreign hostilities. So technological innovations that suppress such risks—now bringing them to zero—validate (in their view) the exclusion of both Congress and the public from decision making. This outrageously antidemocratic concept was formally ensconced in Department of Justice opinions[8] supporting the president's right to make unilateral decisions to use military force overseas without consulting Congress.

A third policy strategy involves reconfiguring forces deployed in combat settings. Over the past four administrations, America has witnessed a radical but seldom discussed transformation of the forces sent abroad to fight. Military contractors have figured in since the Revolutionary War, when boat-making contractors helped General Washington ferry his men across the Delaware. But historically their numbers have been fairly modest. By the time of the Afghanistan War, however, the number of civilian contractors deployed actually came to exceed the number of uniformed service personnel.[9] National security elites assume that the American public is less concerned about the death or dismemberment of a contractor than of a serviceman or -woman. They also feel no particular compunction to collect or provide that information. The turn to contractors is justified as a cost-cutting measure, but there is no convincing evidence of that. To the contrary, available evidence suggests, unsurprisingly, that an ethos of profit rather than national service leads to consistently higher costs to the nation's treasury.

One particular aspect of the new surge in military contracting presents a special challenge, the rise of private security companies (PSCs)—mercenaries, though the legal definition of the term is so narrowly drawn that almost any organization can navigate around it. These companies sell governments the ability to deploy quickly into hostile areas, use lethal force aggressively and without the limitations that the professional military is trained to respect, and do so in total secrecy.

Contractors are also private companies. They can shield their activities from congressional oversight by claiming business confidences. One of the most important benefits that PSCs sell is the ability to skirt the political concerns that surround a decision to send soldiers into harm's way. Americans may well be concerned when their spouses, sons, and daughters are sent abroad to fight a war. Do they have the same concern when the risk and the brunt of conflict are managed by Academi (formerly named Blackwater) or Triple Canopy?

The world has now developed a $100 billion private security industry.[10] Private security contractors can fill a gap that opens when a democratic government wants to deploy forces to some dangerous corner of the world but does not want to face questions from its population motivated by concern for the safety and well-being of young men (and increasingly also young women) in its armed forces. But heavy reliance on contractors rather than on troops may also enable national security elites to skirt the duty of public debate and democratic decision making surrounding complex foreign entanglements. It dilutes democracy further.

Generations of Americans were schooled in another adage: you can't have both guns and butter—the population faces privations in wartime to meet the burden of the effort. There was a moral element to this—those at home should also suffer: war should be associated with pain for all. Their suffering would be financial. After all, the cost of wars should be borne by those who fight them. Otherwise, the nation is mortgaging its future—one generation is loading the burden of its political decisions on following generations.

This fact had obvious repercussions for democratic process. As the greatest conservative political theorist of the Anglo-Saxon world, Edmund Burke, once reasoned, the proponents of a war need to demonstrate that the foreseeable outcome of a war is sensible in terms of its cost. Some wars are existential in nature and the cost must be borne whatever it may be; others result when the nation is attacked. Still other wars are essentially wars of choice (though their proponents rarely acknowledge that fact). In this category, the cost element is important for democratic accountability—rulers who spend the nation's treasure foolishly should suffer the consequences.

The cumulative effect of these developments—a volunteer military, robotic warfare, and private security contractors—does not remove the legitimacy of democratic interest in decisions about war and peace, because that is a basic element of sovereignty, which in America's case has always rested in the people. But it does lower the interest of the American public in questions about going to war. There will always be pockets of interest: communities that are attached to foreign countries affected by strife, for instance; pacifists who instinctively oppose military intervention; industries that support and supply the military effort and those attached to them. But the experience of recent decades shows clearly that deeper and broader public interest in conflict—of the sort that accompanied wars in the period from World War II to Vietnam, for instance—is fading quickly. This may give the American executive in the twenty-first century broad latitude to engage in military campaigns.

That power may be exercised wisely. But we should ask the more fundamental question of whether this arrangement is consistent with what we mean by democracy today and what the founding fathers meant when our republic was launched. My object here is to probe what democracy means in the context of making decisions about war and peace, as well as to examine how this idea was developed in America and how the American process has evolved over time.

. . .

In the chapters that follow, I offer some analytical tools for understanding the role of citizen knowledge and public debate in a democratic society, the threat presented by secrecy, and some thoughts on how this menace has unfolded in American society in recent years, particularly in the post-atomic era. Chapter 2 looks back to the origins of democracy during the golden age of Athens and draws on democratic *mythos* and practice to consider the role played by national security decision making in the democratic process. I then chart how this concept of knowledge-based democracy has influenced political thought down to modern times, and the paths by which it came to influence America in the Age of Enlightenment.

Chapter 3 looks at the seminal contributions made by sociologists, starting with Max Weber and Georg Simmel and ending with Edward Shils and Daniel Patrick Moynihan, to our understanding of how secrecy has paralleled the rise of bureaucratic institutions and been used by bureaucrats as a tool supporting the accumulation of power and influence. I then apply theories advanced by sociologists to the conduct of national security elites in America over the past decade and demonstrate how these case studies vindicate the sociological theory of bureaucratic use of secrecy.

Chapter 4 charts the evolution of the national security state in America following the discovery of nuclear weapons and the recasting of the government during the cold war. I then track the birth and expansion of the lords of secrecy, the elite professional leadership of the national security apparatus, as an aspect of this evolution of political structures, and focus on how secrecy has been used to heighten their power and authority. I examine how these elites adapted to the trauma of the Vietnam War, in which their authority was systematically challenged, by identifying and acting against the major touchstones of public interest, starting with the elimination of the draft.

Chapter 5 considers the role played by war-making technologies in this process, and cites the armed Predator drone as the new weapon of choice among the lords of secrecy. I note the use of drones in connection with covert warfare by intelligence services as the national security state's preferred strategy in the counterterrorism warfare of the last decade, and I highlight the fundamental policy issues for American democracy, particularly as the use of drones may trigger broader and more sustained warfare.

Chapter 6 looks at the conflict between whistleblowers and the lords of secrecy. I consider how whistleblowers undercut the position of national security elites and shine a light on their dubious activities, then challenge the government's claims about its enforcement measures and examine the tools that the national security state has honed to use against whistleblowers, as well as the viciousness of their application.

Chapter 7 looks at how the Obama administration decided to launch a military campaign in Libya in 2011, as well as its failed effort to undertake a retaliatory mission against Syria in 2013. Both illustrate how Congress and the public are circumvented in national security decision making—and how the authority and control of the lords of secrecy are growing.

The last chapter explores the churning sea of secrets that is engulfing America today: the offspring of the rise of the lords of secrecy and the key to their power and influence. I then look at the legal edifice on which these developments are based and discuss approaches to rolling back the sea of secrets by forcing national security information that is essential to democratic discourse into the public domain, concluding with a useful role that Congress, the public, the media, academics, and whistleblowers can play in this process.

KNOWLEDGE-BASED DEMOCRACY

These things my spirit bids me teach the men of Athens:
that Ill-governance brings evils a thousand-fold for the
    polis,
but Noble-governance yields a city where all things are
    decorous and sound,
thickly enfolding in fetters those who are unjust.

    —Solon, Fragment 4 (c. 580 bce)

NO MODEL OR VISION OF DEMOCRACY is more powerful than that born 2,500 years ago in Athens. Yet an Athenian of the classical era coming to America in the first years of the new millennium would probably have difficulty with the notion that the American system is a democracy. No doubt he would see some institutions associated with democracy. But he would find little of the citizenry's direct engagement with affairs of state that he would understand in the term *dēmokratia*: the ability of the people (*dēmos*) collectively and through mediating institutions to exercise political power to fix the law and make other essential decisions about themselves. He would also be surprised by the diminished role of the people in taking responsibility for their own collective security and in decision making in regard to it—the dilemma at the core of this book. Moreover, he would detect the rising forces of oligarchy at work, as the voices of a tiny elite empowered by money and position drown out the *dēmos* in key aspects of decision making for the state.[1]

The Athenian might suppose that this was once a democracy, but with time its commitment to democratic principles eroded—a phenomenon known in classical Athens as the *kyklos,* or cycle. Greek political theory of this era, reflecting its own historical experience and the enormous diversity of governance systems then found in Greece, assumed a process of routine change that took certain recurrent paths. Democracy was an exciting development of this era, but it was just one of the forms of government known to Greece, introduced in response to tyrannical and oligarchic governments that sometimes bribed, and other times repressed, the masses.

The rise of democracy in Athens was an almost miraculous leap in human history. Humankind achieved enormous strides in philosophy, the arts, and the sciences. These accomplishments centered on a historically unprecedented confidence in the worth of individuals—in their capacity to govern themselves and contribute to the construction of a more secure, wealthier community. In so doing, it emphasized human freedom and individual choice as ideals that society existed to promote and protect. Moreover, Athens rose to the fore of the Greek city-states as a democracy competing with other states that were generally more authoritarian in nature, some extremely so. In retrospect it seems clear that Athens' status as a democracy nurtured its rise over its rivals in the Aegean world.

To be sure, Athens had troubling shortcomings that detract from its luster as a historical example, and some of them probably contributed to its fall. While the franchise of citizenship was extended dramatically compared with many of Athens' peers in the world of the Greek *poleis,* or city-states, it excluded women, and a significant part of its population lived in bondage. Even with respect to the male citizenry who held the franchise, Athens failed to live up to its rhetoric promising political equality. As Athens reached its zenith, it was increasingly parsimonious in granting citizenship rights, ultimately requiring proof that both parents were Athenians.[2] Athenians sometimes demonstrated clear leadership within the Hellenic world, but on other occasions they resorted to bullying, threats, and physical force to win resource concessions from their neighbors.

Finally, and most disturbingly, Athenians developed a penchant for overestimating their own capabilities and perhaps valuing too highly their own exceptional qualities. *Hubris,* extreme pride or arrogance particularly in the exercise of political power, contributed to a chain of flawed tactical decisions, such as the ill-fated Sicilian campaign of 415–413 BCE, which undermined Athenian power and prestige and dramatically undercut Athens' ability to function as a leader and build alliances within the Greek world. As the mother of democracy, Athens seemed destined to emerge as the leader and unifier of the Hellenic world, but its shortcomings led to disappointing failures that tended to tarnish democracy's reputation as a form of governance.

But for all of this, Athens in the golden age (fifth century BCE) is a historical jewel that continues to challenge presumptions in favor of governance patterned on the dominance of elites and projects a strong, clear alternative vision of what humans can achieve in the realm of self-governance. It is also underappreciated by contemporary political theorists, particularly those of the international relations school, who remain locked into outdated understandings of the classical period and accept with insufficient critical analysis assumptions about the natural ascendancy of elites and the impracticability of direct democracy that were popularized a century ago. Contemporary classicists have, on the other hand, developed a deep and rich understanding of Athenian democracy, patiently stripping away layers of distortion.

For generations, scholars turned to the contemporaneous accounts of Plato, Aristotle, and Thucydides to understand the Athenian constitution and internal politics. But they neglected the fact that these important thinkers opposed Athenian democracy and may not have presented democratic institutions in the most favorable, much less accurate, light.[3] Other sources of classical antiquity, particularly of the Roman era, likewise stressed the bickering and indeterminacy of Athens as a means of showcasing the superiority and grandeur of Rome and its emperors. Finally, the German historical school of the nineteenth century produced prodigious classics scholarship that strongly influenced generations of political scientists, but much of it was laced with the Caesarist and antidemocratic prejudices that were common to German intelligentsia during that nation's Second Empire.[4]

Stripping away this thick varnish has uncovered a more authentic understanding, constructed painstakingly from primary historical records, of how democracy actually worked in Athens. These data in turn have given new insight into the rise of Athens on the world stage—politically, economically, militarily, and, in a more enduring fashion, intellectually. It was not so much the rise of the trade in olive oil, nor the development of a strong merchant marine, that led to Athens' rise as a vision of democracy and its realization in institutions and civic culture. Recent scholarship makes clear that Athenian democracy allowed the city-state to tap a deep source of knowledge and ingenuity among its citizens. Athens established itself in short order as a vital marketplace in the eastern Mediterranean. It also built the alliances and relationships that were essential for its rise as a political and military power.

Could a nondemocratic Athens have accomplished as much? That seems unlikely. Our own age shares this question with one posed by Pericles: Is real democracy an efficient system of government in regard to security and defense?

. . .

America at the beginning of the new millennium is the greatest military power in human history. American taxpayers fund nearly half the military spending in the world, and America has built a global network of military installations and infrastructure that knows no historical precedent. America projects its military might around the globe and into space and, compared with other periods of US history, with remarkably little self-doubt. It is hard to see a small city-state in distant antiquity standing as any sort of relevant model for the militarily stupendous, ethnically complex, and diverse nation that is today the world's paramount power. Yet there is a remarkable strand that connects them across time—the answer to the ancient question *why do we fight?*

American rhetoric suggests that its warriors engage around the world not merely for their own security and that of their families and fellow citizens, but for a greater ideological cause—for democracy and freedom. Moreover, these commitments are not particularly divisive within America's political culture. George W. Bush's second inaugural address used the word "freedom" and its permutations forty-nine times in twenty-one minutes. This mantra was a justification for two significant wars led by President Bush.

Barack Obama's Nobel Peace Prize speech from 2009 justified the use of military force in the interest of peace, drawing on rhetoric often indistinguishable from that of his predecessor. Obama argued, for instance, that American service personnel around the world fight from a conviction that "their lives will be better if others' children and grandchildren can live in freedom and prosperity." He spoke of sacrifices made in the interest of freedom. All of this resonates remarkably with the rhetoric used by political leaders of the first great democracy when it went to war, suggesting a timeless element to these concepts.

On the other hand, the differences between Athenian and American ideas of democracy are striking. America's concept of democracy has evolved steadily since the nation's founding. Some changes have opened up the electoral franchise, once limited to white male property holders, and expanded it over time to include a much broader spectrum of its population. On the other hand, the scope of democratic participation in decision making is open to question. In this book, I focus on democratic participation concerning national security matters. As we will see, for the Athenians direct democratic participation in questions surrounding war and peace was the very essence of the institution.

Athenians valued the social and technical knowledge of their citizenry, and they called on the citizens to debate and decide essential questions of strategy. They recognized from the outset that the essence of their democracy lay in making decisions about their own security as a state: When should wars be waged and peace made? Who should be given command over their armies and navies? Should returning generals and admirals be honored for their victories or forced to give account for their failures? The importance of security matters was obvious from many perspectives. The existence of the state depended on it, but also the freedom of the citizenry: in classical antiquity a conquering power would routinely impress a defeated people into bondage. But Greeks also recognized an enemy within. Bands of oligarchs and tyrants had repeatedly come to power by gaining authority over the military in time of conflict, and often by connivance with neighboring authoritarian regimes. Indeed, Athens' failure at the end of its long struggle with Sparta can be linked directly to a series of betrayals by disloyal members of the Athenian elite, who resented democracy and firmly believed their wealth and ancestry gave them a right to rule. It is not surprising therefore that the notion of giving that authority, conditioning it, and holding those given authority subsequently to account was seen as part of the essence of rule by the *dēmos*.

In the world today, few nations would forbear the claim to be democratic. Even the most repressive and autocratic regimes, North Korea or Uzbekistan for instance, create superficially democratic institutions and organize sham elections. They do this so their leaders can claim legitimacy through popular mandate. It is hard to ground the legitimacy of any state today without claiming to be "democratic." But in America, and in many other nations widely if not universally recognized as democratic, a strong tendency has emerged to centralize power in the executive, consolidate control over agencies of power such as the military, police, and intelligence services, and impose greater secrecy, particularly by restricting the information available to the public about security matters. This is routinely coupled with the negation of the privacy rights of ordinary citizens through the development of increasingly subtle, but nevertheless universal, surveillance. These measures make these societies less democratic, dilute the people's ability to address questions of national security through democratic processes, and chill the willingness of citizens to express any viewpoint at odds with the current government.[5]

Leaders of the democratic states today, most notably America, have mimicked the historical critics of democracy in each of these moves. They have mobilized the language of fear historically used by authoritarian states to foreclose questioning. And in their obsession with secrecy and surveillance technologies they implicitly present democracy as something weak, as a "soft underbelly" of society that renders it more vulnerable to its adversaries, as neoconservative critics have argued.[6]

These developments reveal a fear or distrust of democracy, as well as a lack of faith in the most fundamental of democratic values: that by mobilizing and involving the entire citizenry, by putting their knowledge and skills to use for the benefit of the entire community, democracy can prevail over its rivals without compromising its internal commitments to personal freedom.

Knowledge-based democracy is deeply rooted in Greek philosophy and literature of the Classical period (fifth through fourth centuries BCE), yet we have no real democratic manifesto that spells out how democracy was understood at its zenith in Athens. A few texts, like the celebrated funeral oration that Thucydides attributes to Pericles in his *History of the Peloponnesian War*, provide some clues. Pericles, noting what made Athens different from its rivals, stressed the importance of democratic dialogue: "Instead of looking on discussion as a stumbling-block in the way of action, we think it an indispensable preliminary to any wise action at all."[7] In order to gain insight into what democracy meant to the Athenians who prized and cultivated it, modern scholars distill it carefully from many records, including the writings of authors who were not unqualified advocates of democracy. Into that category we can, with some hesitation, place Socrates and his follower Plato—writers who had ambiguous ties to oligarchs and tyrants. They left the advocacy of democracy to others whom they in turn questioned and sometimes ridiculed.

Several of the Platonic dialogues give us tracings of Athenian thinking about democracy. One of the dialogues, *Protagoras*, contains the most passionate and inventive justification for democracy to survive from that age. Following the dialectical process of the time, it first gives us democracy in the form of a myth and it then extends this with argument showing how the myth should be construed and applied. In *Protagoras*, a conversation unfolds, in 433 BCE, between Socrates and a sophist philosopher, the dialogue's namesake.

The word "sophist" in English has a bad odor about it—and much of that can be traced to Plato's hostility to the sophists. But contemporary scholarship has tended to paint the sophists of the Athenian golden age in a far more positive light, as the champions of democracy. Protagoras, while still little known, has started to emerge, some 2,400 years after his death, as a hero for democracy theorists. He has recently been labeled the first important democratic theorist[8]—a distinction tied to this very conversation. At this point we cannot say that the words Plato ascribes to Protagoras were actually uttered by him. On the other hand, they do appear consistent both with Protagoras' historically reported thinking and with democratic theory as it was being shaped in Athens in his age.

Present for Socrates's conversation with Protagoras are key figures of Athenian democracy of the era, the sons of Pericles and the young Alcibiades among them. Most of their dialogue goes to a single issue: whether virtue is vested by nature or can be acquired through learning. This issue may seem abstract, but it goes directly to the core issue that divided democracy's advocates and its critics. The question was whether the *dēmos*, the many, were really capable of forming valid judgments on the key issues facing society. Protagoras not only argued this proposition in the affirmative but committed his life to training young men who came to him to learn how to reason and argue clearly. In his view judgment can be learned with patience and application and can be communicated to fellow citizens in a way that further develops the judgment into a community understanding superior to the judgments of individual citizens.

Like many Platonic texts, the conversation wanders and fails to reach any obvious conclusions. But its high point to modern audiences comes in a tale (*mythos*) presented by Protagoras. He seems clearly irritated at Socrates' elitism and refusal to accept a fundamental

premise of the Athenian democrats—that all citizens, even fisher-
men and carpenters, have something important to contribute to the
discourse surrounding public affairs. Protagoras' tale is like the Prometheus or Pandora myths that can be found in Hesiod, Aeschylus,
and several other writers. But following a practice conventional to his
age, Protagoras has tailored it for his own purposes.

Protagoras' version can be understood as a democracy creation
myth. He starts with the dawn of human existence, a presocial era, and
tells us of the perils humankind faced then:

> Humans dwelt separately in the beginning, and cities there were none;
> so that they were being destroyed by the wild beasts, since these were
> in all ways stronger than they; and although their skill in handiwork
> was a sufficient aid in respect of food, in their warfare with the beasts it
> was defective; for as yet they had no civic art, which includes the art of
> war. So they sought to band themselves together and secure their lives
> by founding cities. Now as often as they were banded together they
> did wrong to one another through the lack of civic art, and thus they
> began to be scattered again and to perish.
>
> So Zeus, fearing that our race was in danger of utter destruction,
> sent Hermes to bring respect and right among the humans, to the end
> that there should be regulation of cities and friendly ties to draw them
> together. Then Hermes asked Zeus in what manner then was he to give
> men right and respect: "Am I to deal them out as the arts have been
> dealt? That dealing was done in such wise that one man possessing
> medical art is able to treat many ordinary men, and so with the other
> craftsmen. Am I to place among the humans right and respect in this
> way also, or deal them out to all?" "To all," replied Zeus; "let all have
> their share: for cities cannot be formed if only a few have a share of
> these as of other arts. And make thereto a law of my ordaining, that he
> who cannot partake of respect and right shall die the death as a public
> pest."
>
> Hence it comes about, Socrates, that people in cities, and especially
> in Athens, consider it the concern of a few to advise on cases of artistic
> excellence or good craftsmanship, and if anyone outside the few gives

advice they disallow it, as you say, and not without reason, as I think: but when they meet for a consultation on civic art, where they should be guided throughout by justice and good sense, they naturally allow advice from everybody, since it is held that everyone should partake of this excellence, or else that states cannot be.[9]

The Greek Prometheus myth changed significantly from its first appearance in the dark, conflict-ridden age of Archaic Greece until its final recounting. Critical to this change was the attitude that Zeus, the king of the Olympian gods, bore toward humans. In the early recountings (such as Hesiod's *Works and Days*), a vengeful Zeus is prepared to wreak havoc on humankind, which subsisted in a brutish state. This telling provides some of the sinister framing of Ridley Scott's film *Prometheus*, which offers a twenty-first-century Prometheus overlapping to a certain degree with that of Archaic Greece.

By contrast, Protagoras' telling gives us a benevolent Zeus, keen to see humans succeed, though insisting on their reverence. But Protagoras' object is not theology as much as political science. He wants to explain why humans banded together to form states. Greek writers of this era offered many different explanations for the formation of states, prominently including the benefits that came from specialization. But in Protagoras' telling, the reason is far simpler: humans banded together for *collective security*. He tells us that man in isolation was in peril from nature, wild beasts, and other men. Humans assembled together in communities for their own protection—that was the first reason. There were other advantages to a social environment, of course—more people provided the opportunity for specialized work and the development of trades, artisanship, knowledge, for diversifying production and sharing the resulting plenty. But collective security is presented as the essential reason for the state.

The Protagoras narration then proceeds to a second question: Why democracy? Why is it inherently in humankind's interest to turn to a democratic form of governance? This choice is divinely ordained, we learn. Zeus' decision to share gifts with humans is described as egalitarian, "for cities cannot be formed if only a few have these arts."[10]

The specific words he uses are interesting. He speaks of political art or craft (*politikē technē*)—the term *technē* was used to refer to a situation in which a human used his faculties to acquire mastery over an area of practical utility both to himself and to his community.

It has taken some time for scholars to settle on what Protagoras meant by that, particularly because his meaning has to be deduced from the political practices of his own day in Athens. From what we now know, this would have included political speech—the right of the citizen to speak his mind in assembly as part of an extended civic discourse. But a subset of *politikē technē* is the art of war (*polemikē technē*), how humans band together to defend themselves from, or overcome, their enemies. Protagoras calls democratic dialogue and the arts of war divine gifts and insists that they are given to all humans (or at least free men of the *polis*), not just to certain factions, certain communities, or even just to Greeks. In this way, he tells us that questions of collective or state security make up the very essence of political discourse in a democracy.

Protagoras' message is further developed by understanding the two gifts that Zeus associates with *politikē technē*, namely, justice (*dikē*) and recognition of the dignity of fellow humans, sometimes translated as shame (*aidōs*). For a city to survive and prosper, it has to foster respect and justice. But it cannot do this without drawing on the skill and resources, indeed on the knowledge of, its citizens. In Protagoras' telling, each citizen has labor and treasure to contribute to his city as well as political knowledge to share. The process of sharing is both a right and a responsibility. So being endowed with political skills, citizens must also exercise a political franchise—the city's survival may depend on it.

Protagoras' vision of democracy was not universally shared in his age. While the Platonic Socrates respects and defers to Protagoras, he clearly does not share Protagoras' love for democracy, nor his sense that it is divinely inspired. He implicitly challenges the competence of a democratically governed state. He disdains the idea that a carpenter or a fisherman could contribute to decisions about the conduct of affairs of state. Plato's perfect state is governed by carefully selected, specially educated elites, the philosopher-kings.

Even so, it is clear that Protagoras, not Socrates, speaks the vision of the Athens of his day. Protagoras' creation myth reflects the city's political credo and its promise of full citizen participation, especially on questions of national security. Socrates is by contrast an elitist with political ideas that seem at times suspiciously close to those of Sparta, Athens' nemesis, and maintained a series of politically unfortunate associations with the Spartan camp that likely led to his arrest, trial, and death.[11]

Historical accounts provide some critical context. We know that the vital democratic deliberations of Socrates' day focused heavily on questions we would today associate with national security. Was war to be made on a certain state? Was a military alliance to be agreed on with another? Who would be given command over armies and fleets? These issues could be deliberated by the whole citizenry in an enormous assembly. Moreover, the democratic process focused heavily on questions of accountability for national security decisions.

The Athenian way did not embrace "look forward, not back." To the contrary, it rigorously examined the performance of leaders in times of conflict and demanded accountability for errors in judgment and the betrayal of principles, even from a military leader who was successful in battle. That parallels the idea of *mnēmosynē*, the special state of consciousness that empowered a poet or a great political or military leader to speak with gravity and authority to the people. But *mnēmosynē* also meant memory, a power of recollection, an engagement with the past. A Greek hero lived for the present, to be sure, but he was also engaged with the errors of the past, struggling to set them right or remedy their consequences if he could.

While the Greek notion of an afterlife was poorly developed, it clearly involved *mnēmosynē*. The path to the Elysian Fields was open to those who commanded it; those incapable of a rigorous critical retrospective examination were condemned to pass to the land of the zombies without memory, Hades.

• • •

Today there is a tendency to relegate direct democracy to the periphery of New England town meetings. It is quaint and makes for a great Norman Rockwell painting. But how could an assembly of citizens cope with the massive complexities of a modern society where advanced expertise in a large array of fields—economic, commercial, scientific, military—is required? Is it reasonable to assume that a large assembly of citizens can muster the patience and brainpower needed to cope with such matters? Don't societies invariably move to intermediating institutions, to the election of powerful leaders, who, drawing on trusted advisers, can make the decisions for us? Athens was a state of considerable size and complexity for its age, and its historical example suggests that the answers to these questions are not so obvious. Athenians drew on the skills and knowledge of their citizenry and successfully resisted the formation of political institutions with self-accreting power. And by any reasonable measure, the Athenians did extremely well, clearly outperforming their peers.

Stanford political scientist and classics scholar Josiah Ober has authored three important works examining Athens' performance as a knowledge-based democracy.[12] Drawing on an impressive array of primary materials, he has constructed a detailed model of how Athenian democracy actually worked, showing that it did indeed achieve a mobilization of citizen knowledge in the service of democracy that few thought possible. Athenian practices resulted in a strong set of shared values and an impressive base of common knowledge. This formula was clearly important in the long string of sometimes daring military successes achieved by the Athenians during their democratic heyday.

Ober's work sustains his thesis that "democratic Athens was able to take advantage of its size and resources, and therefore competed successfully over time against hierarchical rivals, because the costs of participatory political practices were overbalanced by superior returns to social cooperation resulting from useful knowledge as it was organized and deployed in the simultaneously innovation-promoting and learning-based context of democratic institutions and culture."[13]

The assumption that modern democracies cannot continue the knowledge-based democratic legacy of Athens is flawed, especially in regard to questions of war and peace. As the Protagoras democracy myth suggests, this is the most fundamental complex of issues in a democratic society, and community-based knowledge can be of great service.

The concept of knowledge-based democracy is gaining popularity in academic circles today largely on the basis of the work of Ober, economic historian Joel Mokyr,[14] and a handful of other scholars. However, it is an ancient concept that is deeply wired in Western political thought.

Closely analogous ideas of knowledge-based democracy helped inspire the Enlightenment, paving the way for the reemergence of democracy as a form of government as well as the industrial revolution and the rise of market economics—the three developments that define the modern age.

The core of Enlightenment thought was a systematic rejection of secrecy and an embrace of openness. On the political side, this can be linked directly to aspirations for democracy. To have a say in public affairs, or to contribute meaningfully to the arts and sciences, people needed access to basic information and critical interaction with others to shape and hone their views. Of course, the Enlightenment view was arguably more elitist than the classical Athenian one. Immanuel Kant wrote about "the reading public,"[15] whereas Jeremy Bentham divided people into three groups: one has neither the time nor the aptitude to form judgments; the second believes and accepts the judgments of others; and the third is composed of individuals who form judgments for themselves on the basis of the information available. Still, Enlightenment thinkers also saw this as an unfolding process, with universal literacy, education, and an emphasis on reading likely to produce a judgment-forming class that grew larger in each successive generation.[16]

Few visions better reflect the eighteenth-century Enlightenment paradigm than the coffeehouse, the salon, and the local academic or scientific club, where people with leisure time could gather, read, and engage in open and critical discussion. And no project better represents the Enlightenment than the great undertaking led by Denis Diderot to publish a comprehensive encyclopedia of the sciences, arts, and professions, a massive compendium of human learning that would be accessible to all and would constitute a record for posterity. Diderot famously wanted to "change the way people think," but most importantly, he wanted to agitate them to think about themselves, their lives, and society, and then share what they learned. "Discoveries are only valuable and secure when they circulate among the general mass of people," Diderot wrote. "I am impatient to take them there."[17]

These ideas developed as a response to notions of divine-right governance, under which the exercise of political power came wrapped in claims of mystery and prerogative based in religious authority. As the era drew to its conclusion amid demands for broader participation in government and then for democracy, the rhetoric of revolution demanded freedom of thought, expression, and information, opposing an entrenched state that maintained itself with secrecy.

The American founding fathers presented their adversary as a secretive conspiracy of ministers of George III, riven with corruption and intent on depriving the colonists of the ancient rights of British free men.[18] Similarly, leaders of the French Revolution railed against the secretive, privileged dealings of corrupt aristocrats in making the case for the inalienable rights of citizens.[19] Openness was thus the instrument of democracy, just as secrecy was the natural state of tyrannical government.

John Adams, whose political writings in the revolutionary period presented a typical blend of Greek and Roman sources with Enlightenment writers, argued that

> Liberty cannot be preserved without a general knowledge among the people, who have a right, from the frame of their nature, to knowledge. . . . But besides this, they have a right, an indisputable, unalienable, indefeasible, divine right to that most dreaded and envied kind of knowledge, I mean, of the characters and conduct of their rulers.[20]

This is sharply set against the notion that rulers can, usually in the guise of national security, surround their dealings with secrecy. Moreover, Adams saw the great advantage of democracy in promoting public debate and discourse on all issues: "let every sluice of knowledge be opened and set a-flowing."[21]

The new American state was born out of this philosophy of openness or publicity and incorporated it as a guiding principle. This is not to say that it excluded secrecy. To the contrary, the new culture of openness required secrecy for its own protection. It would actually be far easier to make the case that the founding fathers secretly conspired against George III and Lord North than the other way around. Secrecy was accepted as an essential aspect of diplomacy and of military affairs; it was also recognized as important in certain commercial situations—to protect the rights of authors and inventors, for instance. On the other hand, the principle of openness required that those holding the democratic franchise in America have access to a sufficient amount of information that would allow them to make suitably informed decisions on the major issues before them, a category that included essential questions of war and peace.

· · ·

The most powerful and seemingly implacable obstacle to the realization of knowledge-based democracy in America today is, however, the rise of a national security state obsessed with secrecy. What would the Athenians make of this? Secrets played a powerful role in many Greek societies, including Athens. They were associated with religious rites, particularly rites of initiation used to build a sense of community. Some secrets played an important role in the mythology of the state. Indeed, many secrets of classical Greece were kept so well that modern classicists can only guess about them. Those initiated into secrets who violated their oath of secrecy could face severe punishments, including death.

Yet the officially sponsored and enforced secrets of classical Greece bear little resemblance to the systematic hoarding of intelligence of all sorts by the American national security community today. The Greek system of secrets may be called "mysteries." It is similar to thinking about individuals, society, and religion—not about the dangers of the political and military world, which in Athens would have been openly and fully discussed in citizen assemblies.[22]

Moreover, in the world of politics, the Greeks generally and the Athenians in particular harbored strong suspicions about those who kept secrets, who were often suspected of being agents of an authoritarian state for that reason alone. The Athenian view might be summed up best by Euripides, who authored a brilliant play, *The Suppliants,* in which the virtues of democracy are defended against an advocate of the supposed efficiency and dexterity of the authoritarian state. In the end, Euripides writes, democracy's commitment to openness makes it inherently a more just state: "Nothing does greater injury to a city than a despot; where he rules, there are in the first place no laws applicable to all, for one man is tyrant, keeping the law to himself, and in that case equality is at an end. But when the laws are written down, rich and weak alike have equal access to justice, and the weaker citizen with the better argument may yet prevail."[23]

Secrecy was inherently a tool of the enemies of democracy, of tyrants who ruled by caprice and plotters and conspirators who sought to topple lawful authority. It was not a tool worthy of a democratic state. Moreover, Greek political theory also used the distinction among publicity, privacy, and secrecy to distinguish various state forms.

As Aristotle taught in his *Politics,* in a democracy, the affairs of state are public for all citizens to know and discuss, but the affairs of individual citizens are shielded from unreasonable scrutiny. Conversely, in a tyranny, the tyrant personalizes affairs of state and can therefore in his discretion cloak them (particularly his ignoble deeds and mistakes) in secrecy, as it suits his needs and concerns for his personal safety. Fearing ordinary citizens, a tyrant routinely intrudes into their private affairs to detect hostility. Recourse to secrecy was not, of course, unheard of, but its use in public affairs was viewed as antidemocratic and inherently delegitimizing. Secrecy would of course be used for tactical purposes in a military setting. But in a democratic state it would not encompass questions of long-term strategy or law.

. . .

A key set of examples shows that the notion of knowledge-based democracy had become widely accepted by the mid-twentieth century. Friedrich August von Hayek and Karl Popper, both Viennese men who built their careers at the London School of Economics and developed an important friendship, offer widely differing views of political thought in the English-speaking world. Hayek is linked to modern libertarianism and is routinely and sometimes dogmatically cited by politicians on the American political right, such as Republican congressmen Ron Paul and Paul Ryan. Popper, on the other hand, has historically been associated with social democratic politics and is a driving philosophical force behind the open society movement. Notwithstanding these differences, the two share an enthusiastic embrace of knowledge-based democracy.

Here's Hayek, writing in *The Use of Knowledge in Society:*

> The problem is precisely how to extend the span of our utilization of resources beyond the span of the control of any one mind; and therefore, how to dispense with the need of conscious control, and how to provide inducements which will make the individuals do the desirable things without anyone having to tell them what to do. The problem which we meet here is by no means peculiar to economics but arises in connection with nearly all truly social phenomena, with language and with most of our cultural inheritance, and constitutes really the central theoretical problem of all social science.[24]

Hayek goes on to discuss a passage in Joseph Schumpeter's *Capitalism, Socialism, and Democracy,* in which Schumpeter argues that consumer products can be valued even in the absence of a market "from the elementary proposition that consumers in evaluating ('demanding') consumers' goods *ipso facto* also evaluate the means of production which enter into the production of these goods."[25] Hayek rebuffs this idea, pointing to the essential role of the marketplace in providing an exchange of knowledge: "The practical problem, however, arises precisely because these facts are never so given to a single mind, and because, in consequence, it is necessary that in the solution of the problem knowledge should be used that is dispersed among many people."[26]

Hayek is repudiating the suggestion that lies at the heart of twentieth-century communism, that a small group of highly trained economists can ever know enough about the value of and need for a commodity to determine efficient pricing. He says that this small body of experts will always be an inferior judge to a marketplace made up of a large number of consumers whose knowledge is broadly dispersed. While he posits this as a concept of macroeconomics, he also says that this is "a central theoretical problem of all social science," and thus presumably also applicable to political theory. Thus Hayek endorses and underscores the basic premise of knowledge-based democratic theory.

Popper's embrace of the knowledge-based democracy concept is more direct and enthusiastic. As a philosopher of science, Popper's view of social and political theory reflects his devotion to scientific methodology. He accepts democracy as the political form best suited for human advancement, but he focuses his thinking on human fallibility. Just as progress has been achieved throughout history through the rigorous scrutiny of scientific theories to identify errors, so must we constantly and critically examine political and social tenets, subjecting them to continuous and public debate and discussion. To facilitate this, Popper advances the notion of the "open society," in which individual citizens are free to study government policies, measure the consequences of their implementation, and advocate for their modification or repeal if they are found wanting.

Popper's open society is not a utopian model but a political environment that can be realized by many different political systems, provided that they open sufficient space for study and discussion and forbear excessive secrecy. Its roots in classical Athens are obvious from the initial volume of Popper's *Open Society and Its Enemies,* in which he brands Plato one of the enemies for his elitist views and opposition to the humanitarian principles that were unfolding to craft the democracy of his age. Popper plainly accepts Athens as the direct forerunner of the open society he envisions.[27]

. . .

The thinking of both Hayek and Popper was dominated to a considerable degree by the struggle with socialism and later by the cold war. Their thinking, and the notion of knowledge-based democracy, found strong resonance among intelligentsia on the other side of the iron curtain. In particular, Andrei Sakharov must be cited as an example. One of the greatest physicists of the last century and the father of the Soviet hydrogen bomb, Sakharov is more likely to be known to future generations for his bravery in challenging the brutality of the Soviet state and his relentless advocacy of human rights as the basis for overcoming the cold war. Both his attitude toward science and his political thought are strongly influenced by questions of process and by a clear sense of the proper roles of both secrecy and free information if humankind is to survive.

It is not surprising that the voice raising this banner of knowledge-based democracy emerged from the Soviet Union's scientific enclave, where free thought and the critical exchange of ideas were preserved to an extent largely unknown in Soviet society. Moreover, the path that brought Sakharov intellectually to accept the premise of knowledge-based democracy started with his anger at the adulteration of proper scientific inquiry and method that began with Trofim Lysenko, the author of a series of pseudoscientific theories on genetics that gained official recognition and support under Stalin.

Sakharov recognized the risks that ideology and party discipline presented to the real pursuit of knowledge and was among the few prominent scientists of his day to stand his ground against it: Lysenko "is responsible for the shameful backwardness of Soviet biology and of genetics in particular, for the dissemination of pseudo-scientific views, for adventurism, for the degradation of learning, and for the defamation, firing, arrest, even death, of many genuine scientists."[28] But with time, Sakharov became convinced that the qualities that contribute to valid scientific inquiry—the rigorous formulation of theses, the imperative needed to subject them to vigorous questioning, the elaboration of counterproposals, and efforts to draw on the broader knowledge resident in the community—also served the interests of the society and its governance.

In his memorable 1975 Nobel Peace Prize speech, Sakharov considered the vast arc of human experience, starting where Protagoras had, with man's first emergence as a social animal:

> Thousands of years ago, tribes of human beings suffered great privations in the struggle to survive. In this struggle it was important not only to be able to handle a club, but also to possess the ability to think reasonably, to take care of the knowledge and experience garnered by the tribe, and to develop the links that would provide cooperation with other tribes. Today the entire human race is faced with a similar test. In infinite space many civilizations are bound to exist, among them civilizations that are also wiser and more "successful" than ours. I support the cosmological hypothesis which states that the development of the universe is repeated in its basic features an infinite number of times. In accordance with this, other civilizations, including more "successful" ones, should exist an infinite number of times on the "preceding" and the "following" pages of the Book of the Universe. Yet this should not minimize our sacred endeavors in this world of ours, where, like faint glimmers of light in the dark, we have emerged for a moment from the nothingness of dark unconsciousness of material existence. We must make good the demands of reason and create a life worthy of ourselves and of the goals we only dimly perceive.[29]

Sakharov spent much of his life confined in the world of secrecy, the world in which the atomic and hydrogen bombs were born, a world in which he was a star of the highest order. He fully appreciated and bore the weight of responsibility associated with these secrets, whose divulgence threatened the annihilation of humankind. And he treated the undertakings he gave to maintain secrets with the utmost gravity.

Nevertheless, Sakharov recognized the fundamental fallacy of the culture of secrecy that the Soviet Union had created and soon came to realize that it presented a false choice for humankind. Moreover, he drew a strong sense of personal responsibility from the fact of the secrecy—a need to overcome his initial hermit-like instincts and stand up and speak on matters of public concern, particularly as they were affected by the secrets to which he had access. This led to his important work on the severe and underappreciated health hazards of nuclear testing and to his astonishingly brave decisions to challenge and defy those in authority over their management of nuclear testing programs, and ultimately to his resolve to become a public dissident.

It also led Sakharov to embrace universal information, not secrecy, as a guiding principle for human progress and evolution—much as did thinkers of the Enlightenment. In 1974 he foresaw the development of the universal information system (UIS), a massive database accessible from computer terminals available to tens of millions around the globe, which would include files of all books, magazines, and newspapers ever published, to academic papers and scholarly and commercial compilations of information. UIS is now becoming a reality. It is now called the Internet. Sakharov saw its utility not simply for science but for human society generally: "The true historic role of the UIS will be to break down the barriers to the exchange of information among countries and people."[30]

Secrecy fostered suspicion, distrust, and war. Information sharing was essential to building trust, confidence, and peace. This did not mean, of course, that Sakharov believed that the instructions for building a hydrogen bomb should be published online. He appreciated the need for closely guarding the secrecy of such weaponry. On the other hand, he was adamant that information surrounding the effects of the use of such weapons, whether in anger or simply in testing, should be widely understood so that the public was fully conscious of the existential danger it faced and the shared interest in bringing it under control.

Sakharov's harsh critique of Soviet society and his prescriptions for greater candor and willingness to share information had a profound effect on key thinkers in the final years of the Soviet Union. No one could better expose the fallacy of the cult of secrecy than a person who was born into it and exercised its highest privileges. It was the relentless demand for an end to the culture of secrecy that brought the cold war to an end, not missile programs or Star Wars satellites.

. . .

In this chapter I surveyed a few of the important thinkers who have explored and developed the notion of knowledge-based democracy. The writings of John Stuart Mill, particularly *On Liberty* and *Considerations on Representative Government*, probably constitute the most comprehensive statement of liberal democracy ever produced.[31] John Dewey, whose philosophy of education focused on the construction of a more genuinely democratic society in America;[32] Jürgen Habermas, whose authoritative study of the principle of publicity in the Enlightenment[33] allowed us to better understand both its indebtedness to the Athenian model and its consequences for industrial society; and Richard Rorty, whose critical engagement with Dewey and Habermas led to a new and peculiarly American view of knowledge democracy, could be added to this list.

This cascade of talent demonstrates both how fundamental the idea of public discourse, debate, and citizen engagement are to any reasonable conception of democracy and why democracy has achieved its position of global preeminence in the modern world. As Winston Churchill put it:

Many forms of Government have been tried and will be tried in this world of sin and woe. No one pretends that democracy is perfect or all-wise. Indeed, it has been said that democracy is the worst form of government except all those other forms that have been tried from time to time.[34]

Churchill's intentions are ironic, but his stress is right. Democracy has succeeded precisely because it lays no claim to perfection. Rather, its superiority lies in its very plasticity, its ability to test and reject political ideas that ultimately prove ineffective, and its emphasis throughout on the essential role of citizens in making the call about what works and is best for them.

The threat of ever-creeping government secrecy is therefore fundamental: it robs public discourse of the knowledge that is essential to make informed judgments about whether government actions are effective or are failures. While secrecy in some measure may be necessary for the security and protection of democratic states, unbridled secrecy is a dagger pointed at the heart of democracies, threatening to invalidate their claim to be democracies in the first place.

BUREAUCRACY AND SECRETS

> A case can be made . . . that secrecy is for losers. For people who don't know how important information really is. The Soviet Union realized this too late. Openness is now a singular, and singularly American, advantage. We put it in peril by poking along in the mode of an age now past. It is time to dismantle government secrecy, this most pervasive of Cold War–era regulations. It is time to begin building the supports for the era of openness that is already upon us.
>
> —DANIEL PATRICK MOYNIHAN[1]

IN A PARTICIPATORY DEMOCRACY—in which the enfranchised populace periodically discusses major issues and takes decisions following public deliberation—secrecy has only a modest opportunity to influence the situation. In Athens, those who had secrets and withheld them from the assembled populace risked falling under suspicion, becoming politically marginalized or facing ostracism (*ōstrakismōs*)— the process by which Athenians exiled citizens who posed some vague threat.

On the other hand, when democracies turn to intermediating institutions—as in modern times—issues surrounding secrecy invariably develop. This occurs through the appointment of officers to whom decision-making power is transferred—executives, legislatures, and courts, for instance—and through the creation of bureaucratic institutions that operate under the nominal authority and control of elected officials.

Bureaucracies are instituted to provide services to the state and its citizens, but they quickly assume their own rationale and become powerful players in the political process. Moreover, the steady process of the modern age has been toward ever larger and more powerful bureaucracies around the world.

Whereas philosophers and political scientists have developed and advanced the idea of knowledge-based democracy over centuries, the field of sociology has helped us understand how bureaucracies work and how they use secrets to advance their own power and influence outside of democratic systems.

Two Germans acknowledged as the founders of sociology—Max Weber and Georg Simmel—have provided penetrating insights into bureaucracy and secrecy. Their work has been complemented by the sociologist and Sen. Daniel Patrick Moynihan, who is the most important scholar of bureaucratic secrecy in American history. Their message has been remarkably consistent throughout this period: bureaucrats love secrets. If they are given unchecked power to create secrets, they will find the temptation to use this power irresistible. They will use it to cover justified cases, for example, to preserve diplomatic and military secrets that are important for national security, or to protect the privacy of individual citizens (the information contained on tax returns, for instance). But at the same time bureaucrats use secrecy to obscure from public sight anything that might embarrass them or reduce their political power and influence, for instance, innocent mistakes, evidence of incompetence, evidence that the policies they have made or implemented do not work or have unforeseen negative consequences, corruption, or even evidence of criminal conspiracies and dealings.

Bureaucrats are not driven by an antidemocratic ideology per se—though their use of secrecy may indeed be profoundly antidemocratic—but they invariably develop a desire to grow in size, wealth, and influence. Bureaucratic leaders naturally seek not merely to retain their staff, but to expand it; they seek to justify a larger budget, and to achieve greater influence in core decision making. (Think of the covert motto of the Central Intelligence Agency at its founding: "Bigger than State by forty-eight!" Incidentally, this aspiration was easily realized.)[2] Secrecy, in the bureaucratic context, quickly becomes an essential element of the bureaucratic culture, and keeping secrets from the public becomes the path of least resistance for ordinary bureaucrats.

John Henry Wigmore, the champion of democracy and great scholar of the law of evidence, described the natural instincts of a bureaucrat presented with a request for disclosure of information: "The subordinate at the lowest point, obsessed by the general dogma against disclosure, prepares a reply denying the application; he will usually not have the initiative or courage to propose an exceptional use of discretion in favor of granting the application."[3] Secrecy is thus an almost reflexive response by any battle-scarred bureaucrat.

In 1906 Georg Simmel authored the first sociological study of secrecy and secret societies. He concluded that secrecy exists to restrict the availability of information in society. He studied small religious sects, such as Orthodox Old Believers who had settled in Alaska and British Columbia, the Ku Klux Klan, Opus Dei, and Freemasons or Rosicrucians. Simmel juxtaposes secret societies against government and suggests that they frequently, whether intentionally or not, "appear dangerously close to a conspiracy against the reigning powers."[4]

However, a significant part of Simmel's analysis can be applied with equal force to government structures delving in secrecy, such as intelligence services and law enforcement agencies. Secrecy, he says, leads an organization to an increasingly pyramidal hierarchical structure, in which the sharing of secrets is restricted progressively from the top to the bottom. This accentuates a latent tendency toward the centralization of authority. Because secrecy affects access to information generally, secrecy as a state practice necessarily leads to an aggregation of decision-making power at the top, among the limited numbers of persons with access to the secret information.

Max Weber, Simmel's contemporary, addressed bureaucratic secrecy in a more direct way. He came to the topic at the end of his stellar career, at a point of political catharsis in Germany. The country had been vanquished in World War I and its institutions had suddenly and unexpectedly ruptured. Weber belonged to the small cadre of German democratic intellectuals who, at the fall of the kaiser, raised the banner of Germany's 1848 revolution and proclaimed the Weimar Republic, drawing on the cherished values of Schiller and Goethe.

Weber approached the postwar period with little optimism. The streets of Germany's great metropolises were filled with fighting between right- and left-wing terrorists. "Not summer's bloom lies ahead of us," he said in a prescient speech delivered to students at the University of Munich in 1918, "but rather a polar night of icy darkness and hardness, no matter which group may triumph externally now."[5]

Weber was already sensitive to Germany's radical right. He knew right-wingers would be attempting to blame parliament for Germany's defeat, as well as imperial Germany's relatively weak democratic institutions. Identifying the weaknesses that had contributed to Germany's military and diplomatic failures became a priority in the last years of his life. Much of his study focused on a pathbreaking investigation of the role and nature of bureaucracies.

Weber viewed the gradual creation of Germany's *Beamtenherrschaft*—rule by bureaucrats—as a major accomplishment of the period since Germany's unification following the Franco-Prussian War in 1871, and he voiced a broadly positive opinion of the performance of the civil service. The German civil servant swore an oath to work *sine ira et studio*—without scorn or bias. He left policy making to the political sector and implemented whatever policies he was given, whether he personally agreed with them or not. And this, Weber suggested, is precisely as it should be. Nevertheless, war and secrecy conspired to bring another aspect of bureaucratic life to the surface.

So, reflected Weber, why did Germany lose World War I? There is no single obvious answer, and the question dominated political discourse in Germany during the period between the wars. For Americans, of course, the answer is simple: the United States entered the war, bringing fresh troops and abundant resources, in the late spring of 1917 and tipped the balance decisively in favor of the Allies. Germany no longer stood a chance, notwithstanding its defeat of Russia and ability to consolidate its forces on the western front. That may well be so. But Weber focused on identifying Germany's structural weaknesses, and he became convinced that Germany was hurt by its obsession with state secrets.

On the eve of the war, Germany was a constitutional monarchy in which elections played an important role. The German parliament had been steadily eroding the power and authority of the kaiser and the aristocratic establishment. The war reversed this situation by bolstering the central authority of the kaiser and the military hierarchy, as wars tend to do. By the end of the war, Germany had been converted into a de facto military dictatorship in which the war cabinet and the *Oberste Heeresleitung*, the general staff, exercised a virtual monopoly on power.

Weber detected a clear pattern in the use of state secrets throughout this period. True, sometimes secrecy was invoked for legitimate military or diplomatic reasons. But with great frequency, the claim was put forward to prevent disclosure of a mistake or even some criminal misconduct—the sort of greed or graft that is commonplace in defense contracting.

Secrecy became a favored tactic as bureaucrats claimed secrecy to deny information about their dealings to other bureaucrats and particularly to parliamentary oversight, which quickly became irrelevant. Secrecy put them in a position of superior knowledge and information, lent an aura of greater authority to their analyses and recommendations, and protected them from criticism. Secrecy was an indispensable tool for internal power struggles and intrigues.

"Every bureaucracy strives to increase the superiority of its position by keeping its knowledge and intentions secret," wrote Weber. "Bureaucratic administration always seeks to evade the light of the public as best it can, because in so doing it shields its knowledge and conduct from criticism. . . . The pure interest of a bureaucracy in power, however, stretches far beyond those areas where unadulterated professional interests might justify the demand for secrecy. The concept of the 'official secret' is the specific invention of bureaucracy, and nothing is so fanatically defended by the bureaucracy as this attitude, which cannot really be justified beyond these specifically qualified areas."[6]

World War I provided cover for rampant growth in claims of secrecy; war checked any attempts to question these claims or even attempt to catalogue them. And it had a powerful effect on the process of government decision making. Those with access to secrets became the decision makers. Those with the right to classify secrets became key sources of information. The rest of the government, including parliament, became irrelevant.

It is very difficult to quantify the effect this had on Germany's war effort, and Weber did not attempt to do so. What was the consequence? On this point we can only speculate. But the evidence points to excessive secrecy making government stupid, intellectually lazy, and corrupt—factors that dangerously undermine, rather than enhance, security.

Democratic deliberation rests on the premise that ideas, once exposed to the public—unfolded, challenged, tested, and disputed—will stand or fall on their own merit. The bureaucratic drive for secrecy rests, in many cases, on a need to keep information out of the hands of individuals who could use it to harm the bureaucracy. The bureaucrat will invariably *say* that an enemy could use the information to harm the country, but more often than not the real concern originates with the bureaucrat personally or the office where he or she works.

The bureaucrat may fear that the exposure of a mistake will damage his chances for promotion or undermine the prestige and influence of the bureaucratic institution where he works, making it vulnerable to bureaucratic rivals. To the extent this is the case, secrecy produces a government that is more poorly informed, dull-witted, and more corrupt than would be the case if the power of classifying secrets were stripped away. This is because information stamped "secret" cannot be tested and challenged in the forum of democratic debate; it goes unquestioned and tends to be accepted as truth. If the secret is nonsense, it will likely be revealed as such once exposed.

Bureaucrats quickly learned that affixing a "secret" stamp to their claims insulates them from critical review, and compartmentalizing the secret—further restricting who has access to it—helps even more. This enables the authors of decisions based on erroneous but "secret" information and analyses to quickly climb through the ranks. They will argue that their mistakes cannot be disclosed because that would reveal even more secrets. Robbed of critical perspective, the duller, less efficient, more corrupt members of the bureaucracy steadily climb to the top of the bureaucratic pyramid. You could climb to the top by being brilliant and successful, of course. But it is much easier to ascend the bureaucratic peaks by being secretive. Thieves and charlatans naturally thrive and prosper in this matrix of secrecy.

. . .

Four recent examples illustrate the validity of Weber's thesis about the degenerative effects of secrecy on bureaucratic institutions.

The first is the career trajectory of the relatively small number of CIA agents who were involved in torture and extraordinary renditions programs between the first quarter of 2002 and the third quarter of 2006. One officer in the CIA's clandestine service told me that she and her peers understood that involvement in the supersecret torture and renditions program was a sort of express elevator to the top of the organization. Notwithstanding the fact that these programs turned out to be perhaps the most harebrained (if not criminal) scheme cooked up by the CIA in its sixty-year history, badly tarnishing the reputation of the organization and of the United States and damaging America's intelligence relationships with key allies, those associated with the program appear to have been promoted well ahead of their peers and are now settling into senior echelons at the spy agency. As noted earlier, one of them, Robert Eatinger, rose to the position of acting general counsel and used the office to wage a campaign of fear and intimidation against a Senate investigation focusing on the process by which the CIA obtained legal opinions from the Department of Justice—in which he was a central player.

Adam Goldman and Matt Apuzzo of the Associated Press probed deeply into the torture and rendition of Khalid el Masri, a German greengrocer who was the victim of gross incompetence on the part of CIA operatives who confused him with an al Qaeda terrorist with a similar-sounding name.[7] The AP reporters discovered the identities of the key CIA team members who were responsible for Masri's mistreatment and imprisonment, which continued for many weeks even after the CIA realized beyond any doubt that it was holding an innocent man. In reviewing the case, Europe's highest court found that Masri had been beaten, sodomized, and drugged and that Macedonian authorities had been remiss in failing to investigate and prosecute those who had wronged him.[8]

The team leader, referred to as "Frances" (her real name is well-known to journalists and scholars of the renditions program, but the CIA continues to threaten all who might publish it),[9] pressed hard for Masri to be imprisoned and tortured even when other CIA analysts doubted that they had the right man and after the German government had confirmed that his German passport was authentic and he was therefore not the terrorist the CIA had been looking for—apparently because her "gut told her" he must be a terrorist. Although a court later found that what was done was criminal conduct, the CIA decided that no disciplinary action was appropriate.

When the *Washington Post*'s Dana Priest was prepared to disclose Frances's role in the fiasco and name her, she was quickly given the status of a covert operative, so that CIA officials could tell the *Post* that they were not free to disclose her name.[10] Frances received choice assignments advancing her consistently ahead of her contemporaries, including a plum liaison posting in London with diplomatic cover (which had to be given up when British officials pointed out that she faced possible arrest in Europe due to her involvement in the false arrest, abduction, and torture of Masri, then still under criminal investigation).[11]

Before the Masri fiasco, Frances had played a troubling role in events leading directly to the tragedy of September 11. Frances had directly supervised another agent who had blocked a cable advising the FBI that one of the 9/11 conspirators had secured a visa to travel to the United States and had likely entered the country. According to the FBI's Ali Soufan, this information might have supported interdiction of the September 11 plotters, and its suppression may well be the single most glaring failure by American intelligence leading up to the attacks.[12]

In an apparent attempt to cover up this horrendous mistake, Frances allegedly misled congressional investigators, claiming she had hand-delivered information about the plotter to the FBI. Subsequently Frances came to run a key CIA counterterrorism unit, Station Alec, one of the most important positions in the agency, that gave her direct access to the White House and the president.[13]

Jane Mayer in *The Dark Side* portrays Frances as a "particularly overzealous female officer" who traveled without permission to attend the waterboarding of Khalid Sheikh Mohammed because she thought "it would be cool."[14]

Frances was apparently deeply involved in one of the greatest tragedies in CIA history, when an al Qaeda triple agent detonated a suicide vest at Camp Chapman in Afghanistan on December 30, 2009, killing seven of her CIA colleagues and leaving six seriously wounded. Contrary to established CIA protocol, the suicide bomber had been waved through a series of checkpoints and allowed to proceed directly to a meeting with his CIA handlers without ever being given a security check. An internal CIA investigation apparently cited Frances in connection with the procedural failures that led to the Camp Chapman incident.[15]

Frances commanded the respect of her superiors, who seemed impressed by her daring, enthusiastic, and even voyeuristic embrace of the torture program. However, more critical eyes could see in her career a trail of serious errors, misjudgments, and criminality. But

Frances suffered no repercussions. Instead, she benefited consistently from secrecy, especially the high wall of secrecy erected around the torture program by its authors, who zealously promoted the advancement of their collaborators. Snippets of Frances's career have now been exposed to public view through the exceptional work of a small group of exposé journalists. These disclosures suggest the consistent use of secrecy for self-protection and career advancement, to avoid disclosure of serious mistakes, and to withhold information from other government agencies in order to preserve interbureaucratic tactical advantages for the CIA.

Goldman and Apuzzo also identified other CIA officers, including two officers named Matt and Paul linked directly to the brutal death of a prisoner in Afghanistan, and another named Steve involved in the death of a prisoner in Iraq. Matt went on to become the head of the CIA's Near East division, while Paul, the Afghanistan station chief for the CIA, was given responsibility for sensitive assignments in Pakistan. Steve received a reprimand, retired, and then returned to work for the CIA as a contractor, presumably significantly increasing his compensation arrangements.

A second case involves the aptly named Dusty Foggo, who concluded a twenty-four-year career in the CIA as executive director. Foggo had played an important role in ensuring that personnel involved in rendition cases that went awry never faced meaningful discipline and, to the contrary, were advanced ahead of their peers. Foggo was until recently an inmate at a federal correctional facility in Pine Knot, Kentucky, after being charged with fraud, conspiracy, and money laundering in relation to his dealings with defense contractor Brent R. Wilkes and accepting a guilty plea on one of thirty counts.[16]

Foggo was a protégé of CIA director Porter Goss, a CIA agent turned Republican congressman appointed by George W. Bush to replace George Tenet. He had vaulted from a midlevel management position to the number three slot at the agency, where he wielded immense power over personnel and logistics. Among his signal accomplishments was the construction of a system of secret prisons used in extraordinary renditions, which were quickly scrapped after the CIA took stock of the track record of the program in 2006.[17] Ultimately Foggo was not tripped up by his wrongdoing in the clandestine service, expansive though that may have been, because it was effectively shielded by state secrecy. His problems were exposed in the routine Washington world of pork belly contracting, where they became fair game for investigative journalists and federal prosecutors. There he learned that bribing political figures by purchasing prostitutes for them, a routine gambit for a company man, might be viewed by a humorless federal prosecutor as a crime.

One of the many jaw-dropping moments in the Foggo prosecution occurred when prosecutors submitted a sentencing memorandum—a document laying out various peripheral considerations for the judge in the course of passing sentence. It revealed that Foggo had a twenty-year career of alcohol abuse, physical violence, philandering, and corruption, including forcing the CIA general counsel's office to hire Foggo's mistress. It also showed that as the criminal investigation leading to his conviction began, Foggo had been busily planning to return to his native San Diego to run as a Republican candidate for Congress, with the apparent support of Congressman Duke Cunningham.[18] Cunningham, a powerful Republican on the appropriations and intelligence committees, fell in a related corruption scandal.[19]

How could a rogue like Foggo work his way to the top of the CIA, particularly in view of a long career of boozing, petty corruption, and philandering? Secrecy. Because of the culture of secrecy at the agency and its almost manic efforts to suppress public knowledge of wrongdoing by its operatives, particularly the more senior among them, no one was in a position to challenge Porter Goss when he picked his friend Foggo for the sensitive senior post.

A third case that demonstrates the negative effects of secrecy on bureaucratic institutions allowed a con artist to feed off America's bloated national security apparatus: Dennis Montgomery, a former hospital technician from Mena, Arkansas.[20] He purported to be a scientist with highly specialized abilities in signals cryptography, but in fact had neither a formal scientific education nor experience in the intelligence community. Instead, he had street smarts and a keen ability to figure out what people wanted to believe and then sell them the confirmation of their suspicions.

Montgomery knew that the Bush administration reviled the Qatar-based Al Jazeera news service, which had reported on American military operations in Afghanistan and Iraq in a harshly critical way. Defense Secretary Donald Rumsfeld had accused the broadcaster of "vicious, inaccurate, and inexcusable" reporting on April 16, 2004.[21] According to a secret British protocol published in 2005, the next day President Bush, in a meeting with British prime minister Tony Blair, raised the possibility of a military strike on Al Jazeera's headquarters in Doha, but was talked out of the idea by the prime minister. Assessing the situation, Montgomery knew that the administration would be eager for intelligence that established some connection between Al Jazeera and al Qaeda, and that's what he offered: a claim that al Qaeda had devised a system of encrypted communications to its sleeper agents transmitted within Al Jazeera broadcasts.

In short order, Montgomery's pseudo-intelligence was fed to the CIA, the Department of Homeland Security, the US Special Forces Command, the Senate Select Committee on Intelligence, and one of its most enthusiastic consumers, the office of Vice President Dick Cheney.

Because of the high security classifications imposed on Montgomery's projects, exactly how it affected US security arrangements remains unclear. Apparently some of Montgomery's mysterious analyses of Al Jazeera broadcasts led the Department of Homeland Security to breathlessly impose a Code Orange alert across the United States in December 2003, with secretary of homeland security Tom Ridge announcing information "from credible sources—about near-term attacks that could either rival or exceed what we experienced on September 11."

Dozens of commercial air flights between the United States and Mexico, Britain, and France came under suspicion as the Bush administration forced airlines to put US air marshals on board and canceled at least six flights. While journalists at the time speculated that

Homeland Security was acting on the basis of intelligence intercepts, all of this had resulted from an outrageous scam that duped the intelligence community.

It remains unclear exactly how much the US government was scammed in this caper because the principal contracts were concluded with the CIA's Directorate of Science and Technology and all information surrounding them is highly classified. Montgomery made statements to the effect that the United States had paid about $30 million on one contract and had appropriated another $100 million within the secret intelligence budget. In fact, he began to live a flamboyant and extravagant lifestyle: he drove a Porsche Cayenne and started dropping thousands of dollars at gaming tables, including $422,000 in a single day at the Agua Caliente Casino near his home in Rancho Mirage, California. This is odd conduct indeed for a person engaged in highly classified intelligence-gathering operations for the US government, unless, as seems likely, he had come into enormous government contract revenue.

Two traits of the US intelligence community enabled Montgomery to pull off his scam. The first is gullibility—the irrepressible desire to find its suspicions and prejudices against Al Jazeera confirmed. The second was pervasive secrecy. Montgomery effectively turned secrecy against the CIA and Defense Department, insisting that he could not share with them because the specific algorithms he had devised were his intellectual property and he was afraid it would be stolen from him if he shared them with the government. Secrecy also protected Montgomery's preposterous claims from being punctured and ridiculed through public exposure.

At one point Montgomery became involved in a bitter feud with a former employer, which led to subpoenas and discovery requests directed to the US intelligence community, and even the joinder of the Defense Department as a defendant. Director of national intelligence John Negroponte intervened, insisting that disclosure of the commercial dealings between Montgomery and the US intelligence community would produce "serious, and in some cases exceptionally grave, damage to the national security of the United States." Negroponte invoked the state secrets privilege to end the government's involvement in the litigation.

In retrospect, it is hard to see how the claim of state secrecy could be viewed as anything other than bogus. Still, it was readily accepted by the judge. Disclosure of the government's dealings with Montgomery would have been hugely embarrassing to the numerous high-level government officials who were suckered by him. The United States never pursued claims against Montgomery. In fact, figures in the government who pushed for an investigation suddenly found themselves cut off and fired from their jobs—including an FBI agent, an assistant US attorney, and the US attorney for Nevada who supervised them. Why were senior figures in the government mortified at the thought that their dealings with Montgomery would be exposed and willing to take extreme steps to block it?

The most compelling explanation for the government's willing victimhood is what Max Weber posited a century ago: to avoid the embarrassment that would result if its flawed judgment was exposed. Still, corruption is so pervasive in this story that concern about exposure of criminal wrongdoing cannot be ruled out.

The fourth and final case involves an Afghan financier, Pacha Wazir. His name became widely known in June 2006, with the publication of Ron Suskind's best-selling book *The One Percent Doctrine*. Much of Suskind's book was given to a flattering narrative of a secret effort launched by the intelligence services to destroy al Qaeda's financial network. Suskind reported that a massive multiple-agency task force had scored dramatic successes in this effort.

The signal success had consisted of the capture of Pacha Wazir, a man breathlessly described as "the main money-handler for Osama bin Laden."[22] Pacha Wazir's banking operation had been penetrated and vital information about the terrorist organization's financing had been seized. Wazir was not cooperating with CIA interrogators, Suskind noted at the time,[23] but they had seized his brother as part of an effort to make him more talkative. If Suskind's report on Wazir were true, the case would indeed have marked an enormous intelligence breakthrough for the United States.

Unfortunately, however, Suskind, who had no access either to Wazir or to his CIA case officers, was dealing with information provided by persons keen to promote imaginary victories. The claims about Pacha Wazir were false. In fact, the CIA case officer assigned to cover Wazir, Glenn Carle, subsequently published a book laying waste to the claims Suskind published about Wazir (which were no doubt faithful reports of what Suskind was told by his sources in the intelligence community).

As *The Interrogator: An Education* details, in the fall of 2002, Carle was the CIA case officer for a man he identifies only as CAPTUS—in reality Pacha Wazir[24]—who had operated an informal money-changing and transfer business, known as a *hawala* system, that may have had customers with terrorist ties. As the man who handled Wazir's interrogation and attempted to draw conclusions as to who he was and what he was up to, Carle concluded that his prisoner cooperated with his interrogators and told the truth about his operations, on the whole.

The suggestion that Wazir was consciously managing bin Laden's financial affairs was then, and remains today, utterly baseless—somewhat like claiming a clerk at Grand Central Terminal who unwittingly sold a train ticket to Osama bin Laden was al Qaeda's transportation logistics officer. Indeed, after learning of the accusations against him, Wazir traveled to Dubai, determined to meet with FBI agents to explain to them why they were mistaken. Instead, he was kidnapped and taken to a detention facility north of Rabat, Morocco, run by the Moroccans for the CIA, and later to the CIA's Salt Pit prison north of Kabul.

Law enforcement and intelligence agents frequently make mistakes about their subjects. What is remarkable in this case is that two successive case agents dealing with Pacha Wazir told their superiors that a mistake had been made. Pacha Wazir was not the man they thought he was, and he should be released. Their reports and recommendations were ignored. American intelligence officials similarly resisted appeals by the Afghan government, ultimately including a 2008 order by Afghan president Hamid Karzai directing his release. Not until February 2010, after eight years of American captivity, much of it on Afghan soil in defiance of the Afghan government, was Pacha Wazir finally set free and sent home.

When Carle published his work, the CIA insisted that he not identify Pacha Wazir or divulge any clues that would disclose the facts that he had been held in the joint CIA-Moroccan facility near Rabat or at the Salt Pit prison north of Kabul. Why did the CIA work so hard to disguise the operation involving Pacha Wazir, who was by then a free man and capable of corroborating and confirming the account himself? Moreover, a court action had been brought on Pacha Wazir's behalf that included much of this information, and Afghan government officials were only too happy to fill in the blanks. Perhaps the CIA was afraid to acknowledge that it had wrongly held and mistreated a legitimate businessman for eight years, without access to the legal system, and under harsh and illegal conditions. Or perhaps the CIA was concerned that claims about the greatest success of its financial intelligence program would be exposed as puffery, as indeed they were.

The tale of Pacha Wazir clearly demonstrates the malicious and self-serving manipulation of secrecy classifications. Fantastic and unsubstantiated claims were leaked to a prominent journalist with plausible agency approval for purposes of burnishing the reputation of a new program targeting the financial dealings of terrorists. This would have served to advance the careers of key figures, one of whom was promoted to a key national security position in the Bush White House. It would also have advanced the institutional lock-in, in terms of staffing and budgeting, for the new counterterrorism finance task force.

Following the leak, there was fierce resistance at the highest levels of the intelligence service to correcting the false information provided, which would have proved embarrassing to those whose careers advanced through the leak. This helps explain why the agency refused to accept the reports and recommendations of two successive case agents who had deeply explored the claims about Pacha Wazir and found them to be inaccurate, and why government attorneys consistently made false or misleading statements to federal courts when a habeas corpus petition was filed for Wazir.

Finally, the publication of Carle's book was consciously undermined through the CIA review process, with some 40 percent of the text being struck by censors, generally for no apparent reason other than to render the book incomprehensible—a favored tactic when dealing with publications by former employees who criticize their superiors. On at least one occasion, a CIA public affairs officer also placed a call to a major broadcast network considering an interview with the author, belittling his book and describing him as a "disgruntled" former employee. All of this appears to have been a sustained effort to avoid correction of the earlier false reports about Pacha Wazir—and another striking example of the use of secrecy for bureaucratic game-playing rather than national security purposes.

• • •

It remained for two of Max Weber's most important followers in the mid- and late twentieth century—the Anglo-American scholar Edward Shils and the Harvard sociologist and later US sen. Daniel Patrick Moynihan—to develop his thoughts about bureaucracy, extrapolating it onto American conditions, and advancing it into the post-atomic age.

Shils and Moynihan found what Weber would have anticipated: that bureaucrats used secrecy tactically in the struggle for resources and power in American democracy. Both appreciated that secrecy spinning out of control presented an existential threat to America's democratic institutions, while probably actually undermining its security.

Shils noted that studying secrecy on its own is not analytically useful. Rather, in a modern society, a triangle exists consisting of:

Secrecy—matters that for security or public safety reasons must be kept from the public, with access limited to a handful of persons with a clear need to know.

Publicity—matters that the public has a right to know and government has a duty to disclose, knowledge of which is useful for public discourse, education, science, and commerce.

Privacy—matters that persons and institutions are entitled to shield from public view because only the persons holding this information have a legitimate right to know it.[25]

In every modern society each of these concepts is present, and how the elements balance out reveals the inner nature of the society. American society, in the Shils view, had been the historical fortress of publicity—championing the right of Americans to know in wholesome measure the inner workings of their government.[26] The Progressive movement at the beginning of the twentieth century, advocating open meetings, obligations to publish and share information, rights of initiative and recall, and abhorrence of the smoke-filled room as a crucible for political decision making, is taken as a demonstration of how American democracy has "luxuriated in publicity" from the outset, as Alexis de Tocqueville observed.[27]

Americans were historically suspicious of secrets and secret societies, linking them to privilege and even disloyalty to democracy.[28] Britain, on the other hand, was the "bulwark of privacy,"[29] a nation that inherently valued aristocratic privilege and only grudgingly accepted limited democratic rule. As Shils saw it, the widespread acceptance of hierarchy and its attendant sense of privilege in British society allowed a much higher measure of secrecy than would ordinarily be possible in a democracy; this was to be understood as a historical legacy.

On the other hand, the power of secrecy is dominant in authoritarian and particularly in totalitarian states. Indeed, totalitarianism can be defined using the Shils triangle: it is the expansion of secrecy to its utmost and the minimization both of the privacy rights of the individual and of the public's right to know. The totalitarian state presents itself as a paternalistic institution, attending to the essential needs of its citizens and promising them security. Rights of privacy and information must be surrendered as a part of this pact.

Shils further recognized that the secrecy triangle is dynamic—constantly shifting in the face of political and social developments. Perceived threats to state security, whether internal or external, invariably lead to a tilt in favor of secrecy and a corresponding reduction of privacy and publicity rights. Shils left no ambiguity about his preference for the traditional American model as one more likely to preserve individual liberty and foster advances in science, technology, commerce, and the arts. But he was troubled by the rise of hyperpatriotism, xenophobia, isolationism, and fundamentalism—all phenomena that had been present in some form in American politics of the last hundred years, which he saw amplified in the rise of Sen. Joseph McCarthy and the paranoid right.[30]

He associated this with a rise into the higher levels of state secrecy he equated with Britain. It might be a temporary phenomenon, such as most countries experience in times of perceived threat. But a sustained distortion of the triangle would inevitably affect the inner nature of the state—pushing it down the scale from democracy to authoritarianism when the secrecy axis prevailed, and robbing America of some of its strong advantages on the international stage.

Moreover, the arrival of nuclear science produced a particularly troubling set of problems for American democracy. There was no denying the need to carefully protect nuclear secrets. Falling into the wrong hands, they could constitute an existential threat to the country. But the heightened demands for secrecy that arrived with the nuclear age presented a sort of stress test for American democracy. Shils believed that the American political system is well structured to prevent the abuse of secrecy.[31]

The first layer of protection against secrecy is an internal control within the organization itself that can exist from published standards and review procedures, as well as a compliance officer. In the United States, this has generally taken the form of an inspector general, often appointed by the president and subject to Senate confirmation, charged with auditing security procedures and looking into claims of misconduct, waste, fraud, misappropriation, and certain categories of crimes. Under American statute, the inspectors general are often given a special report to and relationship with congressional oversight committees.

The second layer is the one that preoccupied Max Weber: parliamentary oversight. For Weber, the logical check on unjustified bureaucratic secrecy was parliamentary inquiry. When that inquiry is managed properly, involving committees of members with suitable background, experience, and a proper sense of government secrets, supported by a professional staff with similar qualifications, it provides a useful and independent check on the claim of secrecy. Parliament would also be able to use its powers of appropriation to address specific shortcomings by voting or withholding funds. It could use its investigatory powers to establish facts and publish them. Bureaucrats who misuse secrets can be hauled before an open congressional hearing and hit with probing questions. In this fashion, even without disclosing the secrets, parliamentarians can signal to the public that something is amiss and that they may have been misled.

The third layer consists of the courts, where claims of secrecy may be tested and challenged by individuals or by public advocacy organizations.

But the final and most resilient protection, according to Shils, is the work of professional investigative journalists. As Shils notes, the British press was filled with scandal-mongering and remarkably little responsible investigative journalism. British press lords generally quaked in deference to government claims of secrecy and devoted much energy to dealing with political figures who sought to influence their pages. Lord Northcliffe, who founded Britain's *Daily Mail,* wrote, "It is part of the business of a newspaper to get news and to print it; it is part of the business of a politician to prevent certain news being printed. For this reason the politician often takes a newspaper into his confidence for the mere purpose of preventing the publication of the news he deems objectionable to his interests."[32] By contrast, America developed the tradition of the watchdog journalist, the muckraker, who sifts through public records and interviews key actors in order to uncover truths that may have been under our noses all along—as well as dark secrets that were carefully and wrongfully obscured.[33]

Nevertheless, Shils believed that in the coming decades America would face a serious struggle to maintain its tradition of a well-informed public in the face of the powerful encroachment of secrecy: "For the balance to be maintained, there must be a perpetual struggle to keep publicity and a nervous worry about secrets, good and bad, from inundating individual and corporate privacy."[34]

In 1957, shortly after the publication of Shils's book, *The Torment of Secrecy,* another eminent American social scientist, Francis E. Rourke, looked into the role of secrecy in American bureaucracy.[35] He found an amazing proliferation of secrecy in American bureaucracy since the beginning of the atomic age. The government's internal public relations function had led to some particularly questionable practices in which information was released only to the extent it made "a constructive contribution to the primary mission" of the government agency—a serious subversion of the government's traditional publicity function.

Rourke also examined government secrecy practices and found senior political figures regularly weighing in to ensure that sufficient information was available to the public to maintain a fair basis for public discussion and debate, even about strategic questions surrounding the nuclear industry and the use of nuclear weapons. He surveyed federal court decisions dealing with secrets and found that the courts were willing to press and probe government figures who claimed secrecy to assure themselves that a good-faith basis for the claim existed, although they regularly struck a balance in favor of the government's claims of secrecy. He noted that even while deferring to the government's position, Justice Frankfurter had said he could still envision circumstances in which a government bureaucrat might be forced to produce documents notwithstanding a claim of secrecy. And he pointed to the well-known opinion of Learned Hand in *United States v. Andolschek* concluding that government claims of secrecy might well preclude the government from bringing criminal claims.[36]

Rourke concluded that, even at the height of the cold war, and taking into account the concerns raised by Weber and Shils, the United States was still, on the whole, striking a fair balance in favor of publicity. This was attributable to effective measures by the government to impose self-restraint, but more importantly to a free and vigorous press that established the transcendent character of the people's right to know.[37] Press disclosures had been an irritant in the side of the government, perhaps. But the government had not taken steps to encroach on the press's performance of its essential publicity function, even in the area of national security.

• • •

Daniel Patrick Moynihan offers a unique perspective as an academic with a deep understanding of the professional literature on the behavior of bureaucracies and as a Washington insider, senior White House adviser, and one of the most highly regarded figures in the history of the Senate.

One aspect of Moynihan's unique career was his ability to transcend the partisan divides that are a defining fact in modern Washington. He was a key figure in four successive administrations, those of John F. Kennedy, Lyndon B. Johnson, Richard Nixon, and Gerald Ford. He arguably made his most powerful contributions in the Nixon White House, designing a major redefinition of social policy that has proven to be Nixon's most enduring legacy. He then served as US ambassador to India. In 1976, after his distinguished career in the executive branch, Moynihan stood for the Senate from New York and won—as a Democrat. He attracted young staffers who reflected a wide array of political views and perspectives, and closely mentored many of them. National security issues were Moynihan's passion throughout his professional career, and the postures he adopted often proved difficult to pigeonhole in partisan or ideological terms.

Moynihan brought a keen, critical, and scholarly eye to what he observed. He differed from other scholars in that he had a high-level security clearance and, as a senator deeply engaged in oversight of the intelligence community, was able to access classified material and draw his own conclusions as to the merits of the classification system. His observations constitute the most penetrating and systematic analysis of American secrecy practices, particularly in the period after World War II. And he found Weber's theses fully and lamentably borne out by American practices.

One of the high points of Moynihan's long career came with his chairmanship of the Commission on Protecting and Reducing Government Secrecy, created by act of Congress in 1994, which produced a unanimous report in 1997. The Moynihan Commission report remains the single most authoritative government assessment of its own secrecy practices. Its principal conclusions fell under four headings:

SECRECY IS A FORM OF GOVERNMENT REGULATION

When administrative agencies of the government classify something as secret, they are in effect regulating that information. Normally when they issue regulations, they are required to do this in the public sector. Hearings are held, drafts are circulated for comment, and proposed regulations are published. Individual citizens and legislators have an opportunity to weigh in, persuade the bureaucrats that they're making mistakes, urge them to take into account factors they may have missed. This is a core aspect of democratic governance. But this is not true with respect to security classification. How and why government agencies classify is largely undisclosed.[38]

In addition, government agencies can grant personnel access to certain levels of secrets, and possession of such clearance may be a precondition for employment. This allows agencies to fire employees in a manner that may be beyond the normal scope of employment law review and may be arbitrary and capricious. In this fashion, secrecy provides both a means of limiting knowledge available to the public, other agencies, and oversight bodies and a means of disciplining employees that is free from review and oversight.

SECRECY KEEPS INFORMATION AWAY FROM DECISION MAKERS

In a democracy, the ultimate power to fix policy and law lies with elected officials in conjunction with the voting public. But when bureaucratic agencies classify information, they remove it from the information base available to the public, as well as from lawmakers and sometimes even the executive. Moynihan documents a number of instances in which critically important intelligence was withheld from the government decision maker who most needed to know it.[39] The most striking example relates to the Venona project.

In the middle of World War II, the Army Signal Intelligence Service (which subsequently became the National Security Agency) worked closely with the FBI on a project that penetrated and decoded cables sent by Soviet intelligence agencies to their operatives in the United States. By 1947 this project had gained a sense of the actual extent and depth of Soviet intelligence penetration of America's nuclear efforts, as well as of the number of operatives the Soviets had fielded and their trusted contacts.

All of this information was hugely important for a realistic assessment of the threat presented by the Soviets in the critical first years after World War II, as the foundations of the cold war were being laid.

However, Moynihan established that the Venona project and its key findings concerning both US personnel and Soviet actors were never shared with President Truman or key White House aides. Instead, it had been a tightly guarded secret of the Army and the FBI. Moynihan wrote:

> Here we have government secrecy in its essence. Departments and agencies hoard information, and the government becomes a kind of market.
>
> Secrets become organizational assets, never to be shared save in exchange for another organization's assets. Sometimes the exchange is in kind: I exchange my secret for your secret. Sometimes the exchange resembles barter: I trade my willingness to share certain secrets for your

help in accomplishing my purposes. But whatever the coinage, the system costs can be enormous. In the void created by absent or withheld information, decisions are either made poorly or not made at all.[40]

Truman felt that vital intelligence was being kept from him as a consequence of secrecy classifications.[41] In addition, the events surrounding September 11 show that the practice of withholding classified information from those who most need to know it, most plainly demonstrated by the intense interagency rivalry between the CIA and FBI, continue to menace national security.[42]

SECRECY THWARTS ACCOUNTABILITY

A hallmark of democracy, and indeed of any rule-of-law state, is that persons who act under the guise or authority of law are held accountable when they abuse their authority, make mistakes, or commit crimes. Authoritarian regimes typically use the aura of government authority to construct a shield against accountability. So what happens when bureaucrats or government officials make serious errors, exceed their authority, behave corruptly, or engage in criminal misconduct while they are handling secret matters?

Moynihan and the commission found that security classifications were frequently manipulated by persons engaged in serious misconduct in order to thwart oversight and criminal investigations and thus escape accountability for their mistakes and wrongdoing. Eisenhower's attorney general, Herbert Brownell, reported in 1957 that the classification process was "so broadly drawn and loosely administered as to make it possible for government officials to cover up their own mistakes and even their wrongdoing under the guise of protecting national security."[43] A few years later the House Committee on Government Operations declared that secrecy had become "the first refuge of incompetents."[44]

Moynihan cites a number of cases in which a government employee avoided accountability due to secrecy. One of the most intriguing involves William W. Weisband, an Army corporal and cipher clerk, who betrayed to Soviet authorities the fact that their codes had been broken and were being read. The Army never reported Weisband to law enforcement authorities, nor did it take any action of its own. Why? That's not entirely clear. Weisband was discovered in 1950, when public concern over communist agents infiltrating the government was rising and came to a head with the Army–McCarthy hearings in 1954. The Army was clearly concerned that public exposure of Weisband's perfidy might damage its position in intragovernment rivalries with other intelligence branches.

Conversely, a striking recent example of this phenomenon involves the government prosecution of a senior NSA official, Thomas A. Drake, which will be discussed in more detail in the chapter on whistleblowers. Drake was charged with violating the Espionage Act in a failed prosecution, which ultimately produced stinging criticism of the government by the trial judge. His offense had been disclosure of a massive case of contract mismanagement and fraud relating to the NSA's multibillion-dollar Trailblazer Project. Senior figures at NSA pressed for him to be prosecuted as retaliation for these disclosures, and to silence and discredit him. The Drake case thus demonstrates an escalation—secrecy used not simply as a shield but as a sword to attack those who disclose corruption or criminal wrongdoing.

SECRECY UNDERMINES DEMOCRACY

By far the most fundamental problem with secrecy identified by the Moynihan Commission was the highly corrosive effect it was having on American democracy. "American society in peacetime began to experience wartime regulation," Moynihan wrote. "The awful dilemma was that in order to preserve an open society, the U.S. government took measures that in significant ways closed it down."[45] Americans had historically made their choices following robust public discussion in which alternative viewpoints could be debated and deliberated. But with the arrival of the atomic age and the regime of secrecy that attended it, this entire process was undermined.

. . .

The cold war is over, and in retrospect we can assess the performance of American intelligence in dealing with the Soviet bloc. The consensus judgment is clear: it was abysmal, a colossal waste of money, and it produced egregiously inaccurate assessments. How was that possible? Moynihan answers that question with a single word: secrecy. He writes:

> The national security state developed a vast secrecy system which basically hid from us our own miscalculations. The mistakes, you see, were secret, so they were not open to correction. My favorite is the presidential commission chaired by H. Rowen Gaither, a founder of the Rand Corporation, entitled "Deterrence and Survival in the Nuclear Age." It reached President Eisenhower a few weeks after the launching of *Sputnik* in 1957. The report warned of a missile gap, concluded that the Soviets had surpassed the United States in terms of military effort, and projected a rate of growth for the Soviet economy which would have them passing the United States by 1993. . . . The document, replete with profound error, remained classified until 1973. This is what presidents in the grimmest years of the Cold War knew, and what they knew was mostly wrong.[46]

Throughout the cold war, American intelligence grossly overstated the capacity of the Soviet military and the strength of its economy. The *CIA Handbook of Economic Statistics* showed the Soviet Union not merely as a great nuclear power but also as a leading producer of dairy products and meat (at a time when both were in short supply in major urban areas and the subject of constant joke making).[47]

Could these mistakes have survived had the entire process been subject to public scrutiny and discussion? That seems unlikely. CIA claims couldn't be reconciled with firsthand observations of visitors to the Soviet Union or the observations of émigrés. Had the CIA assessments been publicly exposed, they would have been challenged and even ridiculed for their false assumptions and unsustainable conclusions. But kept secret, these assessments could be swallowed whole by other key players of the executive, by the president himself, and by Congress appropriating funds.

Secrecy contributed to a situation in which powerful incentives existed to inflate numbers, presenting a Soviet Union that was economically healthier and with greater military prowess than the facts allowed. Bureaucratic pressures focused not on getting the numbers and projections *right*, but on getting the biggest numbers that could conceivably be justified. The larger the apparent Soviet threat, the larger the likely budget for Soviet analysts, the more staff positions to be filled, the greater the number of fat contracts to be awarded, and the greater the opportunity for advancement.

Indeed, Moynihan singles out one particularly shameless analyst who rode this process to the top: Robert Gates, who became, in succession, chief Soviet analyst, director of the CIA, president of a major intelligence service contractor, and secretary of defense. The analysis of the Soviet economy and military that he vouched for turned out to be outrageously inaccurate,[48] but it ended up being a brilliant career move for him.

Of course, defenders of the CIA's sorry track record will respond that no harm resulted from this, and they will take comfort in the ultimate US success in the cold war. But this really misses the point. The chief function of the CIA was to collect and assess intelligence and to furnish it to other branches to support vital national security decision making.[49] Negotiators and strategists should have gone about their work armed with an intimate understanding of the Soviet Union's economy, its economic potential, its military position, and the doctrine and modes of thought used by its leaders. Instead, they were fed false information about the current situation, an absurd projection of future capabilities, and a terrible distortion of the mind-set of the leading elites.

In retrospect it is clear that the United States misunderstood the internal problems that weakened the Soviet Union and failed to understand the centrifugal forces that ultimately tore it apart. In other words, the CIA failed in its fundamental mission, notwithstanding a lavish budget and resources that allowed it to tackle the project in a more grandiose way than social scientists could ever imagine.

Moreover, by focusing heavily, almost exclusively, on the military threat from the Soviet Union, the CIA failed to assess and develop a number of other genuine threats that were growing on the horizon, notably including the rise of Islamic militancy. Indeed the CIA's initial engagement with militant Islamists—including Osama bin Laden— had come in the context of the cold war. It had outfitted, trained, and funded them, sensing that they could be a useful ally in the battle against the spread of Soviet communism! The cost of the mistake was severe.

This is not to say that democratic process was circumvented entirely. For instance, Moynihan concedes, "vigorous public debate about nuclear strategy did occur, principally at various universities and think-tanks. But within government, decision making proceeded on the basis of tightly held (unless deliberately leaked) classified information and analysis."[50] This points to two other aspects of secrecy: the false assumption that classified information, by virtue of the aura of exclusivity surrounding it, must be better and more accurate than information readily available in the public sector; and second, the tendencies of secrecy initiates to forbear public discussion and publicly accessible information for the very reason of its "commonness" and presumed inferiority.[51]

There are important psychological and sociological reasons for this process—as both Weber and Simmel tell us—that have to do with the cultic qualities that arise in organizations that generate secrets and live by them, as well as the intellectually corrupting nature of power gained by withholding knowledge from others. Secrecy, particularly in national security affairs, was therefore inherently corrosive of democracy.

If secrecy contributed to the success of the western allies in the cold war, then it was not really so much because secrecy procedures kept America's strategies and weapons systems hidden from the view of its enemies. Rather, it is because the Soviet Union was even more secretive and suspicious than the United States. Secrecy harmed the West. But the communist bloc suffered far more. Secrecy ate through the fiber of the Soviet state like an acid, fomenting suspicion, producing a bloated state security system that severely taxed a struggling economy, blocking the implementation of technological discoveries for commercial or civilian use, and producing analysis of its adversaries that was even weaker and more poorly reasoned than was the case in the West.

. . .

With the close of the cold war, many thought the age of secrecy would wane. Without a vast technologically sophisticated adversary armed with weapons that could ensure the annihilation of the country, and indeed of the entire world, what justification could exist for the extraordinary secrecy regime of the cold war era? A conscious decision was taken to reduce the size of the officer corps, the intelligence sector struggled to maintain its budget, and the Moynihan Commission recommended sweeping reforms and a sharp reduction in the scope of secrecy. Moreover, President William J. Clinton issued Executive Order 12958, which tightened national security classifications while liberalizing declassification. The Clinton order established a presumed shelf life of twenty-five years for most government secrets, mandating their disclosure unless specific steps were taken to retain the classification.

But if you thought these steps would lead to a shrinking world of government secrets, you would have gravely misassessed the ferocity with which bureaucrats hold to their secrets. In fact, the opposite occurred: the lords of secrecy began to wield their weapon even more savagely. Indeed, that was the case even before the events of September 11, 2001, provided them with a plausible pretext for doing so.

In the year following the reforms, 1996, the number of classified documents and the rate of classification actually began to *accelerate.* Moynihan observes, "The CIA accounts for 52 percent of all classification decisions, the Defense Department for 44 percent. It is hard to see how *fewer* military officers and *fewer* classification authorities result in a stunning 62 percent *increase* in new secret documents—almost 6 million documents in all, and all of them deemed threats to national security if ever disclosed."[52] And five years later, entering into the post–September 11 era, the process of classification achieved yet another lunge in magnitude. "In the year following the September

11 attacks, the government classified 11.3 million documents, which jumped to 14.2 million the following year, and 15.6 million the year thereafter."[53]

Today, Washington and its democratic institutions are drowning in a sea of secrets.

THE RISE OF THE NATIONAL SECURITY STATE

Wars may be divided into two classes; one flowing from the mere will of the government, the other according with the will of society itself. Those of the first class can no otherwise be prevented than by such a reformation of the government, as may identify its will with the will of the society. . . . The other class of wars, corresponding with the public will, are less susceptible of remedy. There are antidotes, nevertheless, which may not be without their efficacy. As wars of the first class were to be prevented by subjecting the will of the government to the will of society; those of the second, can be controlled by subjecting the will of the society to the reason of the society; by establishing permanent and constitutional maxims of conduct, which may prevail over occasional impressions, and inconsiderate pursuits.

—JAMES MADISON[1]

DOES A DEMOCRATIC NATION always make decisions about going to war in a particular way? Obviously there are many different styles of democracy in the world, with different constitutions and varying institutions. The amount of power placed in the hands of central authority varies from nation to nation, but democracies have largely ceded enormous power to their presidents and prime ministers when it comes to making war. Invariably there is a power to defend, to repulse an attack on the state. Customarily this requires no special consultation. But the same cannot be said for a war of choice—a war that has not been triggered by an attack, where there is plenty of time for a comprehensive public discussion of the issues facing the nation.

A democracy distinguishes itself from other forms of government in that its citizens are not the pawns of an autocrat. They must be given access to a reasonable amount of information and their views must be paid deference, whether or not there is a formal process of consultation or consent seeking.

Many Americans, and not just Washington policy wonks, love to argue about military conflicts and debate about the allocation of power between the executive and Congress. This has been a core part of American political culture for at least a century. During the George W. Bush administration, advocacy of presidential war-making authority reached a high-water mark with claims of a right to act and deploy troops without the need for specific congressional authority. Congressional leaders pushed back against these claims. But while the contours of presidential power will continue to be debated and will be the subject of tactical skirmishes in which precedents can be mustered for opposing views, both sides have generally observed some standards of deliberative democracy—until recent years.

Because these decisions about war and peace are the most important ones a nation faces, the process used to make them can also be called constitutional. In this case the term "constitutional" refers to a collection of historical practices that are considered binding, much as the British mean when they talk of their unwritten constitution, or Aristotle meant when he spoke of the unwritten constitution of Athens, the *politeia*. And indeed, each of these elements can be found in the deliberative process in Athens at the time of Pericles.

There should be a dialogue that seeks and secures clear reasons that support or oppose the notion of going to war. These reasons must entail a substantive case for or against war. In modern times the proponents of war must attempt to justify their views. They may refer to just-war theory, with its origins in Christian theology. Proponents of war discuss the circumstances or reasons that make the cause for war a just one, demonstrating the restoration of peace as an important objective of military action and other just intentions, and arguing that victory is a likely outcome of the hostilities or at least that there is a reasonable prospect of success. The case for war may also address legalities—why the war is proper as a matter of American law and the law binding on nations. The argument for war should be tested carefully in public debate, and there should be an opportunity for a full airing of responsible views.

There are at least two independent reasons for this process. Most importantly, it aims to achieve the best possible decision on a fateful question. The outcome of a war is rarely apparent at the beginning. Accurately projecting and anticipating the costs, in terms of blood and treasure, are almost impossible. A public debate can force those who seek war to take careful measure of possible costs, and then the public weighs those costs against the supposed benefits the war would present. Fundamentally, this aspect of debate opposes secrecy and requires that proponents of state action present the public with a full, coherent, and reasonably detailed set of factual assumptions that underlie their conclusions. They may of course still say there are certain things that they must keep secret and present the reasons for their secrecy.

However, if the claims of secrecy go beyond the means and sources of securing intelligence—circumstances in which secrecy will be broadly accepted—they may face skepticism. And human experience has shown that this skepticism is well warranted. Public debate affords room to assess the moral, political, and economic aspects of a course of violent action. It recognizes that each area is important and may be weighed by different parts of the society against a different set of standards. It may force the government to confront and deal with skepticism and doubts about motive. Challengers may reveal flaws or weaknesses in official analysis.

Debate may also offer an opportunity to probe and assess whether the benefits claimed from a certain course of action are realistic and whether they can justify the anticipated costs. Edmund Burke was a powerful proponent of military action at various points during his storied parliamentary career. Burke thought deliberative process was needed to expose the costs of proposed action and ensure that a measured and prudent decision was taken. His views were summarized by John Maynard Keynes:

> It can seldom be right . . . to sacrifice a present benefit for a doubtful advantage in the future. . . . It is not wise to look too far ahead; our powers of prediction are slight, our command over results infinitesimal. It is therefore the happiness of our own contemporaries that is our main concern; we should be very chary of sacrificing large numbers of people for the sake of a contingent end, however advantageous that may appear. . . . We can never know enough to make the chance worth taking. . . . There is this further consideration that is often in need of emphasis: it is not sufficient that the state of affairs which we seek to promote should be better than the state of affairs which preceded it; it must be sufficiently better to make up for the evils of the transition.[2]

First, the *substantive* purpose of democratic deliberation is thus to arrive at a decision that best reflects the interests of the community, taking into account its moral or ethical considerations, its political goals and aspirations, and a prudent weighing of likely costs and potential benefits. It is, as James Madison put it, to "subject the will of the people to the reason of the people."

The second purpose of engaging in democratic deliberation before going to war is to build a consensus to cement the cohesiveness of the democracy. Whatever it decides, a democracy must avoid the factiousness that may result from overheated public debate. If it cannot do this, then a democracy may prove weaker than authoritarian forms of governance in this vital area. By soliciting debate, the government is saying to the people: *Your voice matters, your views are respected. You are not mere subjects to be ordered about. We will not go to war without giving you an opportunity to speak and taking your perspective fully into account. In offering your views, you are a participant in the formation of our nation's decision.* The object of this aspect of consensus building is to secure the support of the faction that *failed* to carry the day in the public debate.

Deliberation in a public forum tells all citizens that their viewpoint is important and that it will be weighed fully on a matter as momentous as that of war and peace. It shores up the bond between citizen and state, even if the citizen's particular viewpoint is not the one accepted at the end of the day. When politicians call for full and vigorous debate followed by national support for the decision taken, they are speaking of this aspect of the democratic process.

This effort to build democratic cohesion is a modern approximation of what Protagoras meant when he spoke of *aidōs.* It has been translated variously as respect, modesty, or shame, but for Greeks in the classical era it usually meant avoiding error associated with excess or failing to recognize the limitations of the human condition. The spirit of *aidōs* means that citizens refrain from unnecessary harshness in public debate. All may feel passionately about their views, but in presenting them they should refrain from consciously divisive comments or questioning the good faith of others who do not share their views. The Greek view was that democratic society must guard against excesses that hinder finding consensus for action after debate.

Hence a measure of modesty is woven into the discussion as each side recognizes that it does not possess ultimate truths or supreme wisdom, and neither side should question the patriotism or good intentions of the other by raising charges of treason or disloyalty in the absence of genuine reasons. When politicians state during a national war debate that they will abide by the decision made—for instance, that they will "support the troops" even if they strongly oppose intervention—they are reflecting this important aspect of the democratic process.

The third aspect of democratic process relating to decisions about war and peace has to do with the immediate consequence of a decision. While democratic deliberation aims at reaching an important decision and uniting the community behind that decision, it does not aim to do so indefinitely, nor does it preclude revisiting the decision even while the conflict or military campaign is ongoing.

In modern democracies this translates into an understanding that debate concerning a war never ceases to be legitimate, even after a war has been approved or is being fought. Once a decision is reached, the government has authority to implement it, and the nation must close ranks. The decision must be viewed as binding for some time but not indefinitely. Even while the decision is binding, however, citizens remain free to question the wisdom of the conduct of the military effort, its results, and the representations made to secure consent.

On the other hand, those questioning the war effort may be criticized for undermining the morale of the nation in wartime or suggesting that citizen-soldiers are making sacrifices in vain. The public forum is also open for such points, and those criticizing the government's conduct of the war should take care to present their views in a constructive fashion. The principle of *aidōs* requires that both sides exercise restraint in their arguments, not that they be silent.

Political leaders often attempt to "wrap themselves in the flag" in wartime and insinuate that questioning their judgment is like an assault on the troops. This is a predictable attempt to chill political speech that can be found throughout human history. It is noteworthy, however, that some of the most effective criticism of the conduct of the Second Iraq War came from retired American generals like John Batiste and Paul Eaton, both veterans of the Iraq conflict. Their criticisms focused on the incompetent political stewardship of the war effort and presented a devastating critique of assumptions advanced by political figures as they made a case for war.

In antiquity, military men played a central role in public discourse about security affairs. The modern American model of democracy, however, subordinates them to civilian direction. This severely limits the space given to military men to speak in public discourse. Generals and admirals testify before Congress and field questions and occasionally make public speeches. But they are expected to take supervision at least to some measure from their civilian bosses. No such limitations exist for retired military, however, so that statements like those made by Batiste and Eaton were welcome contributions. This criticism must be appreciated as constructive, since it aims to hone tactics and give the public a better sense of what can and cannot be accomplished through military force. This follows from one of the most fundamental premises of knowledge-based democracy: decisions may be mistaken, and remaining beholden to mistakes compounds the error.

The fourth aspect of democratic deliberation in national security matters is essentially retrospective. The Athenian model of democratic deliberation about issues of national security envisioned that a decision would be taken and implemented with minimal discussion while it was in process. But at the *conclusion* of a military campaign, the *strategoi*, or military leaders, were expected to render account for their stewardship. They might then be subjected to harsh criticism, particularly from citizens who had suffered a loss, for instance, through the death of a relative or friend.

A good example is contained in the history of the Peloponnesian War, the battle of Arginusae in 406 BCE. Several of the participants in the *Protagoras* dialogue played roles in the battle or the controversies that erupted over it later. Athens achieved a dramatic naval victory over Sparta at Arginusae, and the people rejoiced over it. But a few days later word arrived of a tragedy: a storm at sea had taken the lives and bodies of Athenian sailors on two dozen wrecked ships that had not been saved by the balance of the fleet. Relatives of the deceased charged that neglect by Athenian admirals had cost the lives of the lost sailors and that they had failed to retrieve the bodies for proper burial. (As readers of the *Iliad* know, respect for the bodies of those who fell in battle was an emotional point for the Greeks.) The military leaders were brought back to Athens to account for their dealings before a jury of five hundred.

The most interesting fragment of the surviving historical record of the trial is that Socrates vigorously attempted to thwart it. But Socrates was clearly out of touch with his contemporaries on this matter. Athens of the golden age had a clear concept of democracy: the broadest possible participation by the citizenry in questions of war and peace was essential to the democratic franchise. The records reveal that it was not enough for a general to win battles. *How* he had won and how prudently he had managed the precious assets given to him—men, money, and ships—would be questioned.

Athenians of the assembly set tough standards for their military leaders and were unforgiving to those who made serious mistakes, whether they returned as victors or not. This process could be attacked as retributive and unproductive, but it served as an after-the-fact assessment: Whose arguments to the assembly had been vindicated, and whose proven false? Who had demonstrated ability in battle? Had the society's values been upheld? Those who stood this test would be rewarded and gain influence in the democratic process. Those who failed could be punished or exiled.[3]

This is something akin to the process of introspective self-criticism that the US military goes through following major campaigns, known as "lessons learned." As a matter of long-standing practice, the American army collects, analyzes, disseminates, and archives records of specific operations in order to adopt changes that reflect the battlefield or other operational testing of specific tactics.[4] The objective is to identify and avoid errors in the future and assess how well existing training programs prepared American soldiers, sailors, and airmen to fight in the conflict.

However, lessons-learned exercises have become scarce during the deliberative process in America, as public opinion makers argue that they serve no apparent constructive purpose—just as the circumstances provided a compelling case for a postconflict reassessment. Iraq was invaded on the basis of claims that it possessed weapons of mass destruction (WMDs) and there was an imminent threat to the United States and its allies from their use. These claims proved to be false.

Moreover, the invasion appeared to be planned and staged without appropriate attention to the likely consequences of this action for Iraq and for the political stability of the region. Advocates spoke, with remarkable naïveté, of a democratic groundswell that this would unleash, producing natural American allies not just in Iraq but in neighboring countries as well. But by taking early and ill-considered steps that smashed Iraq's well-grounded secular state without immediate hope for repair, a very different set of developments ensued. Sectarian differences quickly bubbled up and the Iraqi state soon began to unravel, with the more numerous Shias seeking a natural alliance with Tehran, while Sunnis divided among remnants of the Baath Party, tribal groups, and various Islamic radical organizations. It is appropriate for a democratic state to examine closely the dealings that led to the invasion of Iraq, focusing, among other things, on claims for the existence of WMDs and then questioning whether enough attention was paid to the consequences of destroying the Baathist state in Iraq.

Political leaders have suggested that any such review would only undermine the nation's reputation on the world stage. But that is nonsense. The tradition in democratic societies is that political figures who use misrepresentations and distortions to persuade the nation to make grave missteps face accountability for what they have done. This demonstrates the accountability principle. The arguments and claims that propelled the country into the Second Iraq War, for instance, might have rested on honest mistakes or on conscious distortions of the available evidence—the difference is an important one.

Resistance to an accountability dialogue lies with powerful figures in both political parties who endorsed the flawed case for an invasion of Iraq and would be embarrassed by revisiting it. The press normally provides an alternative engine to drive such a dialogue, and some publications have played a notably important role in doing so.[5] However, the nation's leading newspapers for national security matters—the *New York Times, Washington Post,* and *Wall Street Journal*—acted as cheerleaders for the war effort. The same is true of major television news organizations. Consequently, after failing to play the role of skeptical inquiry that a democracy expects, the media has been unenthusiastic about reexamining the mistakes it made in the buildup to the war.

In this case, once more, secrecy claims serve to avoid democratic dialogue and accountability. The public was told that the basis for WMD claims rested on highly sensitive intelligence that could not be publicly disclosed. But in a retrospective review, the question becomes whether the intelligence really was as represented, and whether the analysis of the intelligence was reasonable.[6] Developing this analysis is difficult without delving deeply into the secretive work of the intelligence services. Were they pressured by politicians to produce a certain result? America's failure to grapple with such issues is also a failure of the principle of democratic dialogue on national security matters.

. . .

Sometimes a commission of inquiry can ignite democratic deliberation in the context of an after-the-fact assessment. Taking different forms in various jurisdictions, commissions of inquiry are often impaneled to study a historically significant development and assess the performance of differing agencies and organs of government in this context. The commission may be outfitted with quasi-judicial powers, including the right to subpoena persons to appear before it and give evidence and to require the production of documents—sometimes including classified documents.

The commission of inquiry can perform an explicit public information role, so it commonly convenes and holds hearings in public so that the people can examine the pertinent evidence and form their own judgments. It generally renders a report offering conclusions and recommendations, supported by factual findings. This is a legitimate and sometimes useful device typical of parliamentary democracies, particularly in the English-speaking world. It can facilitate democratic deliberation, but not always.

In the case of subsequently disproven claims made in the run-up to the Second Iraq War, for instance, a number of commissions were created in the United States and the United Kingdom to address these issues, including the Iraq Intelligence Commission, cochaired by Charles Robb and Laurence Silberman in the United States (2004–2005), and the Butler Review (2004) and the Iraq or Chilcot Inquiry in the United Kingdom (2009–2011). These inquiries largely became an exercise in political misdirection, which is not surprising. They were constituted by the very politicians whose actions should have been studied.

The Robb-Silberman and Butler reviews were tasked to look at presumed failures by the intelligence services, avoiding the question of the role of political actors in the process, which any reasonable observer would conclude was actually the legitimate focus of the inquiry. Moreover, by conducting their work largely in secret and issuing a heavily classified report, the largely discredited Robb-Silberman effort[7] avoided sparking meaningful public discussion of the underlying issues, instead drawing criticism for the toothlessness of the review.[8] The Robb-Silberman report acknowledged that the intelligence community had erred in most of its essential preinvasion judgments about Iraq, but by focusing its inquiry straight down the line of command, it failed to grapple with the key question: the role of Bush administration policy makers in these false judgments. This was, if anything, even more the case for the Butler Review. The public reaction to it was well summarized by the headline of the London *Evening Standard* reporting on its outcome: "Whitewash (Part Two)."[9]

Of these inquiries, the Chilcot review has come closest to stimulating democratic dialogue about the underlying issues. It has yet to render a report, and there is skepticism that its report will be of much consequence. However, by conducting public hearings, largely broadcast live on radio and television, the inquiry put leading political and bureaucratic figures in the crosshairs—forcing them to answer difficult questions about their conduct. This fueled penetrating press reportage and public discussion.

In the end the inquiry revealed that British decision makers were highly skeptical about American claims of Iraqi WMDs, but were convinced that the country's long-term security interests lay in a tight relationship with the United States. This in turn necessitated following America into Iraq whether or not a legally or morally cognizable basis for such action existed. The British government has resisted sharing with the commission extracts of conversations between Blair and Bush during the critical period,[10] but many of these extracts were leaked and government resistance only highlighted public interest in those interchanges. On May 29, 2014, the Cameron government agreed with the Chilcot commission that a summary reflecting the gist of these discussions could be released, but the actual notes would not be.[11]

The US government apparently had concerns that the Chilcot Inquiry would both spark democratic dialogue and reveal embarrassing facts about how America had led its ally into the Second Iraq War. Among the cables published by WikiLeaks was a secret report from a British minister that he had "put measures in place to protect your interests" with respect to the Chilcot process.[12] Revealingly, the cable reflected satisfaction with the idea that interest in the launch of the Second Iraq War had gone dormant in the United States but concern that the Chilcot Inquiry might trigger democratic dialogue in Britain, which was apparently highly undesirable from the perspective of the two diplomats.

In fact, the British government had previously barred the inquiry access to all the key documents pertaining to the Bush-Blair meetings to discuss action in Iraq, including the minutes of cabinet meetings at which the American agenda had been discussed—meaning that the inquiry was not able to examine the best available evidence of the very matters it had been commissioned to study. Chilcot had pressed for release of these materials, and the issue had held the inquiry's work open for three years beyond its mandate.

This is a striking example of secrecy being invoked by the intelligence services of one democracy to thwart democratic process in another democracy, because it might embarrass individual politicians and figures in the intelligence service. It demonstrates the utility of diplomatic secrecy as a cover for all failings, because the premises and use of diplomatic secrets are rarely questioned. In the case of the Chilcot Inquiry, however, diplomatic claims of secrecy were used reciprocally by politicians and intelligence officers in the United States and United Kingdom to block disclosure of matters that the American and British publics had a common interest in knowing. The use of diplomatic secrecy in this context was fundamentally illegitimate but essentially unchallenged.

The final aspect of democratic dialogue respecting national security, the accountability dialogue, has gone dormant in America today.

Indeed, the complete failure of accountability is one of the most striking features of the emerging national surveillance state. In his superlative book on American military command practices since World War II, *The Generals*, Thomas E. Ricks notes how generals were regularly cashiered and shuffled throughout World War II as a tool of discipline and to demonstrate disappointment with performance. In contemporary Washington, the aversion to any form of accountability is so intense that this almost never happens—save for abjectly improper reasons, as when a general inadvertently demonstrates that a political figure has said something foolish.

Similarly, no criminal proceedings were commenced against intelligence service personnel linked directly to the torture-homicides of prisoners in the Iraq and Afghanistan wars, even though such prosecutions are mandatory under international law. I have elsewhere documented the nearly complete failure of prosecution or other forms of discipline for military contractors in Iraq and Afghanistan involved in murders, rapes, and other violent crimes.[13]

As already noted, many of the advocates of democratic dialogue, such as James Madison and John Stuart Mill, were concerned that broad-based democratic societies could be misled by demagogues. As Madison put it, in a passage that appears to discuss the Athenian assembly over the battle of Arginusae, "in very numerous assemblies, of whatever characters composed, passion never fails to wrest the scepter from reason."[14] This leads to a strong preference for allowing the best-informed, most astute thinkers to lead the debate.

However, reliance on "experts" is a challenge-laden process for a democracy. There is a natural tendency in democratic states for elites of various types, whether formed by education, experience, or, most crudely, wealth, to rise to the top and exercise disproportionate power and influence. There is also a tendency among these elites to progressively exclude the participation of a broadly based citizenship in essential political decision making. This thesis was first put forward by the Greek theorists who described the cycle (*kyklos*) of governments, but was refined by the German sociologist Robert Michels. It has come to be called the "iron law of oligarchy."[15]

Michels wrote specifically about what happened within political parties starting in the late nineteenth century, but he ultimately argued that no democratic society would be able to resist the internal rise of elites. Recent discoveries about Athenian democracy defy the Michels rule, and some critics have argued that his law is less "iron" than a rather thin aluminum alloy.[16] Nevertheless, a vast body of literature supports Michels's thesis and it can be fairly considered a part of the modern social science bedrock.

The process of national security decision making offers a test for this phenomenon. Most citizens would agree that critical decisions concerning national security matters require guidance from military and intelligence professionals. The essential question is whether their perspectives *inform and lead the debate* or whether decisions are made by senior political leaders, drawing on the advice of experts, without benefit of any public discussion. In this regard, it is also important to differentiate the scope of the issue. For instance, tactical issues arising in a pending conflict would not ordinarily be subject to any reasonable expectation of public debate or deliberation. By contrast, broad and long-term strategic plans would be.

• • •

In the period following World War II, and rapidly accelerating in the new millennium, the proliferation of secrecy has acted as a gate mechanism. It has moved ever more subjects off the public stage, ensuring that these issues are managed not through democratic discussion but through a bureaucratic-technical decision-making system.

This process can be linked to both political and technical innovations—starting with feverish efforts in the high desert of New Mexico at Los Alamos in the last years of World War II and continuing to the development of robotic warfare today.

The bomb was "born secret," as Daniel Patrick Moynihan said. The atomic bomb marked a powerful turning point in America's stewardship of national security affairs. After its arrival, Garry Wills argues, "the power of secrecy that enveloped the Bomb became a model for the planning or execution of Anything Important, as guarded by Important People."[17] But the first stop was a radical restructuring of the government itself, to account for the development and expansion of a nuclear arsenal requiring special means, staffs, oversight, and a stringent and novel regime of peacetime secrecy. The national security state was born.

Previously America had ramped up its military in times of war or crisis, and allowed it to languish in peacetime. It had a War Department for land forces and a Navy Department for forces at sea. The rivalry between the two occasionally reached comic levels. Intelligence gathering was something of a hit-or-miss proposition as well, with many figures taking a rather dismissive attitude toward the spying industry as a whole. "Gentlemen do not read each other's mail," Secretary of State Henry Stimson recalls having noted in 1929 when he withdrew funding from a communications interception and decryption program. But after being appointed secretary of war at the outset of World War II, Stimson changed his attitude, and when he assumed direct supervision over Gen. Leslie Groves and the Manhattan Project, Stimson became an enthusiastic advocate of secrecy and intensive surveillance to manage its secrets.

The post–World War II redesign was intended to provide a posture of constant military readiness for the country, smoothing out interagency differences and strongly emphasizing the scientific and technical innovation that had served the country so effectively in the war. America had mobilized 12 million men and women by the end of World War II. In 1949, after demobilization, the number stood at 1.5 million. However, that was three times the size of the military America fielded before World War II.

The most striking change was a focus on lethal technologies. America's emergence on the world stage as the paramount military power had rested substantially on its striking innovations in military technology. The Truman administration was determined to hold and expand that edge, and it was committed to spending whatever it took. The new architecture of the security state, the heart of which is contained in the National Security Act of 1947, was built around this assumption. It therefore gave formality to the new culture of secrecy born at Los Alamos, and stretched it into peacetime.

By 1949, the uniformed services were united under a new Department of Defense, which was to retain the core of the nascent intelligence community formed during the war. However, recognizing the need for a peacetime civilian intelligence service that did not operate in accordance with the laws of armed conflict, a new intelligence service, the Central Intelligence Agency, was formed. President Truman later insisted that his intention in introducing and signing the act had simply been to provide a central point for information gathering and analysis that could serve other agencies, notably the new Defense Department and National Security Council—not to promote espionage, or as he put it, "strange activities."[18]

However, the act explicitly authorized the CIA to engage in "covert action," which it defined as "an activity . . . to influence political, economic, or military conditions abroad, where it is intended that the role of the United States Government will not be apparent or acknowledged publicly."[19] While it risks seeming tautological, this would prove a vital and, in contemporary Washington, increasingly powerful point: the CIA could dabble in operations abroad, even paramilitary operations, but they had to be *secret.* Absent such a finding, the project had to be managed by the Pentagon or another agency.

Recognizing the long history of embarrassing shenanigans involving spies around the world and the risk that covert operations could be used to pursue private agendas rather than those of the government, the architects of the new national security state imposed important restrictions.

First, the ability to run a covert operation depended on express presidential authority. The president was to issue a written "finding" that the covert action was "necessary to support identifiable foreign policy objectives of the United States" and "important to national security."[20] Second, it made clear that the finding could not violate the Constitution or any statute of the United States.[21] The CIA director was to "keep the congressional intelligence committees fully and currently informed of all covert actions which are the responsibility of, engaged in by, or are carried out for or on behalf of, any department, agency, or entity of the United States Government including significant failures."[22] Last, it stressed that secrecy classifications could *not* provide a basis for withholding information from congressional oversight committees.[23]

The national security state that came into existence in 1947 thus reflected deep concern about the unchecked spread of secrecy and a need to reconcile the pervasive secrecy that had existed during World War II with the needs of a democratic society. The people had a right to know a good deal about this new power. They had a right to know, broadly speaking, what it could accomplish and what risks it carried. On the other hand, secrecy served a vital public interest of limiting proliferation of this powerful new weaponry that had for the first time given humankind tools that it could use to extinguish most advanced life on the planet.

The architects of the national security state were keen to ensure that space for public debate was cleared and sufficient information was provided to fuel it, even in connection with strategies for use of the new arsenal and delivery systems. This deliberation may have been limited largely to universities, think tanks, and congressional committees, but it occurred, and it was important to the preservation of democratic process. Without it, the dangers of nuclear testing would have gone unrecognized for years, with great harm to the planet and millions of humans.

The rules laid down in 1947 were far from a uniformly negative development in US history. Harry S. Truman had been an important player in looking into waste and corruption in military contracting during World War II, and he fully appreciated the importance of Congress's role. If anything, he was suspicious that claims of secrecy flowed too smoothly in Washington's security establishment.

Truman, Dean Acheson, and other architects of the national security state were interested in consolidating the authority and power of the executive branch and in securing a huge budget. They wanted to perpetuate the advantages America had at the outset of the cold war.

But they also understood that this vast new defense establishment existed to protect more than the people, fields, and factories that were America. It also existed to protect a set of democratic values that marked America and distinguished it from its totalitarian adversaries. From this perspective, secrecy was a powerful and necessary tool that presented serious threats if not kept under control.

Weber, writing at the end of World War I, saw one potential effective check on overblown claims of secrecy: parliamentary oversight. This provided a means for independently checking the works of bureaucrats and forcing them to account for mistakes and wrongdoing, notwithstanding claims of secrecy. This requires of course that secrecy not be invoked against congressional oversight. The new national security state built off this premise and expanded upon it. But the bureaucrats had different ideas.

The crisis of secrecy that exists in America today cannot fairly be laid at the doorstep of the new government system that was introduced in 1947. Planners had foreseen the problem, drawn reasonable protections against it, and laid out a course to preserve democratic dialogue. But the architects underassessed the power of secrecy. They failed to see how the newly created institutions of the national security state would use secrecy to expand their power and authority beyond anything Congress anticipated. They did not foresee that Congress would be no match for intelligence services commanding enormous budgets and vast staffs and, most importantly, adroitly manipulating secrecy.

. . .

The cold war was waged on new battlefields, and it was very expensive. Universities and research laboratories had taken a leading role developing new weapons technologies during the war, and that role accelerated with the refinement of those technologies after the war. That was still only a fragment of the new empire that was being built. Defense contracting ballooned out of proportion to what had existed before the war. Successive American administrations also provided generous budgets to train and educate an impressive new national security elite consisting of military and intelligence professionals, as well as scientists and other academics skilled in international relations theory and area studies. This was to provide the spawning grounds for the lords of secrecy.

Vietnam emerged as the first war that was designed and run by these elites. Their effort was an embarrassing failure. As David Halberstam wrote, these experts devised "brilliant planning which defied common sense,"[24] and they were averse to subjecting their policies to popular deliberation or discussion, or to accepting the people's view about them. Indeed, among the many mistakes made during the Vietnam War, offenses against democratic process are among the most obvious and egregious.

As has happened on other occasions in our history, this had at least to some degree to do with the war being an unwanted distraction in the mind of the executive. It was *supposed* to be a minor military operation, nothing of particular consequence. Lyndon Baines Johnson was far from an advocate of the war. He had inherited it from his martyred predecessor—or more significantly, in his view, from Kennedy's brain trust.

For Johnson, his presidency was about a great social transformation in America: hallmark civil rights legislation and a series of dramatic social programs that were collectively styled the Great Society. Vietnam was an unpleasant distraction. He didn't want to commit resources to it, and he didn't want it to dominate the public dialogue. But he would be disappointed in both expectations.

Vietnam was in its essence the national security experts' war, and it emerged from their design, prepared by think tanks, academics, and the cream of the government's national security intelligentsia. Much of this occurred, moreover, in secret, subject to high-level classifications, and out of the eye of the public—and to an alarming degree, Congress as well.

It was a striking departure from prior American wars in other ways as well. There was no meaningful public debate about whether the country should go to war and commit its fighting men and resources. The early phases of the conflict were justified as an exercise in training and capacity building for the forces in Vietnam's south: there had been fewer than 17,000 American military advisers on the ground when Kennedy died, and Kennedy had signed a memorandum authorizing a drawdown. In 1965, however, a decision was made to raise the number to 180,000 and take a direct role in the fighting. By the end of Johnson's presidency, 535,000 soldiers were on the ground. Vietnam had become the definition of the term "mission creep."

The closest experience the American people had with a "go to war" decision came with the Tonkin Gulf incident and the resolution that followed. The incident involved a military interchange between US and North Vietnamese naval forces in the Tonkin Gulf in August 1964. This formed the basis for a request by President Johnson for authority to use military force to assist South Vietnam, which a congressional joint resolution granted.

A secret internal government investigation, declassified and released to the public in 2005, concluded that the case put to Congress and the American public had materially misrepresented the facts, falsely claiming that a second North Vietnamese attack had occurred on August 4, 1964.[25] There is no clear evidence to show that President Johnson knew of this inaccuracy, however.

Apart from the dramatic but fleeting days surrounding the Tonkin Gulf incident, America missed a defining moment of public discourse making a case for war and both the American people and Congress buying in to it. This served the interests of national security elites advising Johnson at the time, figures such as Secretary of Defense Robert McNamara and National Security Adviser McGeorge Bundy, and other senior figures at the CIA and within the military intelligence community: they were pressing a war agenda and viewed the democratic process as an obstacle. George Ball stood as a solitary figure in the senior echelon of advisers opposing escalation and pressing for a fuller, more public debate. This failure to engage in a more thorough democratic deliberation would have very serious repercussions since it deprived the war effort of the vested public support that a public discussion and decision can provide.[26]

As the war ground on and became increasingly unpopular, hundreds of thousands of Americans, particularly the young, were brought to the streets in protests and other actions. The war effort was portrayed as immoral and inhumane, and it fueled a counterculture rejection of dominant cultural values, including both the conservatism of the Republican Party and the welfare liberalism of the Democrats. The vehemence of the reaction against the war had precedents in American history, but not in recent memory. At the same time, bitterness developed among the soldiers, sailors, and airmen sent to fight this war. They sensed the public ambivalence toward their military mission, and indeed many shared it. Earlier generations of returning soldiers were greeted with parades and cheers, with civic outreach and special community-based efforts to smooth their reintegration into civilian life. The experience of troops returning from Vietnam was unsettlingly different. The flawed stewardship of the Vietnam War had led to the most serious fissure in civilian-military relations in the nation's history.

It was a traumatic experience for the nation's security elites. They were troubled about the consequence of a political backlash for the nation's security strategy and for its security and intelligence establishments. They were right. Vietnam led to a series of powerful backlashes.

One of the most important immediate ramifications was development of the total force policy. Looking back at the experience of Vietnam, army chief of staff Creighton Abrams thought it essential that no American president again take the country into a sustained ground war without securing support from the American people. In 1973, he created the total force policy ensuring that the regular Army, the National Guard, and the Army Reserve would be treated as a single consolidated force for such purposes—thus heightening the political profile of a sustained deployment and requiring that political leaders follow proper democratic process in securing authority to act.[27]

The second major piece of fallout was the war powers resolution, which became law after Congress overrode President Nixon's veto in 1973. The resolution resulted from an intense debate in Congress about how the country had gone to war in both Korea and Vietnam, circumventing the process of seeking a declaration of war. The experience of the Tonkin Gulf resolution was parsed. A broad consensus emerged that even in the absence of a declaration of war, the Constitution and sound politics anticipated that Congress would play a role in decisions to go to war or engage in hostilities abroad short of war.

Through this legislation, Congress was putting down markers—requiring the president to make reports, allowing him some flexibility for short-term actions, but also requiring him to seek specific congressional authorization whenever Americans were sent into sustained foreign hostilities. Its authors expected that the precedents of Korea and Vietnam, in which the American path to war had involved little timely congressional discussion, would be avoided in the future.

The intelligence services also came under sharp scrutiny in the immediate post-Vietnam era. The Church Committee and the Rockefeller Commission looked into a long list of intelligence failures and gaffes that proved something of a public humiliation, particularly for the CIA. A long history of covert operations aimed at destabilizing and toppling unfriendly governments was publicly aired, as were a number of failed plots, some of which—like assassination plans involving exploding cigars and LSD—provided material for American comedians for years. Strong measures were introduced to rein in the CIA's covert operations, and particularly its penchant for political assassinations.

But the secret stewards of American security slowly developed a responsive strategy. In surreptitious think tanks where the Vietnam War had been planned and its history had been recorded, there were discussions of the "soft underbelly" of democratic society. The notion that the American public might be swayed by what they saw on their evening television screens about a war, that they might be discouraged by high levels of American casualties and increasingly skeptical about claims of military success, that they might elect congressional leaders who challenged the war and committees that demanded accountability for mistakes and failure—all of this provoked acute concern. Democracy, in other words, was recognized as a threat to the national security establishment and the commercial sector that supported it.[28] Some smart strategies were needed to contain it.

• • •

The solution was clear: the government needed to convince the public that it would ensure its security in a way that ratcheted down public concern with questions about military conflicts.

The initial prescription had to do with the forced conscription of young Americans to fight a war they did not believe in. Some among the experts drew a peculiar conclusion from this: sensitivity to conscription and casualties could strongly influence the public attitude toward war and move opinion against a war over time.

For moral philosophers and religious leaders, of course, this is just as it should be. Society should be concerned for the lives and well-being of those sent into harm's way—the cause for which they sacrifice should be worthy of that sacrifice. But for some of the new national security elite, this was a vulnerability, latent in democracy, that an adversary could exploit in wartime. Many of them adopted a perspective that was fundamentally antidemocratic. Their goal was to diminish public concern about conflicts to ensure a wider berth for action by the president and his handful of unelected advisers. It was a subtle but very effective power grab.

As noted earlier, the first step this produced was a decision to terminate the draft and develop a professional volunteer military. This clearly aimed to mute public concern about the deployment of troops—after all, they were now willing volunteers. But it was also a remarkable departure from America's tradition of a citizen army.

The founding fathers had been strongly guided by examples of classical antiquity in their attitude toward an army. "The Greeks and Romans had no standing armies, yet they defended themselves," Thomas Jefferson wrote in 1814 to his friend Thomas Cooper. "The Greeks by their laws, and the Romans by the spirit of their people, took care to put into the hands of their rulers no such engine of oppression as a standing army. Their system was to make every man a soldier and oblige him to repair to the standard of his country whenever that was reared. This made them invincible; and the same remedy will make us so."[29]

Jefferson was wrong, of course, about the Romans—they did have standing armies. But the Greek model was, as usual, the more compelling. It demonstrated how the army was to be reconciled to the notion of democratic governance.

In Athens, notably, things ran pretty much as Jefferson suggested. All male citizens had to do military service when called, though aspects of that service would be dictated by their wealth—owning a horse to be in the cavalry and buying heavy hoplite armor to serve in the most prestigious infantry units. Nevertheless, military service was a great equalizer and socializer for the Athenians. Even a poor citizen could afford to serve and was usually proud to do so. He knew that if he died on the field of battle, the state would attend to his family and guarantee the proper upbringing and education of his son.[30] Military service was therefore an essential aspect of a citizen's duties, and that service was backed with a dense web of social supports, what we know as veterans' benefits. As Aristotle noted in talking of the rise of Athens' naval power, this intimate interweaving of democracy and military service was a distinctive asset of Athens that contributed significantly to her military might and success over nondemocratic rivals.[31]

In a passage of the *Nicomachean Ethics* that was well-known to many of the American founding fathers, Aristotle had distinguished between citizen-soldiers, motivated by a desire to maintain their own freedom and inspired by concerns for the safety and well-being of their fellow citizens, and mercenaries, moved by a desire for fame and fortune. In his view, only citizen-soldiers exhibited true courage and reliability, whereas mercenaries were the first to run away when their on-the-spot calculus suggested that defeat was more likely than victory.[32] Resting national defense on those motivated by profit making rather than by love of country was profoundly unwise.

These may have been self-evident truths to America's founding fathers, but they were rapidly discarded by the stewards of America's burgeoning national security sector as the cold war faded away.

The second step was to shift a growing part of the national security budget from the uniformed services to military contractors. As the cold war faded and political leaders began to clamor for a "peace dividend," Secretary of Defense William Cohen assembled a group of leading executives from the private sector—almost all of them major defense contractors—and sought their advice. What would be the most efficient way for the Pentagon to downsize while maintaining the nation's security? Cohen asked. To the surprise of no one, these titans of industry were quick with an answer: most of the tasks now handled by the uniformed services could be handled better and more cheaply by private contractors.[33] This advice was enthusiastically accepted by the Clinton and Bush administrations. In 2000, the Pentagon spent roughly $133.2 billion on contractors, but by 2008, that figure had grown to $391.9 billion, an almost threefold increase.[34]

Functions performed by contractors were also dramatically expanded. Throughout the last century, contractors had been deeply involved in essential activities directly related, for instance, to war planning, developing, and testing weapons systems and military vehicles. Contractors were increasingly tapped to provide ancillary services—to relieve uniformed military of the need to cover duties related to housing, sanitation, and food services—so that the military could refocus on core activities directly related to combat. As the military grew more reliant on technology to establish its superiority, the role of contractors naturally grew, but it soon came to invade even the most essential military areas.

Throughout the years of the Iraq conflict, contractors took on such core military functions as interrogating suspects, performing intelligence analyses, and furnishing the perimeter security for forward-operating bases. New regulations authorized contractors to carry firearms and to operate other weapons systems and to dress in combat fatigues, rendering them difficult to differentiate from the uniformed military (and violating the laws of armed conflict).

The number of contractors deployed to theaters of conflict as a percentage of the total force has also shifted dramatically. During the Vietnam War, the ratio of contractors to uniformed military deployed to the region was about 1:60. By the time of the Clinton-era Balkan conflicts, the ratio had changed to roughly 1:5. However, in the Second Iraq War, the contractor count grew steadily until it reached rough parity with uniformed military, and then, in the late phases of the Afghanistan conflict, the number of contractors actually came to exceed the number of uniformed military deployed.

With this, the turn from the concept of the citizen-soldier born with the American Revolution to a heavy reliance on for-profit contractors, prominently including mercenaries, was complete. Two hundred years of American military and civic tradition went out the window.

. . .

These changes were rationalized to the public in different ways: as a response to public concerns about conscription, for instance, or as a claim that contractors are cheaper and more efficient than American service personnel (a claim that was never supported by any convincing facts and was insulting to those who wore their country's service uniform). But one consideration that drove those changes came straight from the experience of Vietnam.

Americans react negatively when their young men (and over time, women) spill their blood overseas, are killed, maimed, or disabled. But that reaction is softened when the soldiers are volunteers, the sons and daughters of economically marginal families with less access to influence over media and government. And the response is softer still when the dead are contractors.

Indeed, the Rumsfeld Pentagon was so sensitive to these matters that it took special steps to mute the word of deaths. Photographers were forbidden to capture pictures of the caskets of American service personnel returning from theaters of war at Dover Air Force Base, Delaware. The tradition, followed from the Civil War, by which the president or the secretary of defense penned letters to survivors and attended funerals and memorials ceased. These practices focused undesirable public attention on the deaths.

As the force footprint shifted from men and women in uniform to contractors, the task became easier. The Pentagon failed to keep track of casualties involving contractors or make whatever information it had public. It focused on keeping reports of fatalities and injuries to a minimum, whether this corresponded to the facts or not.

And this critical fact, born of the Vietnam experience, also helps explain the last and most important shift in the American way of war. It paved the way for the era of robotic warfare, which began to emerge with drone technology.

5

DRONES AND THE ART OF STEALTH WARFARE

Cursed be he that smiteth his neighbour secretly. And all the people shall say, Amen.

—DEUTERONOMY 27:24

A CASUAL STUDY OF MILITARY HISTORY points to a tight relationship between form of government and style of fighting. For Aristotle, Athens' rise as a naval power was not coincidental because the navy was the natural tool of a democracy, just as the cavalry served aristocratic states. The political structures of Rome, first as a republic and later as an empire, were firmly embedded in the institutions of the Roman military, which served increasingly over time as a sort of superstructure for the state. The age of chivalry, which blossomed in Europe's gothic age, appeared to make this point even more firmly. In more recent times, waxing militarization and large-scale mobilization have been portrayed as essential elements of an authoritarian or even a totalitarian state, which uses serial emergencies, threats from abroad, warfare, and military discipline to eliminate internal dissent.

After World War II, America found a new formula: focusing on control of the skies and evolving technologies as the keys to securing its power. This approach was cast as essentially democratic, but over time the aura of democratic control and accountability has faded. In its place stands a pact with technology-based elites, whose power and influence have steadily grown.

The lords of secrecy have chosen a favorite weapon that helps identify them and define their power. It is the Predator drone. The armed drone has one attribute above all others that endears it to the national security elites: it is a consummately secret weapon.

America's arrival on the world stage as a global power and ultimately as the preeminent world power has been linked from the outset to development and mastery of the technology of warfare. Investment in this technology has been enormous; since the end of the cold war, America's defense spending has fluctuated between 35 and 50 percent of the global total—with America's closest allies accounting for a considerable share of the balance.[1]

American technological achievements have driven the course of modern warfare—pioneering airpower, introducing the instruments of nuclear war (and making first use of them in anger), and developing missile systems that took the prospect of war into space. Viewed in this context, drone technology seems a rather modest accomplishment (especially compared with the introduction of thermonuclear weapons), but its importance to war fighting in coming decades is dramatic.

American combat casualties were seen in the period after Vietnam as the key trigger of public concern likely to tether the executive to democratic process and accountability. Ending the draft and shifting the footprint of forces deployed to rely heavily on contractors were two important steps in addressing this vulnerability. But technology offered a further refinement that might, with time, almost eliminate the risk of serious harm to American personnel on the battlefield: robotics.

America's air and missile forces were capable of making strikes with modest risk of loss, but occasionally aircraft would be shot down and pilots killed or captured. What if those pilots were not inside planes but in a control room at Creech Air Force Base in the searing desert northwest of Las Vegas?[2] If the vehicle were incapacitated or knocked out of the sky, there would be disappointment, even frustration, but the pilot would simply go home and eat dinner with his family. The risks were limited to property loss and damage.[3]

This explains the extensive investment in the development of tactical weapons, especially a new generation of robotic weaponry, starting with the Predator drone. It was outfitted with cameras and other sensors, and was used for reconnaissance. It was a natural asset for intelligence services, including the CIA. But soon the potential advantage of arming the drone with lethal weaponry, such as the Hellfire missile, was realized.

By November 2002, the drone thus became a key instrument of surveillance and a tool for assassinations. The CIA's interest in drones from the outset was obvious. But the decision to arm drones with missiles raised a prickly concern: it made the drone an airborne weapon that logically would fall under the primary jurisdiction and control of the Air Force.

There is a dark side to what first appears as a strategic advantage. The value placed on an individual human life, particularly in a democratic society, creates incentives to consider carefully the potential unwelcome outcomes produced by the use of force. During the early stages of warfare, as political leaders work to develop a will to fight and depreciate the value of enemy lives, enemies become demonized. But the risk to the lives of fellow countrymen can present a brake against the rush to war.

The development of what is perceived as zero-casualty war technology tends to negate this important brake, and may therefore lead to the initiation of wars with less forethought. This in turn often means a failure to understand the potential unintended consequences of such a war. The introduction of drones continues a trend started with the erosion of the citizen army through the elimination of the draft and the development of a smaller, volunteer military (drawn increasingly from disadvantaged parts of our society) and has continued with the increasing reliance on military contractors.

The Stimson Center convened a blue-ribbon panel of national security insiders to study the evolution of drone warfare. It concluded that "the increasing use of lethal [drones] may create a slippery slope leading to continual or wider wars. The seemingly low-risk and low-cost missions enabled by [drone] technologies may encourage the United States to fly such missions more often, pursuing targets with [drones] that would be deemed not worth pursuing if manned aircraft or special operation forces had to be put at risk. . . . [Drones] also create an escalation risk insofar as they may lower the bar to enter a conflict, without increasing the likelihood of a satisfactory outcome."[4]

The development of drone technology may also be linked to a devaluation of noncombatants in tactical deliberations—particularly when civilians are caught in proximity to ostensibly legitimate targets. Their unintended death or injury may (under Kantian concepts of proportionality that underlie modern law-of-armed-conflict doctrine) be accepted as "collateral damage" provided there is a reasonable relationship between the military objective and the collateral damage inflicted, and provided further that the party launching the attack uses the weapons and tactics available to him that would inflict the least collateral damage while still accomplishing a legitimate military objective.[5] But the application of proportionality rules is one of the great vagaries of international law, and many militaries, including that of the United States, keep many of their interpretive rules a closely guarded secret.

The Obama administration has repeatedly made ambiguous claims of "no" or only "minimal" civilian casualties resulting from the tactical perfection of drone warfare,[6] whereas independent observers have documented substantial numbers of civilian casualties, supported by confirmed killings of women and children.[7] Because of the secrecy surrounding the US drone program and its targeting practice, it is difficult to understand or explain the discrepancy that has arisen between the CIA and its critics on this score. But part of the explanation may rest in the new concept of "signature strikes." For instance, if US intelligence analysis points to a high likelihood that a male between seventeen and thirty-five appearing at a certain bakery in a town in southern Waziristan is a "militant," and facts evolve that match this "signature," then the CIA will view that person as a militant even though there may be no evidence at hand that establishes this fact.[8]

Has the United States made a radical departure from traditional law-of-armed-conflict analysis in determining who is a noncombatant by introducing the "signature strikes" concept? Statements made by Obama administration officials provide good reason to worry,[9] but US secrecy makes it difficult ultimately to judge the situation. The issue of secrecy again raises fair questions about US compliance with international law, and administration actors find it difficult to answer them.

Drones open the prospect for a new kind of warfare that includes targeted killings, known as extrajudicial killings in international law—the ability to strike a target far away from ground or naval forces with a high degree of precision. Throughout history the evolution of military technology has affected the order and nature of states, and it has done so with particular vehemence whenever states fail to take careful measure of these developments and adapt accordingly.

The use of drones involves a significant number of policy issues for the United States:

- Why should the intelligence community control drones as a lethal weapons system rather than for intelligence gathering?

- If the program is secret, what does this mean for our democracy? How will Congress deliberate its use and approve it with some significant public participation—particularly considering that drones may well be used as the first step leading to a war?

- How will drone strikes be accounted for, particularly when mistakes are made and innocent civilians are killed?

- If the decision to use a drone is based essentially on tactical assessments of its utility in any one particular strike, how or when will the longer-term or strategic consequences of its use over a sustained period in a particular theater of combat be taken into account?

- How can we be assured that the right rules governing armed conflict are being applied when civilians operate this system?

- If the United States can use drones to assassinate its enemies, doesn't that mean that Russia, China, or even Iran and North Korea can legally do the same? Wouldn't this be creating a darker and more violent world rather than serving US interests in peace and stability?

These difficult and complex issues evade simple answers. The immediate crisis facing America is that the deliberation necessary to resolve these questions largely hasn't occurred, or not in the ways that our democratic sensibilities expect. This situation is the direct result of the secrecy enshrouding the program, secrecy that has long gone unchallenged but that is fundamentally illegitimate.

Remarkably, only one issue coming out of the use of drones has captured the public imagination in the United States: the covert use of drones to assassinate US citizens abroad. This itself raises disturbing issues and rests on an assertion of executive power that is troubling in some extreme circumstances, but it is hardly the central question raised by the increasing reliance on drones.

The most disconcerting aspect of the drone program has to do with secrecy: What justifies the pervasive claim of secrecy surrounding drones, and what purpose does it serve? This point has gathered remarkably little attention, which in turn demonstrates the power of secrecy as a tool to anesthetize democracy.

. . .

In the past, new weapons technologies became the focus of a well-articulated military doctrine that would be published, briefed, and debated as an important part of the democratic process in our country. Congress would be a full participant, studying, commenting on, and occasionally providing guidance to the process governing the chain of command over, and the conditions governing the use of, important lethal weapons systems. Think tanks would be engaged and would participate, as well as political scientists, ethicists, and legal experts at our universities and colleges.

Secrecy concerns governing some aspects of the technology have always raised problems for this process on the margins, but never as they do today. And the technology involved here is not nearly so secret or proprietary as nuclear weapons or missile systems, for instance. Much of the innovation in robotics that enables drones comes from Japan, Taiwan, Thailand, Singapore, and China, nations that for the most part are not even within our core system of military alliances. The period in which the United States is the exclusive user of this technology is rapidly closing. By the end of this decade, we should expect a half dozen powers to make military use of drone technology.[10]

The development of drones and the tactical and strategic decisions surrounding their deployment are being treated as one of the greatest secrets in the nation's history. The president, the director of central intelligence, and others go through bizarre circumlocutions to avoid even referring to the existence of drones or their use in individual attacks. Consider a speech that President Obama delivered at Fort Myer, Virginia, on September 30, 2011. Only hours earlier, a CIA-operated drone strike in Yemen, taken with White House authorization that was backed by a fifty-page legal opinion issued by the Justice Department's Office of Legal Counsel (OLC), had obliterated a radical Muslim cleric, Anwar al Awlaki.

Born in New Mexico, Awlaki was a US citizen. Obama said that Awlaki's death marked "a significant milestone" and that it was "a tribute to the intelligence community."[11] But the speech was cast in a bizarrely passive voice: Awlaki "was killed," Obama said, excluding the words "drone" and "CIA" or anything else that would suggest the causal connections that the entire world was reading in their morning papers. The text was carefully prepared to reflect the fact that the strike on Awlaki was covert action—a state secret. And so was the law that justified it, apparently.

The legal opinion,[12] crafted by two highly regarded national security lawyers, Harvard professor David Barron (now a judge of the First Circuit Court of Appeals) and Georgetown professor Martin Lederman, had confirmed the president's power to order the killing of Awlaki. But it remained strictly under wraps, as officials like Attorney General Eric Holder stumbled badly in awkward efforts to explain[13] why the president could order the execution of Awlaki with no criminal charges or trial and with only vague and unsubstantiated claims of an immediate threat that he presented to the country.

The essence of the opinion became known in June 2014 after the Second Circuit Court of Appeals rejected the Obama administration's claims to keep it secret, instead ordering that it be declassified and released—with some redactions of factual discussion. When it was disclosed, the OLC opinion was found to carve out authority for a presidential direction to kill Awlaki largely based on established law-of-armed-conflict norms. In essence, it concluded that Awlaki could be assassinated because six conditions were fulfilled:

- Congress had enacted an authorization for the use of military force that clearly permitted lethal strikes against al Qaeda.

- Awlaki was a leader of a group that was either a part of al Qaeda or allied with al Qaeda in its war against the United States.

- Awlaki had participated in attacks on the United States as part of the command of his group and was engaged in planning further attacks.

- Senior US intelligence and law enforcement officers determined that Awlaki could not be captured without an unreasonable risk to the lives and well-being of US personnel engaged in such an effort.

- US intelligence officers also had concluded that Awlaki posed an imminent and continuing threat to the lives of Americans.

- The proposed plans to assassinate Awlaki would have to conform to the laws of war requiring that attacks be necessary and minimize collateral damage to civilians.

This memorandum was therefore hardly a radical departure from prior OLC legal positions, which have consistently sought to put the president's military prerogatives on the broadest possible footing. It had authorized the killing of Awlaki as an enemy commander in the course of an ongoing war. The fact of his US citizenship was not significant in the end. While there was much to question in this memorandum—and particularly the "fact" it assumed that Awlaki could not be captured and brought back for trial because of difficult conditions that prevailed in Yemen—it was ultimately not surprising.

The most disturbing aspect of the opinion was the intense secrecy surrounding it. Normally a government would assert the right to strike and kill an enemy, and it would have little compunction about this. As a passage in Deuteronomy quoted at the beginning of this chapter reminds us, since ancient times stealth attacks have been viewed as illegitimate and immoral. Certainly a government would keep the time and tactics used for its strike a secret, but the public declaration of intention to use lethal force itself serves useful purposes.

However, the Obama administration's posture was hopelessly confused. On one hand, senior figures leaked the fact that Awlaki was a target to American reporters, and defended the decision by then leaking more classified information that had supported the decision to strike. On the other, the legal memorandum was classified and withheld. This created the impression that the Obama team lacked confidence in its own legal position.

The real core of the government's claim of secrecy came, as we will explore in greater depth below, as a result of the legal opinion's discussion of secret agreements between the United States and Yemen.

These agreements were not secret in the normal sense of the word—
they had been fully exposed and discussed through the publication
of WikiLeaks cables, and by admissions in Washington and Sana'a.
In one cable,[14] the American ambassador, Stephen Seche, reported on
a conversation he had with Yemeni deputy prime minister Rashad al
Alimi, in which the two rehearsed the false statements they would
make about drone strikes in an effort to camouflage US operations. To
his credit, Seche expressed doubt that either reporters or the people of
Yemen could be so easily fooled.

A second cable[15] records in detail the substance of a conversation
between Gen. David Petraeus, then heading the US Central Command, and Yemeni dictator Mohammed Saleh, in which they reviewed
the secret agreement on the American use of drones in Yemen. Notwithstanding these disclosures, the Justice Department was required
to treat the cables and the agreement with the Yemeni dictator that
they discussed as if they were secret. This decision was awkward and
served the nation poorly.

Consequently, the attorney general could not explain to the American people exactly why Obama could order the killing of Awlaki by
releasing drones into the skies of Yemen and why he was bound not to
disclose that he had done so, even as reports of this action were leading the news around the world.

Shortly thereafter, on October 15, 2011, Awlaki's sixteen-year-
old son, Abdulrahman—also a US citizen though never implicated in
terrorist activities—was also assassinated by a drone, as Washington
fumbled for explanations.[16] It subsequently became clear that US intelligence was misinformed about both Abdulrahman's age (they thought
he was twenty-one) and US citizenship—errors that proved fatal for
the young man—even though, as journalists quickly discovered, both
facts could easily have been established by Internet searches.

Still, the question of targeting American citizens with drones is a
relatively peripheral one in the overall context of the drone wars. It
appears that American citizens have accounted for no more than four
out of roughly four thousand drone-related fatalities, and in each case
(other than Awlaki's son) the target was viewed as an important player

in a terrorist organization targeting US persons and interests.[17] While this issue has achieved emotional resonance in the United States, it is dwarfed by other policy questions.

The overshadowing issue is secrecy itself. For Washington's national security elites, secrecy is the default state of affairs. If the American public can't make sense of things, too bad. Better that they butt out entirely.

• • •

Secrecy is a critical element of the massive power struggle that played out between the CIA and the Pentagon after 2001. That struggle had its birth in reciprocal jealousy. The CIA had long chafed under the restrictions on its ability to act as a military force in wartime. It had some limited paramilitary abilities, linked principally to covert action and to the protection of its own personnel. These required a presidential finding and oversight by the congressional intelligence committees. However, the CIA was able to play a role in wartime and have a presence in theaters of combat, as well as develop and use proxies for military purposes.

In the Vietnam era, it recruited Hmong tribesmen in Laos and Vietnamese Montagnards to serve as a secret army; it developed tight relationships with military dictators across Latin America, before a wave of democracy sweeping through the region made these relationships embarrassing and unsustainable. And in the decade just past, it helped motivate Ethiopia to invade Somalia, resulting in tens of thousands of innocent civilian casualties—while barely attracting a glance from American media.

Still, when it came to US military activities—calling in an air strike, being picked up by a submarine, arranging to fire a missile against a target—the CIA had been forced to coordinate with the Pentagon. Many CIA leaders were happy with this arrangement and willing to abide by the demarcation set down in the National Security Act of 1947. Others, inveterate empire builders, were anxious to expand the agency's power and influence by converting it into exactly what the act had forbidden: a secret army.

Conversely, some leaders in the Pentagon, including Donald Rumsfeld, were envious of the CIA. In 1947 the agency, which had been pried from the side of the military, was given a report to the secretary of defense, among others, but it saw its role as providing intelligence and intelligence analysis to the White House. The CIA was supposed to collect and analyze data that could be used for defense purposes, among other things. While not directly under the Defense Department, the agency was just one star in a constellation of intelligence services in which the Pentagon was dominant.

Over time, however, the CIA worked hard to build a special liaison with the White House. It delivered the president's daily briefing and sought to position itself as a core part of the White House national security team, with a voice at the table equal to the key cabinet secretaries—state and defense.

Rumsfeld coveted some of the agency's powers, particularly its covert operations in areas far from any military battlefield, which had stretched in the period after September 11 to include an assassination program and a program aimed at snatching suspected terrorists off the street all over the world and "disappearing" them into secret prisons. In these prisons they would be subjected to illegal torture techniques like waterboarding, sleep deprivation, and the cold cell. Pentagon special operations units had some of the same training and programs, but by the traditional military view, a narrower field of conduct.

The Joint Special Operations Command (JSOC), a special unit of the North Carolina–based Special Operations Command (SOCOM), existed before Rumsfeld, but its mission, profile, and budget dramatically expanded during his tenure as secretary of defense in the Bush administration. It effectively became Rumsfeld's clandestine service. JSOC operatives did not necessarily wear uniforms, dispensed with many aspects of normal military protocol, and adopted secrecy as their byword. Consequently, the boundary lines laid down in 1947 were breached on both sides: the CIA got its own army and air force, and the Pentagon got its own CIA.[18]

Washington's national security lawyers, who a few years earlier had no difficulty saying that torture was not torture and finding "legal" ways for the CIA to run secret prisons, apparently also had no difficulty reading the carefully measured distinctions of the National Security Act into oblivion. They found an easy path to authorizing the CIA's covert war in Pakistan, essentially by atomizing a decade-long military campaign into a long stretch of autonomous covert actions.[19] In Washington, it seems, no one dared to challenge the Pentagon or CIA, at least when it came to plans for secret war.

This in turn laid the foundation for the third war waged in the years following September 11, which continues to the present day. The war has three principal theaters of action: Pakistan, particularly in an area the British referred to as the North West Frontier Province, but which today is called the Khyber Pakhtunkhwa, and the Federally Administered Tribal Areas; Yemen; and Somalia. This war has been conducted by the CIA, often liaising with or subsuming JSOC units, using an air force of drones, proxy military forces, and large numbers of contractors.

In the view of the CIA, this conflict is a "covert operation," and indeed the CIA's ability to run it rests entirely on that label.

However, by any reasonable measure, it is a full-fledged war. These operations have involved, over a decade, more than three hundred strikes with perhaps four thousand fatalities, almost all of this in an area that US military strategists describe as the core of the battlefield in the current war.[20] This is definitely not what the authors of the National Security Act had in mind with the phrase "covert operation."

The term "covert" essentially means that the role of the US government is to be kept secret or out of sight. But from whom is the CIA's drone war in Pakistan being kept a secret? From the adversary? Hardly. They watch and track the drones, they know who operates them, and they have a good sense of how they're being used. Al Qaeda and its associated forces in the Pakistani northwest, al Shabaab in Somalia, and al Qaeda on the Arabian Peninsula in Yemen all appreciate that the drones are being operated by the CIA, using bases on the territory of Pakistan, in Djibouti, on nearby islands like the Seychelles, or from American ships at sea. Al Qaeda and its allies understand that they are targets and why. And it serves US strategic interests for them to know this. Moreover, they are essentially powerless to do anything about it.

Or perhaps the US drone war is being kept secret from the people in Yemen, Afghanistan, and Pakistan, where drones are deployed? Again, hardly. They know what's going on, they know this is a US program, they read in reasonable detail about each strike shortly after it occurs, and they see film footage of the results on television. They also understand that the CIA is running this program, and they appreciate that it is being done through some level of consultation with their own government.

Who doesn't know about drone warfare? The people of the United States. A side-by-side comparison looking at the press reports compiled by the Bureau for Investigative Journalism reveals that American news media carried fewer reports and less accurate information about the use of drones than its counterpart in Pakistan.[21] American journalists are largely happy to reproduce what is said in hushed off-the-record briefings provided by the National Security Council (NSC) and CIA and undertake no immediate effort to verify the accuracy of the claims conveyed, least of all by attempting to probe what transpired on the ground in places like Waziristan, mountainous north Yemen, or chaotic Somalia.

Consequently, Americans read in their papers a dumbed-down version of what President Obama reads in the briefing he receives from the CIA, which almost invariably claims that a particular drone has struck a legitimate terrorist target without causing collateral damage. Sometimes these reports are correct. Other times they turn out to be wishful thinking and rather myopic, particularly in their failure to appreciate and report on the unintended but predictable deaths of women and children, innocent victims of the strikes.

This is a hugely consequential point. Secrecy actually made the US intelligence community into the principal source of information for Americans about drone strikes. Rarely do average American citizens or American decision makers get a view of the consequences of a drone strike from ground level, or an opportunity to test the ripples the strike has sent through the society where it struck. American metrics are filled with positive assessments about terrorist deaths, precisely the reassuring information the lords of secrecy would have them know. But US military leaders operating in the theater of combat know that these assessments fall far short of giving a full picture. As the former US commander in Afghanistan, Gen. Stanley McChrystal, stated, "What scares me about drone strikes is how they are perceived around the world. The resentment created by American use of unmanned strikes . . . is much greater than the average American appreciates. They are hated on a visceral level, even by people who've never seen one or seen the effects of one."[22]

Particularly in remote and tribal societies, frequent drone strikes will usually tighten the bonds between Islamist radicals seeking to make inroads and tribal groups, while feeding resentment of the central government the strikes, in theory, support.[23] This sort of reaction may also manifest itself in violence targeting Americans and American interests, and it often does help fuel recruitment for precisely the insurgent groups that the drone strikes are attempting to suppress.[24] It may make drone warfare, particularly when it is pursued as a sustained long-term campaign, self-defeating.

A striking point was furnished on December 11, 2013, when US drones struck a fast-moving convoy in Yemen's Bayda province. The US quickly claimed the killing of an important terrorist leader. Within hours, however, reporters on the scene were streaming footage and interviewing survivors. The drone had struck a wedding convoy. The strike had a clear consequence: Yemen's new parliament voted to outlaw drone strikes.[25]

Much of the systematic and critical investigative work concerning US drone wars has been done by NGO groups operating in NATO allies Great Britain and Germany. In fact, this has been generally true of the conflicts in Afghanistan and Iraq. British commanders have been candid in their discussions with British reporters about the problems they have faced and have rendered open and honest assessments of the accomplishments of their operations.

By comparison, American commanders have been roped into an elaborate public affairs operation designed to present a unified message to Americans about the status of the conflicts. But with respect to the drone war, the wall of silence has been almost absolute. This helps explain why Pakistanis are generally better informed about the drone war and the results it achieves than are Americans. That says a great deal about our obsession with secrecy and the remarkably accommodating attitude that the American media have adopted toward it.

Americans know little about the drone wars because of a US decision to classify them as covert action. And with that decision, for the first time in our history a state-of-the-art weapons system has been placed in the hands of the civilian intelligence service, not the uniformed military, coupled with a mandate to carry out a sustained military campaign stretching now over a decade. Americans seem far better informed about the fact that Amazon hopes to activate a fleet of drones to deliver orders from its warehouses than about the details of the program that has deployed drones to wage war in distant corners of the world in their name.

. . .

It's not my purpose in these pages to critique the use of drones in military conflict or to suggest that the United States shouldn't use them at all. But the country needs to have a well-informed public discussion about the legal rationale for the use of drones as a part of our democratic process. And more than that, we need a broad discussion about the costs and benefits of the drone program, informed by an honest recounting of the facts—not just in the view of the intelligence community stretching to justify itself and hold on to the privileged position it has secured in counterterrorism warfare vis-à-vis the uniformed military. The public needs to hear from other well-informed and potentially less self-interested sources. Much hangs in the balance.

The drone war has undermined the authority of the civilian government in Pakistan and is being used by Pakistan's increasingly dangerous and radicalized military to secure an inner-state control over a nation that George W. Bush designated a "key non-NATO ally."[26] However, because the use of drones is classified as covert action, we can't have this discussion. The Obama administration didn't want us to know the full legal rationale used by the US government to kill Anwar al Awlaki without first seeking his arrest and extradition, or the rationale governing the deployment of drones in Somalia and other nations, because attorney general opinions on these topics have been classified.

Why are these drones not under military control? That is the single most obvious question to pose with respect to the covert drone program. It was raised by Philip Alston, a professor at New York University who studied the growing US reliance on drones for the United Nations.[27] For Alston, allowing this important weapons system to drift into the hands of civilians presented obvious problems. Uniformed military are trained in the law of armed conflict and understand how to operate a weapons system consistently with it. The military also has a clear system of accountability for serious mistakes. None of that is true with respect to the civilians running the drone program.

The same question was being raised at the highest echelons of the military. Even inside the White House, then–director of national intelligence Dennis Blair was pressing the point. He had apparently challenged the decision to give the CIA a fleet of drones and continue its military-tactical mission in Pakistan. He argued vigorously that the success of the program had to be measured by factors much broader than the kill ratio on specific strikes; in particular its broader consequences for the situation in Pakistan had to be assessed.[28]

Admiral Blair came under heavy attack from the CIA for his views, and he was evidently accused of violating the cloak of secrecy for even obliquely suggesting in public remarks that the CIA ran the drone program in Pakistan. He was forced out of the White House. The firing of Admiral Blair in 2010 shows how secrecy can be used in sniping within the national security establishment itself to silence and eliminate critics, particularly those who challenge the CIA's tactics in public. It was far easier to silence the critics than answer them.

Putting drones in the hands of the uniformed military would address many of the most serious objections against the use of drones. By allowing the CIA to control them, Washington has ensured that the drone program is overseen by civilians—often political hacks—and that the lawyers who advise on how it should function become political actors. These matters should all be in the hands of uniformed military leaders who have the specific professional training to address them, and the lawyers who consult should also be military officers trained in the law of war. Blair fully appreciated these shifts and their consequences. He wasn't afraid to point out that the emperor wasn't wearing any clothes. But apparently making such observations publicly was a betrayal of court etiquette binding on the lords of secrecy.

The CIA's drone war in Pakistan is unfaithful to the vision of the National Security Act of 1947, which provided a clear delineation between the roles of the military and those of the CIA. By calling the process "covert action," however, a cloak has been drawn over the new reality: we have built a militarized CIA, reversing the fundamental guidelines laid down at the creation of our national security state at the end of World War II.

But to date the public has been offered no satisfactory explanation of the decision to allow the CIA to wage covert war in this fashion. The most plausible explanation, suggested by a study of the redactions that persist even in documents that have been forced into the public, points to one persistent but hushed basis for the claim of secrecy: diplomacy.

As Pakistani writers such as Ahmed Rashid and Akbar Ahmed have documented,[29] the drone war found its birth in America's difficult dialogue following September 11 with the Pakistani government headed by Gen. Pervez Musharraf. He had seized power following a military coup d'état in 1999, and installed himself as Pakistan's president in 2001. Musharraf exacted difficult terms for the cooperation he afforded the United States in its efforts in Afghanistan and in counterterrorism efforts generally. Among those terms was insistence, worked out in greater detail in a dialogue between the CIA and Pakistan's Inter-Service Intelligence (ISI), that the use of drones would be a closely guarded secret from the Pakistani people, and thus from the world. To help ensure that secrecy, the ISI had insisted that the operations be conducted by the CIA rather than by the uniformed military. The CIA was, of course, well practiced in keeping secrets from the public, but it was a piker compared with the ISI.

This accord, forged between two intelligence services pressing their own institutional interests, provided the essential legal predicate for the CIA's drone war in Pakistan. Remarkably, one decade later, it continues to do so.

. . .

From the earliest days of the republic, American political leaders have recognized the need to keep diplomatic secrets when essential to national security. But the agreements with the Musharraf dictatorship, and the later agreement with the Saleh dictatorship in Yemen, reveal that the logic of secrecy in such a case is not always beyond question. Indeed, the agreement with Musharraf was a consummate fool's bargain for the United States.

While Americans kept quiet about the drone program, Pakistani military and political leaders—many of whom were fully briefed about the secret accord, but not all of whom supported it—did not. Instead, they railed against the United States, charging that the drone strikes were illegal, were unauthorized by the government, and were slaughtering innocent women and children. This steady deluge of criticism accomplished something that in Pakistan's highly factious political environment seemed nearly impossible: political parties across the spectrum became united on a single point, disdain and contempt for the United States.[30] This in turn proved the Achilles' heel of the drone war.

President Obama, vigorously defending his heavy reliance on drones, has argued that "dozens of highly skilled al Qaeda commanders, trainers, bomb makers and operatives have been taken off the battlefield. Plots have been disrupted . . . these strikes have saved lives."[31] The speech was most remarkable for its failure to appreciate the serious problems that the drone campaign had unleashed. But even if each strike was a success based on the purely tactical measuring stick employed by US intelligence, the entire war would be a miserable failure if the upshot was that insurgent organizations were able to bolster their recruitment efforts as a result.[32] Or if Pakistan, the world's fastest-growing nuclear power, was turned from America's ally into an enemy. And both may well be the case. This failure and Washington's extended delay in recognizing it are tied, in turn, inextricably to secrecy.

Officials in Washington also failed to recognize that diplomatic secrecy of the Yemeni and Pakistani variety raised fundamental questions for democratic process. In the Pakistani case, secrecy between the ISI and CIA placed the United States clearly on the side of a military dictatorship and opposed to democratic process within Pakistan, for indeed the Musharraf regime was concerned that, if it was put to the test democratically, the Pakistani people would not countenance their drone war bargain with the United States.

But the flip side was arguably still more significant: by entering into this secrecy accord, the CIA was taking its new war in Pakistan off the table of democratic debate in the United States. There would be no discussion of the war in public, no accounting to Congress (except behind closed doors, in a fashion that Congress could hardly check) or to the American people for the conduct of the war. Democratic process was short-circuited in the face of a Congress remarkably unwilling to assert itself.[33]

Why should the intelligence community have the power to disable democratic safeguards inside the United States by concluding a secret agreement with a foreign dictatorship? And why, particularly, when that dictatorship itself disregards the bounds of secrecy and behaves in a disloyal if not perfidious manner? If ever there was a compelling case for disregarding diplomatic secrecy, this is it.

The only real explanation that emerges is that the use of drones for sustained covert military campaigns serves the interests of the lords of secrecy. It enhances their power and allows them to avoid criticism and accountability for tactical errors, some of them fairly spectacular—as demonstrated by the drone war in Pakistan.

THE WAR ON
WHISTLEBLOWERS

News is what someone wants suppressed. Everything else is
advertising. The power is to set the agenda. What we print
and what we don't print matter a lot.

— MAXIM FOR NEWSPAPER EDITORS[1]

THE AMERICAN INTELLIGENCE COMMUNITY has been rocked
twice in recent years by unauthorized disclosures of sensitive information that are historically unprecedented in scope. The first
came with the publication by WikiLeaks—a nonprofit organization
dedicated to the publication of classified or secret information by
anonymous sources—beginning in February 2010 of a large cache of
classified State Department cable traffic, which had apparently been
leaked by an American noncommissioned officer with authorized
access.

The second wave struck in June 2013, when former NSA contractor Edward Snowden supplied an immense number of NSA documents—including internal briefing memorandums showing how the
NSA explained its own operations to its staff—to major western media organizations. The US government first argued that these leaks

dangerously undermined national security and placed American service personnel and those supporting them at risk. Under challenge, however, US government officials were forced to step back from many of these claims.[2]

The American intelligence community was undeniably injured with its own public, which quickly learned that intelligence community representatives had long made highly misleading or outright false statements on how surveillance activities affected them. The disclosures also embarrassed key defenders of the NSA, including the two congressional intelligence chairs—Sen. Dianne Feinstein and Rep. Mike Rogers—by demonstrating that they lacked a firm understanding of the NSA programs. Most damaging were the NSA's own internal briefing slides, which contained frank appraisals and explanations of NSA programs that often directly contradicted what NSA leaders had given to the public and to Congress, and that congressional leaders had then parroted.[3] These developments point to the critical significance of unauthorized leaks as a trigger to democratic debate about secrecy, and raise questions about the legitimacy and fairness of government measures taken to grapple with the leakers.

For Weber, there was one obvious way to shield democracy from a bureaucracy armed with secrecy: parliamentary inquiry. It could be wielded aggressively to uncover corruption, ineptitude, and criminality that bureaucrats would inevitably try to cover up. But for Weber's American disciples, who had deeper experience with the practical working of legislatures as well as a more practical sense of their shortcomings, this reliance on a single institution seemed naive.

Daniel Patrick Moynihan and Edward Shils appreciated that legislative inquiry can be an effective check only to the extent that other institutions, such as the press and the courts, supported it by allowing a vital flow of information that the lords of secrecy would not willingly release to the public sector. During and immediately after World War II, the US Congress exercised rigorous checks over military spending and intelligence activities. But in an electoral system dominated by the need for large quantities of cash to fuel campaigns, Congress was increasingly held captive by campaign funders. Oversight of the intelligence sector was particularly vulnerable. Its activities were largely in the shadows and thus removed from the realm of public political discourse.

Over time, intelligence came to focus less on traditional spycraft and more on technological innovations that facilitated surveillance on a scale and over an area previously unimaginable. Washington relied heavily on contractors for these innovations, and contractors absorbed constantly expanding chunks of the defense and intelligence budget, often being direct service providers. Oversight became more complex and more difficult just as economic forces were muting the critical watchdog capacity of the press and of Congress.

The Madisonian model of democracy does not assume a zealous Congress filled with idealistic legislators committed to selfless public service. Rather, it recognizes in juxtaposed interests and political friction a useful tool to produce a more efficient state. It assumes that the legislature will vigorously protect and assert its own powers against the executive—even when both branches are dominated by the same political party.[4] But it also assumes the legislature needs to be motivated to act by the political arena. In the American experience, first the press and then, after World War II, the broadcast media have repeatedly spurred legislative action by critical coverage of current events, and particularly by exposing misconduct by persons in positions of trust or power.

The press recognizes, and history has shown, that persons in positions of power will persistently use national security claims and classifications as a tool to cover up their dirty work—a practice that undermines the credibility of the classifications system and thus undermines national security. Media have therefore consistently second-guessed claims of secrecy, and their record over time suggests that they have been far fairer judges than the government, perhaps erring a bit in the government's favor.[5]

The American experience since World War II has demonstrated three potential checks on secrecy: the legislature, the press, and whistleblowers. The fourth potential check identified by political scientists—the federal courts—remains highly problematic because of the supine attitude adopted by most of the federal judiciary toward assertions of secrecy by the executive branch.

The media's exposé work fuels political debate and primes the legislative system. It regularly furnishes the basis for congressional probes and committee hearings. And that work would be impossible without whistleblowers.

. . .

The term "whistleblower" is used broadly in America today, and it is often claimed by persons who leak classified materials under differing circumstances. Properly speaking, "whistleblower" describes a person who owes a duty of confidentiality to his employer but violates that duty in order to serve the greater public interest by exposing serious corruption, ineptitude, or criminality. In the context of national security affairs, it usually describes a person who, as an employee of the US government or a contractor in government service, has access to classified information and divulges that classified information for purposes of exposing corruption, ineptitude, or criminality.

There is a gap between the layperson's use of the term "whistleblower," which evokes a sense of *public* disclosure, and the way the term is used by government spokespeople. The latter internalize federal statutes requiring the whistleblower to operate within narrow governmental channels, so that their disclosures rarely if ever reach the ear of the public without first going through a government filter. This is how federal prosecutors can vehemently deny that some of the best-known whistleblowers of their generation—such as former NSA contractor Edward Snowden—are in fact whistleblowers. Both sides are correct; they simply draw on different definitions.

Federal whistleblower statutes offer protection against some forms of retaliation. But the scope of the laws is narrow and the protection they offer is to some extent an illusion.[6] The true thrust of these laws is to give bureaucrats a chance to fix misdeeds and keep word of them out of the public limelight; they also serve to identify the leakers, or potential leakers, a fact that may undermine the whole process. The whistleblower is allowed to report abuse to his or her agency's inspector general and, under controlled circumstances and through defined channels, also to congressional oversight committees. Particularly with respect to national security matters, federal statutes do not generally authorize or protect disclosures to the public or to the media.

In some circumstances this form of protected whistleblowing has produced important breakthroughs. For instance, the CIA black site program and the authorized use of torture provoked hundreds of complaints by agency personnel to their inspector general—staffers could not believe that some of the practices being used were legal.

However, the federal whistleblower legislation offers so little protection that it has become irrelevant. The most egregious abuser of the statute—now notorious for suppressing whistleblowers who disclose internal corruption and abuses—is the US Department of Justice.

Whistleblowers contend that going through official channels serves no purpose, since complaints rarely result in corrective measures. Moreover, an individual who files a complaint can easily fall into the crosshairs. He will be viewed as disgruntled and a likely leaker. His communications may be monitored. His career may run off the tracks, and, with the typical loss of security clearance, he may find himself out of a job.

Two CIA whistleblowers I interviewed told me that almost immediately after they approached the Senate oversight committee for a dialogue, they were summoned by managers and asked to account for their dealings on Capitol Hill. Was access to congressional oversight being monitored by the agency? Were there moles in the committee staff reporting back on contacts by agency personnel? In any event, approaching and dealing with congressional overseers were widely reckoned as a very risky proposition. This experience shows how whistleblowing following the narrow path permitted by federal statute is rarely a serious option in national security cases.

Nevertheless, recent American experience points to the whistleblower, operating at grave personal risk, as the last and best hope to check antidemocratic abuses of secrecy. The whistleblower's best shot at impact comes from influencing public opinion, usually through the media. This in turn can cause the executive to change its conduct or can influence Congress in its management of legislation or even in the appropriation of budgets for agencies seen to have seriously abused the system.

Whistleblowers have always had a tough time in Washington, with its well-established pattern of repression. An internal investigation is opened, the whistleblower loses security clearance and then is dismissed from the job on the grounds that he or she no longer holds the security clearance that is an essential predicate to the job. The government has worked hard to make these security clearances unreviewable by courts; the result is that a whistleblower can be fired and courts are cowed from exercising their power to step in and protect him or her no matter what the whistleblower protection laws say.

Barack Obama tells us that as a young lawyer he once represented a whistleblower. As a presidential candidate, he pledged to "strengthen whistleblower laws to protect federal workers who expose waste, fraud, and abuse of authority in government."[7] Within a few years, that pledge had been replaced with a starkly different reality.

Under President Obama, the Justice Department's national security division—which is effectively a private law firm for the benefit of the intelligence community—has staked out plans for a prosecutorial war on whistleblowers. It now relies on the Espionage Act of 1917, suggesting that whistleblowers are spies for some foreign power even when there is no evidence to support this. The Justice Department has now brought eight Espionage Act prosecutions, nearly three times the number brought by all prior presidents combined, from Woodrow Wilson through George W. Bush. Indeed, the Obama team picked up and pursued at least two prosecutions that its Bush administration predecessors could not persuade themselves to act on.

The first attempt to use the Espionage Act on whistleblowers was Richard Nixon's prosecution of Daniel Ellsberg and Anthony Russo over the publication of the Pentagon Papers. Many of the markers of the Ellsberg case are still with us today. One is the high level of political direction involving senior government figures who feel compromised by the disclosures. Then come hyperbolic claims about harm to national security resulting from disclosure. Much to his credit,

Solicitor General Erwin Griswold, who argued the case for the Nixon administration, subsequently acknowledged that the claims of threat to national security he presented to the Court were alarmist and untrue.[8] All the initial prosecutions failed in the Ellsberg case. Had the courts become disgusted with the dishonest, unethical, and illegal conduct of government agents?

The techniques used against Ellsberg and Russo were extreme and extralegal. Ellsberg was defamed with scurrilous claims and portrayed as mentally unhinged. Richard Nixon's White House "plumbers," whose break-in at the Watergate ultimately brought down his presidency, also burgled the office of Ellsberg's psychiatrist trying to find compromising evidence. The failed Espionage Act prosecution of Ellsberg and Russo also discredited the use of the Espionage Act in cases not actually involving espionage—until the George W. Bush administration, there was a sole instance of its use. The case in the interim involved Samuel Loring Morison, a US intelligence officer, who apparently leaked satellite photographs of two Soviet naval installations to *Jane's Defense Weekly* in 1984. That prosecution was successful, but it drew heavy criticism across the political spectrum and Morison was pardoned by President Clinton in 2001.[9]

Pentagon Papers–style prosecutions of whistleblowers were revived again by the Bush administration. Its strategy against whistleblowers, which has been carried forward and amplified by the Obama administration, has been criticized as an attempt to import into the United States key elements of the British Official Secrets Act.[10] Whereas American secrecy legislation generally imposes duties on specific persons who have clearance to receive classified information, the British legislation is far broader in the duties it imposes. In essence it is a legal regime perfectly suited to a monarchy, which places its emphasis on rights of privacy—first and foremost those of the Crown. This system is out of place in a democracy that prides itself on free speech, a free press, and a well-informed and sovereign electorate.

Under the Official Secrets Act, secret information can be likened to radioactive material: everyone who touches it is infected and becomes a potential target for prosecution, whether or not the person is under any agreed duty to the state to maintain its secrets. The Justice Department used this theory in the Bush years against two lobbyists with the America-Israel Public Affairs Committee (AIPAC), Steven Rosen and Keith Weissman.

The two were accused of conspiring with a former Defense Department analyst, Lawrence Franklin, who was also charged under the Espionage Act, to steal classified information and pass it to Israel. What prosecutors sought to portray as a serious case of espionage for a foreign power was dismissed by many observers as information horse trading of the sort that commonly transpires with think tanks and lobbying groups in Washington.

This marked the first use of the Espionage Act to prosecute individuals who are not government employees and have no formal duties with respect to classified information.[11] It would have sent a chilling message both to the Washington think tank community and to journalists about their liability stemming from the use of classified information. The judge handling the case, T. S. Ellis III, seemed conscious of the Justice Department's tactical use of the case, and did not approve. Judge Ellis repeatedly issued procedural rulings against the government, causing the prosecution effort to disintegrate.

Undaunted, the Obama Justice Department is continuing to use the Espionage Act in a series of prosecutions against bona fide whistleblowers where no suggestion of actual espionage exists. Moreover, prosecutors now engage in elaborate steps to forum shop for federal judges who are likely to take a sympathetic rather than critical view of the spinning of the Espionage Act.

One Espionage Act case, brought in August 2010, involves Stephen Kim, a contractor for the State Department, who noted during a Fox News interview in June 2009 that North Korea might be preparing to test a bomb. His statement lacked much specificity and was the sort of information that national security policy analysts routinely disseminate to the press. The prosecution was subject to a great deal of sharp criticism.[12] Apparently the Justice Department also investigated Fox News journalist James Rosen, seizing his phone records and emails without notice of a subpoena and tracking his physical movements over a period of time. In an affidavit filed in the case, Rosen was even identified as a "co-conspirator."[13] Kim pled guilty to a single count of the indictment after stating that he could no longer afford to defend himself against the prosecutorial onslaught. He was sentenced in April 2014 to a thirteen-month prison term.[14]

A second case, brought in December 2010, involves Jeffrey Sterling, a former CIA officer who allegedly gave Pulitzer Prize–winning *New York Times* correspondent James Risen details on Operation Merlin, a CIA covert operation that aimed to delay Iran's development of nuclear weapons by providing Iranian scientists with seriously flawed designs. The plan backfired when the Russian physicist the CIA had recruited for the project discovered the design flaws and pointed them out to his Iranian interlocutors.[15]

The project was grossly inept and counterproductive, and disclosure of these facts may or may not have harmed American national security interests, but they were hugely embarrassing to the CIA. Prosecutors secured access to many of Risen's communication records without issuing a subpoena and have demanded that Risen appear and testify about his dealings with Sterling, a confidential source, steps that attracted enormous criticism. The Justice Department has stood behind the prosecution, while openly acknowledging that the decision to call Risen raises serious issues with respect to freedom of the press.[16] The Sterling case is awaiting trial as of this writing.

A third and particularly disturbing case involves Thomas A. Drake, a winner of the Ridenhour Prize, who disclosed to the *Baltimore Sun*'s Siobhan Gorman evidence of corruption and ineptitude in the management of the Trailblazer data management contract by the National Security Agency. Gorman's articles on this subject won her the prestigious Society of Professional Journalists exposé award.[17]

Former NSA head Michael Hayden was obviously concerned about the exposure of mismanagement of the Trailblazer program but was equally troubled by the prospect that the leaker may have disclosed information about still more controversial, and certainly illegal, Bush-era surveillance programs. Hayden and other senior figures at NSA appear to have pressed aggressively for Drake's prosecution, possibly as a way of silencing him and chilling the relationship between whistleblowers and journalists covering the NSA generally.

Disclosing the $1 billion contract cesspool did nothing to harm Hayden's career. To the contrary, applying the Washington rule under which demonstrations of managerial incompetence rarely go unrewarded, Hayden qualified for his next promotion: to head the NSA's still bigger brother, the CIA. Drake's experience validates Weber's core thesis that, given the opportunity, a bureaucratic institution will always use secrecy to protect itself from the disclosure of incompetence or corruption.

The Drake case collapsed under pressure from the judge who heard it, Bush appointee Richard Bennett. The government salvaged a plea bargain based on Drake's "exceeding the authorized use of a government computer,"[18] an offense rarely charged but routinely committed by government workers. However, Judge Bennett decided to use the sentencing hearing to render a verdict that prosecutors hardly expected. He retraced the melodramatic conduct of prosecutors from the opening of the case, noting their loudly touted public charges and how charge after charge had been exposed as false. He compared the conduct of the Justice Department unfavorably with the British practice of general warrants, which had fueled the American Revolution. "It was not proper. It doesn't pass the smell test," he noted. Judge Bennett pressed the prosecutors to know who at the Justice Department had made the key decisions to charge Drake and to publicly humiliate him with bogus (but privileged) press statements and by staging a raid on his home. The prosecutors offered no answer, leaving the culprits to hide behind institutional anonymity.[19]

By contrast, Judge Bennett heaped praise on Drake for his strong record of public service and his clear commitment to the public good. While the judge turned the hearing into a pillorying of the Justice Department, the case was still in a sense a victory for the intelligence community. A whistleblower had seen his career destroyed, not by a legal process involving the judgment of his peers but by the heavy hand of the state.

The Justice Department may not win its cases in federal court. It may even be criticized by a federal judge who gets a clear sense of how the department's national security division abuses prosecutorial powers for the benefit of the national security state. But in the end, it can consider many lost cases as successful just the same: it has chilled the environment concerning classified information and nipped in the bud a great deal of national security reporting that would otherwise help the public understand what their government is up to.

Most significantly, it sends a clear message to would-be whistleblowers: *We will destroy you. You will lose your pension, your savings, your house. You won't be able to send your children to college or find a job commensurate with your education and experience. We will make your life a never-ending hell. And the courts and your attorneys will be powerless to help you in any way.* The Drake case shows us a Justice Department prepared to abuse its massive powers for the benefit of the intelligence community. It also points to the immense imbalance in power among national security prosecutors, the courts, and accused whistleblowers.

In June 2013, a twenty-eight-year-old computer technician named Edward Snowden—who worked for the intelligence community's leading consulting firm, Booz Allen Hamilton, inside the NSA's huge Hawaii operations center—emerged on the public stage when NSA documents he leaked to a media group that included the *Guardian* and the *Washington Post* first began to appear. Apologists for the American intelligence community, led by California sen. Dianne Feinstein, criticized the young former NSA contractor for leaving the country. If he was convinced he was right, they argued, Snowden should return to the United States and face his accusers.[20]

Even in democratic countries, trials in the national security arena tend to be affected by a peculiar type of justice: the state holds the upper hand and is often quick to silence the accused and hobble his or her fair defense. The Drake case demonstrates compellingly that Snowden would be foolish to return without first securing an agreement with the Justice Department, and any nation could find sufficient grounds to accord him political asylum if it chose to do so.[21] Guilt or innocence in the current American system counts for relatively little, because the national security state is no longer willing to accept the risk that a jury will acquit one of its targets. It will find a way to destroy him, and legal due process will not stand in its way.

The use of the Espionage Act has another dramatic side effect: it puts the government in a position to force journalists to disclose their sources. Prosecutors will tell the journalists who published the leak: *You did no wrong, you acted within your rights, but you must tell us who gave you this information. And if you claim confidentiality of your source, we'll put you in prison.* This assumes that the prosecutors don't already know the identity of the source, and as the Sterling and Kim cases witness, that is rarely the case. Today, federal prosecutors enter the courtroom with copious data reflecting the call records and Internet searches run by journalists, among other matters—all information obtained without ever subpoenaing the journalists themselves.

How do they get this information? That of course is often confidential. But it points to the highly collaborative relationship that has emerged between telephone and Internet service providers and the US government. Today it seems the US government doesn't even need to ask, much less subpoena, to secure the data it wants. The challenge it faces is most often not *knowing the facts* but avoiding giving an account for *how it learned them.*

• • •

When challenged about Espionage Act prosecutions, senior prosecutors offer a formulaic set of defenses. Thousands of leaks occur every year, they acknowledge, but only a tiny number ever become the subject of an investigation, and fewer still are ever prosecuted. They claim it is exceedingly difficult for investigators to actually identify the leakers and the leaks. Prosecutors also note the challenge of bringing prosecutions in a sensitive environment—if they are to bring charges, they may have to agree to the disclosure of sensitive information that could be raised in the course of the litigation.

This accurately reflects current federal law concerning the use of classified information in criminal prosecutions, which strikes a fine line between the defendant's right of confrontation and the state's ability to keep secrets.

Finally, these cases almost invariably involve journalists, and prosecutors claim that giving deference to the First Amendment and the free press in the American system leads them more often than not to elect not to press charges.

These statements may be true historically to some extent—and that reflects positively on the American criminal justice system. Prosecutors and criminal investigators *should not* have access to phone and Internet records in the absence of probable cause and subpoenas authorizing the production of material. Further, any prosecutor contemplating a whistleblower prosecution that directly affects the press should be thinking about the political ramifications of the question. *How will it look for me to be challenging a whistleblower and a newspaper for revealing something that embarrasses the government and points to corruption or wrongdoing by government officials? Won't it look like vindictiveness or an attempted cover-up?* Prosecution of whistleblower cases is one of several areas in which political accountability for prosecutorial decisions is both normal and appropriate. And the prospect of that accountability should make a prosecutor think twice about bringing charges.

But one claim frequently made by prosecutors in this regard is utterly untrue. When challenged about the whistleblower prosecutions by the *New Yorker*'s Jane Mayer, then-Assistant Attorney General Lanny A. Breuer said, "You don't get to break the law and disclose classified information just because you want to." He added, "Politics should play no role in it whatsoever."[22] In fact, precisely the opposite is true, and Breuer, the head of the criminal division as whistleblower prosecutions peaked, is fully familiar with that fact. Decisions to prosecute those who disclose classified information are inherently political, and political figures routinely break the law and disclose classified information with no consequences whatsoever.

The official justifications do not furnish an honest appraisal of the situation.[23] It would be more accurate to say, as noted by a character from the British sitcom *Yes, Minister*, that Washington is a "ship of state that leaks from the top." Politics within the Beltway is to a very large extent practiced by the art of leaking. Tens of thousands of such leaks occur in the course of any political cycle, and the leakers often include political personages of both parties and senior figures in agencies of the government. These leaks have a variety of different purposes, many of them well recognized within the established political etiquette of the Washington Beltway.

Parallel to the culture of leaking, we find a culture of raising accusations about leaks—almost invariably driven by figures who are themselves notorious leakers. This is a sort of Beltway political blood sport in which points are scored both by leaking and by proving that a political rival has leaked. It is worth taking some time to explore different kinds of leaks and the functions served by each.

An administration figure might be on the verge of an important decision—to nominate a controversial person to a high office, to seek funding for a sensitive but problematic weapons program, to authorize a tactical deployment of military forces in an emerging crisis, or to implement a new policy not yet known to the public but likely to draw fire from important interest groups. One time-honored form of leak involves testing the political waters beforehand to draw out potential adversaries and understand their possible lines of attack and to assess the viability of a contemplated decision in the forum of public opinion. This invariably involves sensitive information for the administration, and it may involve information that is still classified—such as the existence of a weapons program still in development, or the decision to deploy an aircraft carrier group to a location close to a building conflict. This sort of leak serves as a trial balloon to see whether a sufficient political consensus can be formed to support the initiative. It may also be used to reassure an ally that his concerns are appreciated and being acted on, or, conversely, to send a message to an adversary that the administration is taking steps that may lead to a more forceful and more public response.

Another type of leak has to do with the ego of the leaker. This brings us to the dangerous area of amateur psychology, suitable for discussion in broad terms but rarely an appropriate basis for conclusions in any specific instance without a more comprehensive evaluation. The leaker may be demonstrating self-importance through access to privileged information. Ego gratification is often suggested by prosecutors as the reason for leaks made by low- or midlevel bureaucratic officials. But more frequently, the leaker may be seeking to develop a special rapport or relationship with the leakee—who may be another government official with certain power and influence or a journalist.[24] This may be done through a process of swapping of secrets, and journalists who receive classified information may often be plumbed by their leakers for other pieces of the mosaic of secrecy. While ego gratification may be relevant to the conduct of leakers, a far more compelling case can be made linking it to prosecutors—many of whom are eager to build name recognition with the public and to lay the foundation for a career in politics.

Leaks may also serve partisan political, factional, or institutional interests—and indeed the leak is perhaps the single most underappreciated tool used in struggles between political factions and government agencies. Excellent examples can be found in the struggle to uncover details surrounding the intelligence failures that paved the way to the tragedy of September 11, 2001—with the CIA regularly scurrying to cover up its missteps, and sources close to the FBI repeatedly stepping forward to disclose them. This interagency game of leaks reflected the two agencies' sparring over an ascendant role in counterterrorism operations, but it was also essential in enabling the public and Congress to understand the serious mistakes that were in fact made.

Leaks regularly occur through inadvertence or by mistake. During a visit to wartime Iraq in March 2009, Rep. Peter Hoekstra made tweets concerning the position and activities of the congressional delegation in real time, compromising ongoing operations.[25] When the president made a surprise visit to Kabul in June 2014, the Obama White House issued a guest list for a formal dinner, divulging the identity of the CIA's station chief.[26] There is nothing in either case to suggest that these disclosures resulted from a conscious decision to make public sensitive or confidential information.

The most important form of leak involves whistleblowers. By definition, a whistleblower leak occurs when a person with proper access to classified information discloses discrete information based on a conclusion that this disclosure is necessary to reveal incompetence, corruption, or criminality.

While it is easy to ridicule and dismiss, the culture of leaks serves important functions in the political system. As the American government becomes entangled in secrecy—much of which is illegitimate or at least serves no compelling purpose—there is a healthy need to ensure that political discussion among policy makers and the public is properly informed. The process of declassifying and releasing information is so slow and cumbersome it hardly serves this purpose in a timely way. But sporadic leaks do. Similarly important, leaks frequently occur in the political process to call political actors to account for false or dishonest statements that otherwise would be permitted to stand because of secrecy.

This culture of leaks, what one notable commentator calls the "leaky Leviathan,"[27] does not reflect a dysfunctional government. Rather, it shows how the political system copes with an excess of secrecy that otherwise would stagnate and stultify.

These considerations serve to focus concern on the current war against whistleblowers. The fact that a tiny minority of leaks leads to investigations or prosecutions ultimately must be explained in this context. It has nothing to do with the limited investigative capacity of the government, because the disclosures surrounding the NSA have made clear that these abilities are historically without precedent. But it does have a great deal to do with the recognition by prosecutors that strict, literal enforcement of secrecy rules across the board would be devastating to the nation's political process. Consequently the decision to prosecute is driven not by technology or the law but by internal political considerations. The decision of senior Justice Department officials to mislead the public about this fact, rather than to make public the systematic criteria they apply in coming to decisions to prosecute, is disturbing and only serves to heighten concerns of political chicanery and intrigue that have always surrounded Espionage Act prosecutions of whistleblowers and that seriously undermine confidence in the fair administration of justice.

This insight in turn suggests that the process leading to these decisions to prosecute and the considerations motivating it should be parsed very carefully. Just because a prosecutorial decision is "political" does not mean it is inherently improper or wrong. In this context, "political" does not necessarily mean "reflecting partisan political calculations," which is the most common use in Washington—as Karl Rove would use the term. Rather, it may reflect the interests or concerns of the state at a higher level, reflecting "politics" in the way philosophers since Aristotle have used the term.

• • •

Several different theories have been advanced to explain the war on whistleblowers. One is that the Obama administration, while paying lip service to the importance of whistleblowers, has consciously launched a formal campaign to punish them and intimidate the media. But if such a decision has been taken, there is remarkably little evidence of it. Policy shifts of this sort are usually accompanied by formal policy statements—speeches given by the president or other senior officials. Regulations would reflect the crackdown, with new prosecutorial guidelines to nail them into place. But official statements on the issue of leakers and whistleblowers are infrequent and show little evidence of a conscious shift in policy.

A far more plausible explanation for the rise in the number of Espionage Act prosecutions of whistleblowers is that it reflects the rise of the lords of secrecy—the growing power and influence of national security elites, and particularly the group that sits at the apex of the intelligence system.

If this is the case, then the Obama administration is exercising light or ineffective policy oversight and management in the face of national security elites. The Obama team may say positive things about the social and political utility of whistleblowers, but it lacks the conviction or fortitude to act on what it says or to challenge entrenched elites— figures like former NSA and CIA director Michael Hayden and his successors, Keith Alexander, Leon Panetta, and John O. Brennan, who may well have played key roles in pressing these prosecutions forward.

If we evaluate the Obama administration's response to major leaks, it seems to support this analysis. In the case of the WikiLeaks and Snowden disclosures, senior administration officials rushed forward to stress the harm that these disclosures would do. Obama's national security adviser, Gen. James Jones, stated that "they could put the lives of Americans and our partners at risk, and threaten our national security."[28] Jones stressed that WikiLeaks never sought comment or approval from the US government before making its releases. But curiously, he did not criticize the *New York Times*, the *Guardian*, or other publications that ran or reported on the materials.

Official spokespeople proceeded to identify and stigmatize Pvt. Chelsea Manning (formerly known as Bradley), the twenty-two-year-old soldier who was accused of, and later court-martialed for, having leaked materials, including some 250,000 classified diplomatic cables, to WikiLeaks, which in turn passed them to highly reputed media organizations. Manning was incarcerated in harsh conditions, including enforced nudity, at Marine Corps Base Quantico in Virginia. The brutal circumstances of her treatment provoked widespread international criticism, including from State Department spokesman Philip J. Crowley, who called Manning's treatment "counterproductive and stupid" and was forced to resign.[29]

United Nations rapporteur Juan E. Méndez investigated Manning's conditions of confinement and concluded that they were "cruel, inhuman, and degrading."[30] Department of Defense general counsel (subsequently Homeland Security secretary) Jeh Johnson traveled to Quantico to personally investigate the matter. Johnson was remarkably tight-lipped about what he found,[31] but the Quantico brig commander was replaced soon thereafter.[32] Manning's conditions of confinement then improved markedly.[33]

Private Manning's case for being a whistleblower is debatable for several reasons. One is the sweeping nature of the disclosures and the absence of a strong contemporaneously articulated desire to disclose *specific* wrongdoing, criminality, or corruption.[34] Another is the special interest any government has of maintaining the security of classified information by military personnel in a military setting. The Manning case also reveals the fury, essentially indifferent to law and facts, that the national security state can muster when it feels threatened by leaks.

This seems to reflect a careful strategy developed by the intelligence community for thwarting large-scale leakers. A Department of Defense counterintelligence study from March 2008[35] addressed the threat presented by WikiLeaks. After giving favorable consideration to steps taken by other nations that WikiLeaks threatened (notably China, North Korea, Russia, Vietnam, and Zimbabwe—nations few Americans would consider a comfortable peer group), the authors formulated this tactical plan: "The identification, exposure, termination of employment, criminal prosecution, legal action against current or former insiders, leakers, or whistleblowers could potentially damage or destroy this center of gravity and deter others considering similar actions." In fact, steps taken by the administration appear to follow this heavy-handed advice.

The demonization of leakers and exaggerated claims of harm may lead to institutional lock-in. When bureaucrats make such claims, they often instinctively back them up, even as evidence develops showing the original claims were false or overblown. Lock-in can lead to aggressive decisions being taken against a suspect, even in the early stages of an investigation.

In the case of Drake, for instance, senior figures within the NSA, including General Hayden, suspected—falsely as it turned out—that he had leaked information concerning the "president's program" of sweeping surveillance. This surveillance program, which remains shrouded in secrecy, was retrenched when acting attorney general James Comey, FBI director Robert Mueller, and other senior Justice Department figures who considered the program unlawful threatened to resign if it was extended over their objections in March 2004.[36]

The program was obviously illegal,[37] and senior NSA figures were apprehensive over the consequences of disclosure for their own careers. For the record they claim, of course, concern only about the harm disclosure would have for the efficacy of counterterrorism surveillance efforts. Drake lost his security clearance and his job, and he was subjected to the public humiliation of having his house searched by the FBI. Drake soon learned that FBI agents had raided the homes of several of his colleagues, pointing guns in their faces and pressuring them to give (false) evidence to support his prosecution.

These statements help make a prosecution inevitable by ratcheting up the internal governmental pressure to prosecute, even when a truly independent and objective prosecutor reviewing the facts would never seek an indictment.

The core change that helps explain the sudden proliferation of whistleblower prosecutions is an internal restructuring of the Justice Department. The 2005 USA Patriot Act reauthorization, which came into effect in 2006, consolidated the national security and intelligence functions of the Justice Department into a new national security division, headed by its own assistant attorney general.

Harold R. Tyler Jr., who ran the Justice Department during the Ford administration, explained to me at the time this legislation was proposed that it would inevitably lead to serious misjudgments being made about whistleblowers. He noted that during the Ford administration, the intelligence community had regularly pressed the Justice Department for investigations targeting journalists who published leaks and aggressive investigations and prosecutions of leakers.

Tyler believed that the law should provide tools for both investigations and prosecutions and that the Justice Department should have broad discretion in both areas. But he also felt that only exceptionally rare circumstances could ever justify a prosecution in a case involving a legitimate whistleblower. The attorney general would essentially have to make the call that the harm was grave enough to offset the damage that such a prosecution would likely do to the political system, and he would have to be prepared to account for this decision in the political arena. "[Attorney General] Ed Levi and I would regularly hear out the demands of the intelligence crowd to persecute some leaker, express our sympathy for their position, and then proceed to do nothing," Tyler told me, "not because we felt the leakers were great Americans, but because those were the demands of our political system."

With the creation of the national security division, however, this process was transformed. Instead of a high-level consciously political call, the decision was effectively being taken by lawyers who understood their role fundamentally as serving the intelligence community. They could be expected to press for prosecutions, because that is what their clients would want. The rise in Espionage Act prosecutions shows Tyler's prescience about this process. The intelligence community has effectively established a beachhead inside the Justice Department; it disposes of its own dedicated team of prosecutors. And this has greatly added to the arsenal at the command of the lords of secrecy.

. . .

The Bush and Obama administrations' resort to Espionage Act prosecutions has consistently been overblown and needs to be curbed before it becomes more deeply entrenched as a Justice Department practice. But this does not mean that not punishing leakers is always an appropriate answer either. The government has a wide array of punishments to mete out, many of which may be better measured to the offense.

For instance, leaks—whether justified on some moral plane or not—may ground a decision to revoke the leaker's security clearance. That in turn may lead to loss of employment and forfeiture of benefits. An individual who has lost his employment in this way will probably find it extremely difficult to find a new job with the government or with a government contractor. This can have severe consequences for the leaker's livelihood and that of his family. Indeed, these steps would have precisely the deterrent effect that the government is looking for—without the drama and overkill.

Prosecutorial *Sturm und Drang* over whistleblowers distracts from vital questions that should be posed to the intelligence community. Consider the case of Chelsea Manning. How did an individual with her background and issues come to have unsupervised access to the entire library of classified State Department cable traffic? The leaks that occurred point to serious lapses in judgment—by persons who supervised Manning and permitted her to have access to the materials. The same question can be asked about Edward Snowden. In both cases fundamental errors of judgment were made in granting access to sensitive information to individuals who felt little obligation to keep it. The failure of oversight and control over classified information—a point that consistently escapes discussion—is a major scandal in its own right. A scandal the lords of secrecy are eager to bury.

Public debate in the United States over national security whistleblowers has tended to swing between two extremes: either the whistleblowers are traitors who merit prosecution and long prison sentences, or they are idealistic heroes who have acted selflessly for the public good. In fact neither label precisely fits the figures whose disclosures have rattled the lords of secrecy. Most whistleblowers are guided by a mixture of idealistic and selfish motives.

But such debates are ultimately a distraction. What matters is the information leaked. Was it important to stimulate a public policy debate? Did it lead to change? Did the public learn something that caused it to reassess the performance of its government and take a more critical view? If these questions can be answered in the affirmative, then the whistleblower has made a positive contribution to American society, and he deserves to be credited. In that case, perhaps prosecutors should not be targeting the whistleblower but rather those whose betrayal of the public trust he or she has exposed.

A review of national security whistleblower cases highlights another issue that the lords of secrecy would rather not discuss. In the American empire of secrecy 854,000 Americans hold top secret security clearance, and roughly 5.1 million have secret clearance.[38] Is it reasonable to assume that such an enormous community of persons with access to highly classified materials can keep secrets? In writing of the preparations for the catastrophic Sicilian campaign that marked the beginning of the end for democratic Athens, Thucydides comments that when more than a tiny handful of persons know tactical secrets, they are unlikely to be kept.[39] Benjamin Franklin, in his *Almanack*, wrote, "Three may keep a secret, if two of them are dead."[40] Modern psychology[41] and human experience attest to the wisdom of these observations. But by creating a massive inner state of persons with clearance to share secrets, and allowing great numbers access to highly classified materials archived on central data storage, have the lords of secrecy not in fact crafted a system in which it is unreasonable to expect that many secrets will be kept? The secrecy regime they have created is ill suited to actually keeping secrets precisely because it affords access to so many.

Similarly, for all the discussion of deterrent effect, there is little to suggest that the prosecution of bona fide whistleblowers does anything to help the state keep secrets. When a whistleblower has actually served public interests by providing information that fuels public debate and forces the government to shift its position—as manifestly is the case with Edward Snowden, for instance—his prosecution is likely to enrage well-informed citizens, fuel still more leaking, and undermine public confidence in the fairness and integrity of the criminal justice system.[42] For this reason, the Department of Justice perspective that has controlled most of the last century but has fallen away in the department's recent fit of policy senility—that whistleblower prosecutions should be brought only in the most exceptional of circumstances—is correct.[43] The war on whistleblowers has become a whip that the lords of secrecy use to flog those who criticize them or expose their errors and lies to public scrutiny.

7

THE PATH TO QUASI-WAR: LIBYA AND SYRIA

Our city is thrown open to the world; we never expel a foreigner in order to prevent people observing or finding secrets that might be of military advantage to the enemy. This is because we rely, not on secret weapons, but on our own real courage and loyalty. . . . We are free to live exactly as we please, and yet we are always ready to face any danger. . . . We love beauty without indulging in fancies, and although we try to improve our intellect, this does not weaken our will. . . . An Athenian citizen does not neglect public affairs when attending to his private business. . . . We consider a man who takes no interest in the state not as harmless, but as useless; and although only a few may originate a policy, we are all able to judge it. We do not look upon discussion as a stumbling-block in the way of political action, but as an indispensable preliminary to acting wisely.

—THE ORATION OF PERICLES[1] (C. 430 BCE)

I HAVE ARGUED THAT THE RISING POWER and influence of the American national security elite are attributable mainly to the use of secrecy as a tool. In essence, classification regimes are used to lock in and control analysts down the chain of command and to exclude vital national security issues from effective public debate and hence from democratic process. Instead, only the lords of secrecy and their acolytes provide the vital information and analysis that lead to decisions on war and peace: whether troops should be committed to a struggle on foreign soil, aircraft should be deployed, or drones and cruise missiles used for strikes. This transformation has been gradual.

A serious consequence of secrecy is that the American public is mostly unaware that this change has occurred. The CIA's proxy war in Ethiopia and its drone wars in Pakistan, Yemen, and Somalia, discussed in previous chapters, are striking examples of this process.

This is also true of conflicts that are in the public eye, but with a heavy tilt toward covert engagement and a reluctance to present the issue directly to the American public and to Congress. The Obama administration's management of its deployments in both Libya (2011) and Syria (2012–2014) provides striking examples of a limited military engagement undertaken by the president on the advice of national security elites, without the process of public and congressional consultations that have been characteristic of most prior American governments.

In the United States, decisions about going to war are made in a tradition shaped by the Constitution and prior practice. Still, the rules governing decisions about the sustained use of military force may be one of the most unsatisfactory aspects of our 225-year-old Constitution. What exactly did the framers intend? Clearly there were divergent views among them, and consequently the system they settled on preserved a good deal of ambiguity. Obviously they didn't intend every petty projection of military force to be governed by the declaration of war clause. But just as obviously they believed that sustained use of military force overseas needed to involve the democratic process in some fashion.

George Mason said during the Constitutional Convention of 1787 that he was "for clogging rather than facilitating war,"[2] and he saw a separation of powers as a means to that end. Before he became president, Madison thought that a continuous state of war was poison to democracy.³ His solution was to ensure that the process of deciding to make war was shared among the executive, the Congress, and the people. But does the Constitution actually contain the tools necessary to accomplish this? More than two centuries later, that remains an open question.

It is also fundamentally a political question that may be resolved differently based on the disposition and attitudes of the individuals who populate the executive and the legislature at any given moment. While no one would question the president's authority to defend the country under attack or launch a riposte in response to an attack, the more enduring war power still assumes a process in which Congress is consulted and gives its consent, and this occurs against the backdrop of public debate.

The objective is clear: whenever possible, the decision to wage a war should be borne by the people, Congress, and the president in unity. The decision should not reflect a desire to retaliate in the heat of the moment. It must follow a process that "subjects will to reason," as Madison wrote. The cost of the war and its long-term and unpredictable consequences should be fully explored. The risk otherwise is that the executive will use war making as a tool to enhance his own powers and strip the powers of the other branches.⁴

The spread of secrecy and the growing size and power of unelected national security elites present a serious challenge to this arrangement, however. National security elites instinctively argue against publicly disclosing the essential facts they consider to limit national security options and to drive decisions. They also tend to press for quick action, arguing that an emergency justifies bypassing democratic process. Similarly, they prefer to sidestep the legislature and avoid giving realistic prognoses of costs associated with actions they advocate. They prefer to present a bill based on a fait accompli, placing the Congress in the politically untenable position of having to defund a military expedition already actively engaged if it wishes to show its opposition.

The consequence of these developments is a growing role for the national security elites in all aspects of decision making, and a shrinking role for Congress and the public. The process is, therefore, antidemocratic in its very essence.

Moreover, those who acquire, hold, and use power rarely want to relinquish it. Consider the case of Barack Obama. In 2007, the *Boston Globe*'s Charlie Savage asked then-Sen. Barack Obama whether the president could authorize the bombing of Iran without first seeking congressional authorization in circumstances presenting no imminent threat to the United States. Obama's answer was clear and succinct: "The president does not have power under the Constitution to unilaterally authorize a military attack in a situation that does not involve stopping an actual or imminent threat to the nation."[5]

That statement respects the Madisonian premises of the American Constitution. But let's consider now how President Barack Obama actually acted in two more recent incidents. First, I will consider the decision to commit US forces to enforce Security Council Resolution 1973 in Libya. Then I will discuss White House policies toward the Syrian civil war, specifically the use of chemical weapons against civilians.

. . .

The civil war in Libya that provided the context for American military intervention alongside key NATO allies can be linked to the leaked publication of secret American diplomatic cables. The WikiLeaks publications of 2010 and 2011 had some clear repercussions for global politics. One was in Libya's neighbor, Tunisia, where confidential American diplomatic cables portraying the venality and corruption of the regime of President Zine el Abidine ben Ali resonated strongly with the populace and helped fuel a popular uprising that drove him from office.

Thus began events that were variously called the "Arab Uprising" or "Arab Spring," a series of popular uprisings across the Arab-speaking world from Morocco to the Persian Gulf, each featuring its own particular blend of local grievances and propelled by a combination of oppositional forces of various stripes, running from advocates of liberal democracy to Islamist militants. The complaints of the protesters focused on the brutality and kleptocratic ways of politically entrenched elites and demanded governments that were responsible and accountable to the people.

The Arab Uprising destabilized the region, but it was nevertheless saluted by political leaders across the American political spectrum, who tended to see in it a validation of their own views about democratic governance and even a sign of the regional transformation that neoconservatives had sought in the invasion of Iraq. In the end, regimes fell in Tunisia, Egypt (twice), Libya, and Yemen, while in Morocco, Jordan, and Oman, governments were shuffled in deference to protests.

In Syria, a bitter civil war was unleashed that ground on for years, while other nations were rocked with violent protests. These events presented a significant challenge for American foreign policy elites— some scrambled to cast them as the logical and positive fruit of American intervention in the region, the spontaneous eruption of demands for democracy.[6] Others saw in them a dangerous expansion of radical Islam that would now threaten seemingly stable American allies, such as Morocco, Saudi Arabia, and Bahrain.

The Arab Uprising presented unusually difficult challenges to Americans who sought to form a foreign policy consensus and launched a (sometimes frantic) effort to identify parties the United States could comfortably support.

Two facts at the core of the Arab Uprising were embarrassing to America's intelligence community and had to be swept under the carpet at all costs. The first was that domestic intelligence community partners of American intelligence were in almost every case a focus of popular rage. One of the unifying cries of the uprising was "dignity," and widespread human rights abuses—torture and the systematic humiliation of prisoners—were tightly associated with state intelligence services throughout the Arab world.

As a consequence of the American wars in Iraq and Afghanistan and special counterterrorism operations, these same practices— waterboarding, hypothermia or the cold cell, forced standing, and even more gruesome techniques—were also associated directly with

US intelligence operations. As one astute observer of these regional developments put it, "Denials of fair trials in Guantánamo, CIA black sites, renditions of terrorist suspects to third countries known to torture, and legal formulations paving the way for 'enhanced interrogation techniques' all brought discussion of human rights further to the fore of Arab consciousness. Instead of viewing human rights as a Western imposition, increasingly it became a language that Arab populations embraced to challenge America's post-9/11 policies."[7]

Hence the uprising mingled demands for popular sovereignty and transparency that resonated with American elites, together with a sharp condemnation of the use of torture, which produced muffled embarrassment to them. But the intelligence services themselves, which had become the dominant point of contact for American national security elites, were the real focus of ire whose removal and punishment were being called for.

Second, America's vast intelligence network, which had over the prior decade refocused its analytical efforts from its cold war adversaries to the Middle East, simply didn't see these developments coming. The CIA had witnessed a full-scale and systematic intelligence failure—every bit as astonishing as the intelligence failures in misassessing the Soviet Union during the cold war and being blindsided by the Iranian Revolution in 1979. And just as in the prior cases, it responded by stamping its shortcomings "top secret" to protect itself.

This pointed to two key failings in American intelligence. One was the shift away from human intelligence gathering (intelligence gathered from actual interaction with human beings) to signals and communications intelligence (information assembled through intercepted communications—increasingly telephone- and Internet-based communications), which had been extremely profitable to certain contractors, but left the American oracles with a remarkably weak grip on what the people actually thought. The second was the heavy reliance on local intelligence services for an understanding of what was happening in their countries.

But domestic intelligence services were hardly going to reveal their unpopularity and weakness to their American friends. To the contrary, they could be counted on to do everything in their means to disguise their weaknesses and demonize their adversaries.

Notwithstanding an intelligence community budget that exceeded $80 billion at the time,[8] America was flying blind into a crisis. Perhaps this helps explain why the government didn't want the public to track its maneuvers too closely.

Weeks after the ben Ali government collapsed in Tunis, an uprising began next door in Libya, with large-scale demonstrations in the nation's second largest city, Benghazi. Libya had been the idiosyncratic fiefdom of Col. Moammar Qaddafi since he toppled King Idris in a coup d'état in 1969. Shortly after Qaddafi consolidated his power, he shut down America's Wheelus Air Force Base in Tripoli. He proceeded to chart an independent and unpredictable course, at times using Libya's wealth to help position himself as a leader of the nonaligned movement.[9]

Libya had long been linked to terrorist groups. Washington elites viewed it as a pariah state—a fact that was punctuated by President Reagan's decision to authorize bombing raids on Libya in 1986 following the bombing of a Berlin discotheque in which Libyan intelligence operatives were implicated. That situation had gradually changed under George W. Bush, as the United States and United Kingdom pursued a thaw in relations with Qaddafi in late 2003. Qaddafi took the initial steps necessary for the change by decommissioning his country's nuclear and chemical weapons programs in December 2002.[10]

This rapprochement was led by the intelligence services, and Stephen Kappes (who later emerged as the CIA's number two) was involved in meetings with Qaddafi that steered the turnaround.[11] Qaddafi was concerned about the consequences of being labeled a target in the global war on terrorism, while US and British policy makers wanted Libyan cooperation on counterterrorism planning and access to Libyan hydrocarbons, among the largest reserves close to the European heartland.

A popular uprising against Qaddafi in early 2011 and the dictator's brutal threats against the rebels produced a sudden shift in sentiments. Calls resonated in western capitals for military intervention under a recently coined doctrine of humanitarian law called "responsibility to protect."[12] Military force would be deployed to stop Qaddafi loyalists from massacring the disloyal populace in Benghazi and in other towns and cities that flocked to the opposition. Still, the Obama administration initially signaled great reluctance to become entangled in hostilities on Libyan soil.

Only two days before US aircraft dropped bombs and unleashed Tomahawk missiles over Libya, National Security Adviser Thomas E. Donilon—also widely known as "an unnamed White House source" because of his heavy-on-background briefing practices—was assuring reporters in the White House that the conflict in Libya did not affect essential national security interests. In other words, he was suggesting to them very strongly that the United States would not become involved militarily. Then the administration did a sudden and largely unexpected about-face, with Hillary Clinton, Susan Rice, and Samantha Power apparently persuading Obama that the Pentagon's reluctance to intervene was a mistake, and that the United States should at least provide the initial air support and technical backup requested by NATO allies.

Still, the president delivered no Oval Office speech to the nation explaining what he was doing and asking for the people's support, nor did he or his secretary of state appear before the United Nations to present their rationale (though significantly, they did obtain the Security Council's mandate).[13] The president sought to limit public attention to the Libya mission. This was a political calculus, but it was also driven by secrecy concerns.

The Libya effort, particularly in its first stages, consisted disproportionately of covert action: sending in paramilitary figures to assist in targeting, after-strike assessment, and training of the embarrassingly disorganized but enthusiastic rebels. The covert strategy was a massive, historically unprecedented, and highly successful operation that targeted and peeled away Moammar Qaddafi's inner circle, a tactic that probably contributed far more to his collapse in the end than hundreds of bombing sorties. It demonstrated the White House's continuing reliance on the intelligence services and their paramilitary capabilities over the more traditionally dominant role of the uniformed military.

Congress was not asked to give its assent, and no congressional leaders moved to do so even in the absence of a request. On April 1, 2011, the Justice Department's Office of Legal Counsel issued an opinion finding the president had the authority to act without explicit congressional authorization. Justice reasoned that the "operations in Libya would serve sufficiently important national interests" and the scope of the operations did not amount to "war" in the constitutional sense.[14] Unfortunately for the Justice Department, Defense Secretary Robert Gates directly contradicted both of these conclusions in a congressional appearance a few days before the mission started.

Gates had cautioned that essential national security interests of the United States were not implicated, and he warned that the initial steps necessary to implement the no-fly zone then under discussion would amount to acts of war under traditional analysis.[15] These facts gave the OLC opinion a distinctly hollow, formalistic resonance. It looked like a document drafted after the fact to cover a decision already taken. And that's exactly what it was.

Note that my concern here—as throughout the book—is not whether the Libyan intervention was lawful, or even whether it was wise in terms of national security policy. It is simply whether the consultative process was observed—whether the president made his case for committing military assets abroad in a sustained conflict to the American people and the Congress, built support for the decision, with the Congress voting its assent through some vehicle such as a resolution or authorizing legislation.

Sensible people supported or opposed the military intervention in Libya from a variety of different perspectives. Some argued that the emerging international law doctrine of "responsibility to protect" warranted action to defend Libyan civilians from Qaddafi's forces, the posture that is adopted in Security Council Resolution 1973, others that intervention was warranted from various national security perspectives, including the threat that a sudden surge of refugees from North Africa into southern Europe would present for the Atlantic alliance. But a majority of America's senior military apparently opposed the intervention on the grounds that the military, engaged in land wars in Iraq and Afghanistan, was overextended, and the national security interests implicated in Libya were too remote.

Democratic deliberative process is less concerned in the first instance about who is right on the merits of the decision; rather, it is focused on the need that arguments be developed fully and publicly so that an informed consensus can emerge behind the decision ultimately taken. The president, the Congress, and the people should stand together on this decision.

Moreover, no one ever intends to get into an interminable quagmire. But there is an unwarranted tendency at the start of many military engagements to expect that they will be resolved quickly, favorably, and cheaply. The process of public debate and congressional consultation is intended to check this kind of wishful thinking—and to ensure that there is public acceptance of potential costs and risks in the event of war.

Why did Obama feel he could simply dispense with steps that generations of American presidents had taken? There is no clear answer to that question, but it seems likely that a consensus had formed among the national security elites advising him to that effect. President Obama announced at the outset that the scope of American support for the operation would be limited, heavier at the outset and then more reserved as a greater role passed to NATO allies France and Great Britain. The facts largely bear out this description, though it is difficult to identify the point at which other NATO allies took the lead in operations from the United States.

But there are serious questions about whether the United States and its allies acted within the limits of Resolution 1973. Within weeks, discussion about "responsibility to protect" was supplanted by a demand for "regime change," as presidential advisers insisted that the people of Libya could only be protected by removing Qaddafi from office and installing a new regime.

This is a very important fact from the perspective of fidelity to Resolution 1973. In addition, it means that the political premises of the military operation were changed after the fact. (Similarly, the Second Iraq War was justified to the American people and the world as a strike to eliminate weapons of mass destruction, whose use against the United States was alleged to be imminent; later the war was justified as an operation to install a democratic government in Iraq.) The change from a humanitarian purpose (defending a civilian population threatened by its own government) to an operation focused on nakedly political objectives, such as decapitating the existing regime and installing a new one, also weakened the administration's claim that it was not a war in the constitutional sense. As that term was used around the time of the writing of the Constitution (in connection, for instance, with the Polish partitions of 1772, 1793, and 1795),[16] it is clear that a military operation aiming to topple one sovereign in order to install another would very likely have been viewed as war.

The Obama administration made a clever but troubling argument: the operations in Libya were not war in the constitutional sense because no ground forces were committed and there was little risk of casualty to American forces. Essentially, the administration argued that the development of zero-casualty military technology—beyond the contemplation of the original drafters—drove the definition. But if American technological developments keep apace, then America will be able to project immense lethal force around the globe with robotic and similar high-tech weaponry and there will be ever fewer occasions to deploy large numbers of troops.

Nevertheless, Libya marks a powerful and terrible precedent when it comes to an executive taking the country to war. The constitutional process for decision making was viewed as a sort of irksome formality, ultimately addressed with a rubber-stamp legal opinion.

The conduct of Congress, particularly the Senate, was equally discouraging. Congressional leaders who had advocated engagement in Libya seemed to turn on a dime when the president actually took that step. A series of maneuvers followed, apparently designed to embarrass and isolate the executive, not to deliberate the proposed engagement and approve or reject it. Tactical partisan machinations were the rule of the day.

The behavior of the American Congress was particularly embarrassing when contrasted with America's major democratic allies that shared the operation. In the United Kingdom, the government introduced the question of the Libya mission to Westminster within forty-eight hours; it was fully and publicly debated and Parliament took resolutions expressing confidence in the government to proceed.[17] Even in France— with a far weaker tradition of parliamentary oversight, and under the Fifth Republic, a tradition of strong executive guidance of the armed forces in times of conflict—the government moved the question before the Assemblée nationale; it was the subject of lengthy televised deliberations, and a resolution of support was voted, all within a few weeks of the first hostilities.[18]

By comparison, in the United States, only the House of Representatives took up the question in any meaningful way. The House conducted televised debates in early June 2011 and then adopted H.R. Resolution 292,[19] which noted that "the President has failed to provide Congress with a compelling rationale based upon United States national security interests for current military activities regarding Libya." Section 3 directed the president to submit a report within fourteen days describing the "President's justification for not seeking authorization by Congress for the use of military force." The resolution was adopted by a 268-to-145 vote.

A thirty-two-page report was submitted in response,[20] buttressed by the testimony of State Department legal adviser Harold H. Koh.[21] The administration argued from the outset that the president had independent constitutional authority to direct the Libya operation without congressional authorization. It did not explicitly challenge the legality of the war powers resolution (WPR) but advanced the argument that the Libya operations were undertaken within its terms because they were not "hostilities":

The President is of the view that the current U.S. military operations in Libya are consistent with the War Powers Resolution and do not under that law require further congressional authorization, because U.S.

military operations are distinct from the kind of "hostilities" contemplated by the Resolution's 60-day termination provision.

One wonders what the author had in mind in referring to "further congressional authorization," as plainly the executive had obtained *no* explicit and direct congressional authorization for the operations up to that point (or thereafter).

This is an audacious and worrisome precedent, with the administration essentially arguing that as long as it limited its war-making powers to drones, missiles, and aircraft and put no boots on the ground, it was free to wage war without concern for the restraints of the war powers resolution. But it is now also evident that the White House had to fish deeply in its reserve of legal talent to find someone who was prepared to go to Capitol Hill to defend it. Caroline D. Krass, the acting associate attorney general in charge of OLC who authored the equally dubious April 1 opinion, and Jeh Johnson, then general counsel at the Department of Defense (and subsequently secretary of Homeland Security), apparently declined to do so.[22] The lot fell to Koh. A former dean of Yale Law School and the author of a leading treatise on foreign policy and the Constitution, Koh is widely regarded as the most important scholar of his generation in this field, but his testimony about "hostilities" had even ardent supporters cringing. Both Democratic and Republican leaders in Congress ridiculed this explanation.[23]

Political sniping in the context of deliberating questions of war and peace is inevitable, and a perfectly normal aspect of any democratic political dialogue. But it is not a substitute for full deliberation and a clear decision. Congress notably failed to take any formal action, either to approve or to obstruct the executive's conduct of Libya operations, even after the sixty-day period authorized by the war powers resolution expired on May 20, and the further thirty-day withdrawal deadline expired on June 19.

Congress embarrassed itself in a way that suggested a failure to appreciate the earnestness of the matter. It demonstrated a striking lack of political will to enforce the institutional interests of Congress under the Constitution and it left the war powers resolution exposed as a doubtful or impotent piece of legislation. Conversely, it failed to challenge a presidential claim to the unfettered right to make war, as long as he relied on drones and other breakthrough technologies developed in the quest for zero-casualty warfare.

• • •

Weeks after ben Ali fled in 2011 and his regime in Tunis collapsed, a civil war erupted in Syria—a nation woven from a fragile patchwork of secular and religious Arabs: Sunnis, Shias, and Christians as well as Armenians, Kurds, Alawites, and other groups. The situation quickly deteriorated into a proxy war, with Russia, Iran, and Hezbollah siding with the regime of Syrian president Bashar al Assad, while Turkey, Qatar, and other Gulf states and Saudi Arabia sided with various rebel groups.

The Obama administration criticized the Assad regime for human rights transgressions and voiced sympathy for the rebels opposing his government and opposition to the Russian, Iranian, and Hezbollah assistance flowing to him. However, the White House appeared reluctant to intervene in the conflict militarily. But in the summer of 2012 President Obama signed a national intelligence finding that provided the basis for covert operations designed to support the rebels.[24]

While information about these activities—including training operations in Jordan and close coordination with allies such as Turkey and Saudi Arabia—floated around Washington and were reported heavily in European media, they received relatively modest attention in the American press,[25] suggesting once more its willingness to respect the secrecy of pending covert military operations. Interestingly, one of the major leaks of information about the covert operations came in connection with a secret briefing the White House gave to two critics, Arizona sen. John McCain and South Carolina sen. Lindsey Graham, in an obvious effort to placate them.[26]

An important turning point in the conflict came when reports began to circulate documenting the use of chemical weapons, and particularly the lethal nerve toxin sarin. President Obama then stated that if Assad used chemical weapons during the civil war, this would cross a "red line" and would "change his calculus."[27] In December 2012, he escalated this rhetoric, stating to Assad that "there will be consequences, and you will be held accountable," if Assad's government made use of its chemical weapons, particularly sarin gas.[28]

Further reports of the use of sarin spread in April 2013, gaining increasing support from French, British, and Israeli intelligence services.[29] While the American intelligence community first equivocated on the issue,[30] advocacy for strikes against the Assad forces as a response to chemical weapons use began to mount. The White House seemed to be a model of caution. However, by mid-June the White House was condemning the Assad government for an attack using sarin that cost between 100 and 150 lives; it stated that the attack "crosses clear red lines."[31] The linkage between the sarin gas attacks and the Assad regime continues to be controversial, with a majority view in western intelligence circles accepting that the attacks can be traced to forces loyal to Assad while a minority point to plausible scenarios of intrigue involving the opposition, which clearly wanted to use Obama's red-line rhetoric to extract further support from the western powers.[32]

Immediately thereafter, Obama apparently stepped up covert support to Syrian rebels and began consultations with key allies, including British prime minister David Cameron and French president François Hollande, concerning the use of force against the Assad regime. Discussions evidently focused on coordinated air, missile, and drone strikes on Syrian government forces believed to be associated with the use of sarin, with the United States playing the lead.

Obama is said to have shared tactical plans developed by the Pentagon, and also the cautions raised by American military planners about the operation. It would be very difficult to eliminate the Assad regime's chemical weapons capacity without deploying ground forces to secure the storage areas and manage removal of the materials and some delivery systems, the Pentagon had warned. This would draw American forces directly into the conflict for the first time, and could easily entrap the forces used in a longer ground campaign. Obama is said to have expressed his disdain for the plan and felt frustrated at having been drawn into it through his own red-line rhetoric.

Ultimately this initiative fizzled out, as America and its allies accepted a Russian proposal for the supervised dismantling and removal of Syria's chemical weapons arsenal as a compromise.[33] But what is striking for my purposes is how the three major western democracies went about committing forces for a lethal assault on another state that would have been an unambiguous act of war.

David Cameron, following British precedent, recognized that the British government could not proceed without putting the question to discussion in Parliament. On August 29, 2013, during an eight-hour debate, the prime minister was inundated with skepticism, a good deal of it from the ranks of his own Conservative Party. Ultimately the question went down to defeat, 285 to 272. The debate revealed that public opinion had been "well and truly poisoned by the Iraq episode," as Cameron stated after the vote.[34] At the opposition's core was a lingering distrust of secret intelligence assessments—and particularly those coming from the US intelligence community—and bitter memories of the secret intelligence that paved the way into the Second Iraq War and turned out to be completely false.[35]

Across the channel in France, François Hollande and other political leaders deliberated next steps. While most political leaders felt France's strong-president constitution did not *require* a parliamentary test prior to the commitment of military force in such a context in Syria, there was a strong press for parliamentary deliberation and a vote just the same.[36] A sense of a need to act to show no tolerance for the use of chemical weapons against a civilian population was balanced by popular reservations about the use of military force and questions about the trustworthiness of the secret intelligence that was being cited to sell the move. With Britain having put the question to the test of parliamentary deliberation and a vote, French political leaders were acknowledging the need for democratic legitimacy with respect to any sustained military effort, but the wheels were already coming off the effort. No vote was taken.

The British decision to vote down military action in Syria had immediate repercussions for the Obama administration. Among other things, it put a spotlight on democratic process and made clear how widely distrusted America's national security elites were within the NATO alliance. They had led allied forces into an invasion of Iraq and toppled the government. The invasion had been predicated on false claims of an imminent threat from weapons of mass destruction that rested on unverifiable and highly classified intelligence data that turned out to be completely erroneous. Moreover, once the invasion was launched, its authors had hardly an inkling of what to do. The Bush team had made no realistic plans for a sustained occupation and quickly moved to demolish the secular Baathist state and its institutions without giving serious thought to the consequences this would have for stability and governance in the long term.

In sum, British politicians across the philosophical spectrum viewed the American national security elites behind the Iraq project, and particularly the neocons, as both dishonest in their war drumming and naive vis-à-vis the cultural complexities of the Middle East. The Libya project had revealed that the NATO alliance was prepared to engage with the Middle East when core security and humanitarian interests were raised. Yet the Syria red-line project echoed too much of the Iraq experience for comfort.

While carefully reserving his right to act regardless of the outcome, President Obama made a turn that few saw coming. Two days after the British Parliament voted down a military action in Syria, Obama convened a press conference in the Rose Garden of the White House. He called for a vote in Congress for specific authority to strike Syria over the sarin gas attacks. At first it seemed that a freight train would move the matter through Congress. But when a Russian diplomatic initiative aimed at brokering an independently verified elimination of the chemical weapons capacities offered Obama an escape hatch, he took it.

Obama's move also turned the tables on his congressional critics. When pressed to step up and take a clear position about what should be done in Syria in the wake of the chemical weapons attack, critical voices across the political aisle who had been clamoring for military action in Syria suddenly went silent.[37] Votes were first delayed and then dropped as the push for military engagement sputtered in the face of a Russian-initiated project to simply dismantle and remove Syria's chemical weapons arsenal. In the end, the most striking thing about the incident was that dismantling chemical stockpiles and other more pragmatic and less violent solutions to the dilemma had not been fully explored before the "bomb Syria" train pulled out of the station.

The Syrian incident came closer to the sort of political process that Madison and his followers had in mind, but again Congress failed to pass the military engagement sobriety test of mature debate and action. And again, democratic process concerning the path to war in another Middle Eastern state seemed less "democratic" than it was in the major western allies aligned with the United States.

● ● ●

President Obama's strange dance with his Republican critics in Congress is attributable to several factors. One is Obama's sense that after three wars in the Middle East, the country should strive to avoid another ground war. Another is his desire to stress domestic over foreign policy initiatives. Finally, with the notable exception of the party's growing Libertarian wing, Obama's Republican critics had almost reflexively argued for robust military engagement, even though they often were at a loss to identify a faction they could support.

A consistent Republican political meme throughout this period has been to portray the Obama administration as dilatory and hesitant to take recourse to arms—making it perplexing for them to criticize him when he actually did so. Whatever the utility of this posture as a domestic political instrument, it obstructed lucid geopolitical analysis of crises as they presented themselves, often leading to inconsistent and even embarrassingly contradictory stances.

Nevertheless, it seems likely that two factors lie at the heart of this constitutional crisis. One is an emerging bipartisan consensus in Washington that values robust presidential war-making powers and gives short shrift to the power of the Congress to limit or control their exercise. In the Libya conflict we saw how this was possible: the liberal interventionists who dominate the Democratic Party and the neoconservatives who set the tone for GOP foreign policy joined forces in pushing for action: Susan Rice and William Kristol, Samantha Power and Charles Krauthammer. These two groups have considerable differences regarding the details of foreign policy, but they are united in their vision of a robust American presidency projecting military force around the globe with no need to seek a congressional or popular mandate before doing so.

In essence, their vision opposed the Madisonian vision, which foresees a dialogue and balancing act between institutions. Instead, in America today it is not the people and the Congress, but unelected and increasingly unaccountable national security elites who work with the president in making decisions about the use of force abroad.

The second factor (and in some respects the flip side of the first) is the dissipation of foreign policy statesmanship in Congress. In prior generations, figures like Howard Baker, Robert Byrd, Everett Dirksen, J. William Fulbright, Richard Lugar, Michael Mansfield, Sam Nunn, and Hugh Scott, while holding widely divergent views, had nevertheless extended hands across the aisle to safeguard the prerogatives of Congress on national security questions and had worked to build a nonpartisan consensus at the outset of significant hostilities whenever feasible. By comparison, more recent Republican congressional leaders seem far more fixed on using national security issues as a partisan wedge, while Democrats have generally adopted a softer and more defensive posture.

This reflects a retreat from the guarantee many of the founding fathers saw of democratic participation in decisions about war and peace. As Madison expressed it in *Federalist* 51, each branch "should have a will of its own," each must possess "the necessary constitutional means and personal motives to resist encroachments of the others." The play between these different wills should produce an informed discussion that tests assumptions of fact and produces a democratic consensus—or at least forces a honing of foreign policy.

But the way the political game is played in Washington today re-flects a different reality: we have become a presidential republic in which the powers of Congress steadily recede, especially in the arena of foreign affairs and national security. Capturing the presidency is the highest prize. In the emerging American model, the role of Congress is being reduced and accountability is being systematically eliminated. The lords of secrecy emerge as the major winners in the reallocation of power in Washington, given their key role as expert technical ad-visers to the executive. By keeping their advice secret, they heighten its appeal and immunize it against attack from others—who might otherwise expose the weakness of their reasoning or fallacies in their assumptions of fact.

At every stage in this struggle, secrecy has played a vital role, and it has often been reinforced by claims of emergency, which in retro-spect seem very weak. Indeed, in decisions to commit military forces since the invasions of Afghanistan (2001) and Iraq (2003), as well as in the more limited military commitments to Libya (2011) and the con-templated punitive mission in Syria (2013), a phenomenon we can call the emergency-secrecy cycle kicked in. A national security emergency is cited simultaneously as justification for heightened government se-crecy and urgent action. Of course, if the government determines that an emergency exists in secret, and decides exactly what kind of emer-gency it is and what measures are needed to deal with it in secret, then the secrecy becomes self-justifying. A self-sealing system is created in which the space for democratic discussion and the weighing of options with respect to war and peace contracts or is entirely eliminated. The flip side of this process is that the power and influence of the national security elites expand whenever secrecy and emergencies are present.

Karl Popper saw in a comparable emergency-secrecy cycle, which played out in several European states in the period between the world wars, the essential predicate for the suffocation of a democratic state and the creation in its place of an authoritarian or even totalitarian system. Popper focused on the perceived risk presented by a mono-lithic and highly militaristic adversary state. But the period after 9/11 shows that an ill-resourced but ideologically fervent band of violent radicals, while not an existential threat, could still be used as an external threat of sufficient gravity to drive the emergency-secrecy cycle. In essence, the threat that these radical groups have presented has been severely misassessed because we have failed to take account of the risk that battling these groups presents for our society's democratic values and institutions. This risk of corrosion of democracy at home while fighting abroad is one that many democratic societies have faced in the past, and many will face again in the future. It is a risk that Albert Camus patiently exposed and described in his chronicle of the Algerian Civil War, for in the end the damage that war did to Algeria was matched by a huge rent in the fabric of democratic society at home in France.[38]

These considerations demonstrate why democracy should approach claims of secrecy and emergency with patient skepticism, always probing the bona fides of the claims. The new century has seen entirely too many unjustified invocations of each.

8

DROWNING IN SECRETS

I think that if I were asked to single out one specific group of men, one category, as being the most suspicious, unreasonable, petty, inhuman, sadistic, double-crossing set of bastards in any language, I would say without hesitation: "The people who run counterespionage departments."

—ERIC AMBLER, *THE LIGHT OF DAY* (1962)

THE PASSAGE QUOTED ABOVE comes from a crime caper with an espionage twist by British author Eric Ambler. Two years after its publication, blacklisted director Jules Dassin turned it into a feature film, *Topkapi*, with an all-star cast. The film was a hit around the world and it earned Peter Ustinov an Oscar for his portrayal of Arthur Simon Simpson, a small-time hustler based in Istanbul. Years later, a student in a master's degree program at the Defense Intelligence College quoted it, on a separate page, in his thesis, "Espionage in the Air Force Since World War II."[1] The Air Force Office of Special Investigations classified this specific page, with nothing but the single word, "secret."[2]

The reason for this is not entirely clear, though there is little doubt that someone who runs a counterespionage department (such as the Office of Special Investigations) would take offense to Ambler's remarks. There are thousands of further examples of this kind of practice, but I will demonstrate just two more.

On November 5, 2008, I appeared, together with two recent inspectors general, to testify before the House Judiciary Committee with respect to a report prepared on the case of Maher Arar. A Canadian computer engineer of Syrian origin, Arar was seized by US authorities in September 2002 as he tried to change planes at John F. Kennedy International Airport. He was returning home to Canada from a family vacation overseas. Arar was held in isolation, railroaded through a sham review process, sent to Jordan, and then delivered to Syria, where he was held and tortured for about a year. When the inspector general's report on the incident was finally made public,[3] it had been redacted into senselessness. Too late, Americans and their Canadian intelligence counterparts came to realize that they had nabbed the wrong man.

I was able to establish that among the classified and redacted passages were lengthy quotations from a Canadian inquiry about the case—a public document.[4] I also learned that other passages of the report had been classified and withheld because they would have embarrassed two political appointees directly responsible for the gross errors and abridgement of due process that led to Arar's torture.[5] Here was a case of using secrecy to protect political personages from embarrassment that exposure of their actions would produce.

In documents released in February 2014, the Defense Department deleted as "secret" public information about the resolution of the Cuban missile crisis, blacking out public statements made by Soviet leader Nikita Khrushchev about America's agreement to withdraw its nuclear missiles from Turkey as part of the resolution.[6] This fact, of course, can be found in current high school history texts. This is an example of secrecy being used to influence the popular understanding of historical events—a tactic highlighted by George Orwell in his dystopian novel, *1984*.

Government officials who have responsibility for such things have consistently acknowledged that *most* classified materials should not in fact be classified.[7] One of the most pressing questions the US government faces is how to stem the deluge of improperly classified materials. The production and maintenance of this mass of classified documents cost the federal government $11.63 billion in 2013, according to the National Archives and Records Administration's Information Security Oversight Office.[8] That measure only begins to assess the damage of the secrecy rampage. The more serious costs cannot be calculated in dollars and cents. They go to America's continuation as a democracy that assures its people a fair say about their security and the information they need for an informed opinion.

THREE AREAS WHERE SECRECY IS USUALLY WARRANTED

Even in a democratic state that places a premium on transparency and a well-informed public, there is a legitimate, though limited, role for secrecy. We should recognize three areas where the state has an especially compelling interest in preserving confidentiality.

The first concerns advanced, sensitive weapons systems. It is imperative that this information be kept out of the wrong hands, and aggressive measures to preserve its secrecy are essential. I earlier touched upon the advent of nuclear weaponry in the course of World War II and the years that followed. The United States reacted by adopting a far more rigorous system of military secrecy than it had known before. Later studies have identified many abuses associated with this secrecy, some of them tragic and unjust. Still, even though proliferation was inevitable, few would question that a nuclear bomb merited many of the extreme measures that were adopted—its advent gave the United States a decisive military advantage in the war, but if passed into the wrong hands it could present an existential threat, something hardly known beforehand. Moreover, the nuclear program was in fact the target of sophisticated and well-resourced espionage efforts aimed at gleaning whatever they could for the benefit of foreign powers—not all of them America's enemies.

The same concerns might well exist in other areas. Consider, for instance, a medical research facility that discovers a virus that transmits itself by air or contact, is invariably fatal, and has no cure. If released, the virus could cause the death of billions, or possibly even the extinction of the human race. It would be immensely irresponsible for a government that knows how to create this virus to allow it to become public. It might be replicated by someone with homicidal intent, or even someone who allowed its release through negligence.

Still, concerns about secrecy related to weapons systems are not without reasonable limitations. Major breakthroughs regularly occur in the area of abstract science. These discoveries may have useful applications for weapons systems, which the state would reasonably seek to keep secret. But they may have other applications that advance human well-being in other areas, both in commercial ways and in connection with health sciences, for instance. Indeed, western success in the cold war has often been attributed to the fact that its secrecy barriers were sufficiently flexible to allow for commercial and other uses of scientific breakthroughs achieved in the arms race, whereas the higher secrecy perimeter erected by the Soviet Union did not. Moreover, the public has a legitimate interest in having a general understanding of the risks associated with the use or testing of the weapons system, as well as its costs.

The second category consists of critical signals intelligence and cryptography, disclosure of which might reveal an aspect of the nation's ability to collect intelligence through the interception of communications that are assumed confidential by the persons hostile to the government. For instance, early in World War II, American naval intelligence had succeeded in cracking Japan's codes. This gave the Americans an immense strategic advantage, which would vanish if the Japanese learned that their cipher had been broken. In the days following the Pearl Harbor attack and through the summer of 1942, the *Chicago Tribune*—then run by the arch-isolationist Col. Robert R. McCormick—ran a series of articles about American plans for war with Japan from which American interception of confidential Japanese communications might reasonably have been inferred.[9]

This presented a horrendous dilemma. The information, while ambiguous, was acutely sensitive and its disclosure could have put thousands of lives at risk. The government might well have been justified in taking extraordinary measures against the publication. At one cabinet session, Attorney General Francis Biddle openly entertained the notion of an Espionage Act prosecution. However, President Franklin D. Roosevelt and Biddle probably made the right decision in doing nothing—because a prosecution would have created a stir that would have made it more likely that the Japanese would discover the leak and therefore would have compounded the problem.[10]

Concerns about disclosure of signals intelligence are frequently invoked, but not always legitimately. In the recent controversy surrounding the NSA's sweeping surveillance program, its defenders consistently argued that anything that discloses the full scope of the program would also disclose the NSA's technical capabilities and the extent of its current surveillance, so it should be protected. This argument was used to justify crude acts of intimidation targeting internal critics, and even brutal and aggressive criminal prosecutions of legitimate whistleblowers, as already noted. It was also used to justify misleading the American public about the extent to which their own communications and Internet explorations were being monitored. But this argument is not particularly compelling, in part because it assumes that terrorist operatives and other surveillance targets do not suspect that the NSA is attempting to intercept their telephone and Internet communications—which is hardly the case. However, it would be legitimate to the extent a disclosure revealed a particular modality of surveillance that was not already in the public domain. The government has a strong interest in keeping these capabilities under wraps if they are to be effectively employed.

Third, the identity of covert operatives and foreign informants presents another sensitive case. Particularly in times of war and with respect to operatives working in brutal authoritarian dictatorships, the disclosure of identities could put their lives at risk, and thus the government has a compelling interest in keeping this information secret to protect them.[11] It may literally be a matter of life and death. But this point is sometimes abused by a too sweeping assertion, as we witnessed with the WikiLeaks disclosure of diplomatic cables that frequently noted the names of private persons who provided critical information to American diplomats. The State Department was right to be concerned about these disclosures and to ask that names be redacted before any disclosure. But the experience of disclosure so far at least has shown that concerns were often overstated.

Still, disclosing the identity of a foreign collaborator with a US spy agency operating in a hostile country could put that person's life or liberty at risk. For instance, an inspector general's report on the case of Aldrich Ames, a career CIA officer who was discovered to be doubling for the Soviet Union, found that "unprecedented losses of [the CIA's] most significant assets," as well as the loss of two FBI assets in the Soviet Union, could be linked to disclosures made by Ames.[12]

These concerns are addressed by special legislation that criminalizes disclosure of the identity of covert operatives, designed as a shield to protect them. However, the lords of secrecy have refashioned this gag rule into a sword that can be used to intimidate whistleblowers. For instance, the CIA pressed the Justice Department to probe and threaten human rights investigators with the John Adams Project looking into CIA involvement in torture and other serious crimes in order to advance the legal cases of torture victims.[13] It also persuaded prosecutors to bring charges against former CIA agent John Kiriakou when he disclosed the identities of two CIA agents involved in torturing prisoners.[14] Both of these cases demonstrate the use of secrecy to cover up serious crimes with the complicity of the Justice Department.

The gag rule has also been used abusively to withhold the names of intelligence community personnel, such as several of the persons discussed in Chapter 3, who now serve in policy-making positions, and whose names and identities are widely known within the national security community and among journalists and academics. This includes many figures whose counterparts in other democratic states are properly considered public personages, and who routinely appear and speak at public policy functions. Keeping their names secret serves a notably improper purpose: shielding their misconduct and poor judgment.

• • •

TWO AREAS WHERE SECRECY IS NEVER WARRANTED

Claims of secrecy are inherently suspect and never legitimate in two areas: law and the retroactive classification of public materials.

The notion that legal rules, binding on all citizens and potentially providing a basis for their punishment, can be kept secret violates the fundamental principles of the rule of law and of democratic society. It is a great testimony to the power of the lords of secrecy that they have led the government to utter secret law. And it is not surprising that this secret law, once it sees the light of day, is often subjected to severe ridicule and is unable to sustain itself in the forum of public debate.

These concerns have come to focus on the Justice Department's Office of Legal Counsel, which exercises the attorney general's power, conferred under the Judiciary Act of 1789, to issue opinions that constitute interpretations of the law binding on all agencies of the executive branch. OLC opinions consequently form a type of law, a fact that highly placed figures in the Bush administration seized on as they sought to overcome internal opposition to the introduction of torture techniques as an approved modus operandi in counterterrorism operations.

Two sets of OLC opinions demonstrate why these materials should not have been classified, one under Bush, the other under Obama. Bush administration lawyers issued a series of opinions over several years that were designed to provide legal protection to individuals who used torture or cruel and inhumane treatment on prisoners held in counterterrorism operations in Iraq and Afghanistan, including prisoners captured in conflicts covered by the Geneva Conventions.[15] The CIA and Defense Department sought these opinions ostensibly for the purpose of providing detached legal guidance—but for the actual purpose of overcoming objections raised within the ranks to the use of torture. In the words of one of the former heads of OLC engaged with the opinions, they were designed to create a "golden shield" that would protect any potential torturer or abuser from criminal prosecution under applicable federal statutes or international law.[16]

The ostensible reason for classifying the opinions was that their disclosure would reveal the use of authorized techniques and thus render them ineffective. However, the opinions easily could have been, and ultimately were, redacted to remove the most sensitive information about methodology while fully revealing the legal reasoning behind the advice. When the opinions were revealed, however, it soon became apparent that they had been kept secret—both from the public and even from other government lawyers with special expertise in the subjects covered—for another reason. The legal reasoning contained in these opinions was so thoroughly flawed and weak that it could not withstand public scrutiny. The opinions were subjected to immense ridicule within the legal community and were studied in law schools as examples of substandard or professionally irresponsible legal counseling. The Bush administration was required to rescind them.

The second set of opinions classified as secret, but having the force of law, was issued by the Obama administration. As senator, Obama criticized the torture opinions and offered the conclusion that waterboarding was torture;[17] he questioned the legitimacy of the decision to keep them secret. Once president, Obama ordered the publication of the entire cache of secret opinions addressing the question of torture techniques.[18] But the Justice Department under President Obama has continued its practice of keeping some attorney general opinions dealing with national security matters secret. The best-known example consists of a July 16, 2010, opinion written by Assistant Attorney General David Barron discussing the legal standards for the planned assassination by drone strike of Anwar al Awlaki, an American citizen identified by American intelligence as a leader of an al Qaeda faction linked to a number of attacks and failed attacks on Americans.

The Obama administration, at the emphatic urging of the intelligence community, sought to keep this opinion secret, but the decision was challenged in legal proceedings brought by the *New York Times* and the American Civil Liberties Union. The US Court of Appeals for the Second Circuit rejected the government's secrecy claims, urged clearance of the opinion for release, and ultimately, on June 23, 2014, published a redacted version of the opinion—an increasingly rare disposition in a federal court.[19]

Unsurprisingly, Barron's OLC opinion found a *legal* basis for the killing only if a series of predicate factual findings could be made that tied the act to actual warfare and eliminated the prospect of the target's arrest and removal to face charges. (Conversely, the *factual assumptions* contained in the opinion remain controversial, particularly the notion that Awlaki posed an "imminent threat" to Americans and that his arrest and return to the United States to face charges were not feasible.) Rather, it was the government's decision to keep secret the opinion that inspired the legal controversy. By making a decision to operate entirely in secret and failing to explain how it legally justified its actions, the government was undermining its legitimacy. The decision to keep the legal rationale secret had to be juxtaposed with the Obama administration's decision to go public, in a crude chest-beating fashion, with its decision to assassinate Awlaki.

Since the spring of 2010, a public debate has been under way surrounding the use of drones to assassinate individuals, including US citizens, without charges or a trial. The debate was precipitated by Obama administration decisions to expose to the media the decision to kill Awlaki and to then attempt to justify it with a series of on-background interviews.[20] By keeping the basis for its legal authority a secret, however, the Obama administration made it difficult to fully engage in a serious policy discussion. Instead, it sent most observers a signal of weakness or vulnerability on questions of law. Keeping the legal advice that supported the authorization of Awlaki's assassination secret is a good demonstration of how secrecy can harm national security interests.

The fundamental premise of the decision to keep the opinion undisclosed was also shaky. It assumed that national security interest lay in concealing the fact that the United States felt it had a legal right to use lethal force to assassinate the leader of a terrorist group actively engaged in attacks on American citizens and interests. It is true that the logistical specifics of any particular strike would need to be closely guarded—but such details hardly require mention or discussion in a legal policy memorandum and could be redacted if they were. On the other hand, the nation's security interests are well served by making the intention to strike in such a case known and credible and by confidently asserting that the action can be squared with American and international law.

Publicly accessible and published documents, particularly those of historical significance or linked to pending investigations of wrongdoing or inept conduct, constitute a second area in which classification is never warranted. Over the last decade, intelligence services, led by the CIA, have engineered a new process called retroactive classification. This involves taking materials already released to the public—through publication, release in response to a FOIA request, or deposit in the public sector of the National Archives or in public libraries—and determining that they are now again classified. The process has been likened to "squeezing toothpaste back into the tube"[21] and presents a crisis to academic researchers, journalists, and congressional investigators who gain access to, read, and use the materials—and who may actually face criminal prosecution for doing their jobs under arcane provisions of American national security law.[22]

A few examples show how the process works. In 1978 James Bamford, the foremost historian and critic of the NSA, issued a FOIA request to the Justice Department seeking historical documents on the agency, including its intense program of legally dubious surveillance targeting of Martin Luther King Jr. and other vocal critics of the Vietnam War. He received some 250 pages of documents, which shed light on the NSA's historical role of spying on critics of national security policies, most of it embarrassing to the NSA. However, the political guard in Washington changed, and the incoming Reagan administration decided that the release of the documents to Bamford had been a mistake. It then retroactively reclassified the declassified and released documents. Bamford was threatened with an Espionage Act prosecution should he divulge the information and was pressed to return it.[23] He called the Justice Department's bluff, however, publishing the materials in his book *The Puzzle Palace.* He was not prosecuted.

This struggle reflects a difference in viewpoint between administrations about what historical documents can legitimately be retained as classified. The Reagan administration sided with the NSA in the view that historical materials that would prove institutionally embarrassing to the agency (and to prior administrations, particularly that of Richard Nixon) can be suppressed. The Carter administration had disagreed. But the Reagan administration felt it was not bound by decisions that the Carter administration had made to declassify, and it would not treat the matter as resolved by disclosure or even publication. The law supported the posture of the Reagan administration to a large extent; but as often happens in the national security field, the law was at odds with simple reason.

In 2000, a congressional committee was investigating the progress made on the national missile-defense shield program and secured a report from the program's auditor, including recommendations for improving the testing process. The report and recommendations were discussed in hearing sessions and published in the *Congressional Record*. In 2004, the committee learned that the Department of Defense had retroactively classified the report and recommendations. Committee members understood that the classification had been imposed to block the Government Accounting Office from issuing a report on the subject and to make it impossible for Congress to conduct open hearings.[24] This is an example of retroactive classification to protect a costly, troubled defense program from public discussion and criticism—and to frustrate congressional oversight.

From 1999 to 2006, the CIA and four other agencies retroactively classified 25,000 documents that had been released—demanding that they be removed from the public access areas at the National Archives and from other repository libraries. Most of these materials were historical documents from the period from the end of World War II to the Kennedy administration, and a substantial portion consisted of newspaper clippings. A widely cited example was the CIA's insistence that its 1948 plans to drop propaganda from hot air balloons over nations of the Soviet bloc were still too sensitive for public access.[25]

The idea of forcing the public to forget materials that have been examined by scholars, journalists, and congressional staffers is insulting enough. However, an examination of the specific cases in which the process was applied shows that the purpose for retroactive classification is almost always improper and at odds with democratic principles.

· · ·

Even most critics agree that the rules in their current form—under an executive order issued by Obama in 2009[26]—are methodical, precise, and set out clear criteria to govern the process. Classification is authorized on a determination that "disclosure of the information reasonably could be expected to result in damage to the national security," and the differing base levels of classification—confidential, secret, and top secret—depend on the extent to which damage may result, with top secret reserved for "exceptionally grave damage."[27] Significantly, the order notes that classification should not be used to "conceal violations of law, inefficiency, or administrative error," or "to prevent embarrassment to a person, organization or agency."[28]

Back at the time of the Manhattan Project friction developed between the scientists and their military minders regarding scientific practice. Generally scientists expect to publish and defend the results of their research so that they can be tested and replicated or refuted by the broader scientific community. A large part of human progress over the last two centuries has rested on fidelity to this principle, and the failure of powerful figures in the national security elite to appreciate it led to a great deal of counterproductive conflict in the early stages of the atomic era. On this score, Obama's order states, "basic scientific research information not clearly related to the national security shall not be classified."[29] The order also incorporates an important rule of decision: when in doubt, the decision should be struck *against classification*.[30]

Obama's order embraced and theoretically expanded another important check on abuse of secrecy by providing that all secrets have a "shelf life." At some point these secrets, however legitimate at the time granted, have a historical value that should not be denied. The order provides a default presumption of twenty-five years, though it exempts some categories from this (weapons of mass destruction, for instance, and the identities of covert agents).

A recent case demonstrates the practice of releasing historically important secrets. In October 2010 the United States recognized that from 1946 to 1948 it had conducted experiments on unwitting Guatemalans, under the guise of public health research. They had been infected with syphilis so that the degenerative effects of the disease could be studied together with possible cures. The process, which almost certainly amounted to a serious crime under international law and would have been illegal in the United States, produced eighty-three deaths. The Obama administration decided to make records surrounding the program public and offered formal apologies to the victims and to the people of Guatemala. An expert panel was appointed to study further disclosures and the issue of reparations to victims and their families.[31]

The notion of shelf life is not new. President Clinton tried it in his 1995 order on classification procedures, setting up a default under which documents would generally be declassified twenty-five years after their issuance.[32] Congress undercut this in 1998 with an amendment that required a page-by-page review in some circumstances, particularly when there was reason to believe that nuclear secrets were involved.[33] Nevertheless, these rules provide perfectly reasonable criteria for decision making and they do on their face provide a fair basis for pruning back the total quantum of classified information and reducing what is protected to a much smaller—and ultimately much more easily safeguarded—minimum.

There are several noteworthy failings in these rules. First, they fail to explicitly recognize that circumstances may arise in which information may be legitimately classifiable, but it may nevertheless be in the broader interest of the state for the information to be known.[34] There is no doubt that the government has such authority—all modern administrations have accepted this principle, some taking it more to heart than others.[35] In addition to current controversies, such as those swirling around NSA surveillance practices, disclosures are often made when addressing threats leading up to a war of choice or other military action, where it is in the interest of the state to build a strong consensus in support of action and educate the populace about the seriousness of the threats. In these circumstances it may well be appropriate for elected officials and senior officers to *balance* the potential for harm resulting from disclosure against the benefit to the state of having a better-informed population that appreciates a threat and therefore is more strongly joined behind a government facing a difficult decision.

The order is designed to provide guidance down the line in the national security system, and it plainly does not contemplate such a decision being taken by junior personnel but by those close to the system's apex. Still, this balancing of interests is also a decision that may be appropriately made by others—by jurors and judges considering the case of a whistleblower, or a newspaper's challenge to a government's decision to withhold a document requested under the Freedom of Information Act, for instance. Or by a news editor looking at an explosive story that suggests, based on a leak of classified information, that a political leader has been misleading the public about an important national security issue.

Too often in contemporary America there is a tendency to understand democracy as a beauty pageant among well-groomed personalities seeking elective office. That amounts to a pale imitation of what Athenians in the age of Pericles or Americans in the age of Madison and Jefferson understood by the term. Democracy can only meaningfully exist when the electorate has access to the essential information that enables it to make informed decisions about matters of serious concern. Historically, matters of national security have always topped that list. Consequently, a classification system that leads to the wholesale exclusion of national security information from the public sector also tends to gut the country's core democratic attributes. The Obama order's failure to fully appreciate this dilemma and to explicitly authorize a balancing test is therefore hardly a trivial failing.

Second, the lords of secrecy are now charting an unseemly course in favor of gagging civil servants, making it progressively more difficult for journalists to do their job, and claiming for themselves a disclosure monopoly on classified materials. This starts with restricting what civil servants, who are also citizens, can read in the public domain. Even those with security clearances, for instance, are told not to read classified information that has been published—such as the WikiLeaks and Snowden NSA materials, which have routinely appeared in the *New York Times, Washington Post, Guardian, Der Spiegel,* and other publications—and not to cite or discuss such materials. In fact, the administration has moved to punish those whose actions were as trivial as to cite a website that published and discussed classified materials.[36]

The national security establishment's reluctance to declassify materials simply because they have been leaked is understandable to some extent. But it is difficult to understand how making a virtue of ignorance serves the national interest of a democratic society. Ignorance is viewed as a virtue only in authoritarian states. American diplomats and national security policy makers risk not merely being excluded from public debate as a result of these rules, but appear ridiculous when they are sent into the public fray without leave to discuss headline-grabbing disclosures. Diplomats defending the interests of a democratic society need to be able to engage flexibly with matters that become the focus of public attention. They may need to offer explanations and context, particularly when the disclosures position the government in an unappealing light. On other occasions, they may need to apologize for conduct and statements that are unseemly or harmful to American interests.

Consider the imbroglio that erupted between the United States and the second most populous and wealthy of the NATO allies, Germany, in the summer of 2014. The Snowden disclosures that had cascaded over the prior year showed that the NSA was engaged in data trawling that affected millions of Germans. It also revealed that Chancellor Angela Merkel and more than a hundred other senior German political figures routinely had their phones tapped by the NSA.[37] Moreover, much of this involved NSA personnel and facilities operating on German soil.[38] The disclosures prompted a significant shift in public opinion in Germany against US intelligence services, and the German government began to press for a "no-spy agreement" along the lines of the "five eyes" accord the United States had reached with the four other Anglo-Saxon states.[39]

The United States responded by rejecting the request and denying the existence of comparable protections under the "five eyes" agreements.[40] But Germans were quick to point out that US claims about the scope of NSA surveillance programs and the special arrangements in place exclusively for the Anglo-Saxon states could not be reconciled with the already leaked documents. The situation deteriorated further when two US spies were uncovered and arrested. They appear to have been asked to track Germany's probe into presumptively illegal NSA operations and to keep American intelligence overlords abreast of what the Germans learned.[41] American diplomats and representatives were unable to make any meaningful statements in regard to the controversy, effectively gagged by secrecy rules.

Secrecy in this case, having first failed in its mission of safeguarding the information, ultimately served to sharply undermine the credibility of US diplomats and administration officials, whose statements were effectively limited to hollow formulas that lacked any credibility. German officials concurred on the need to maintain the secrecy of signals and communications intelligence but disagreed with the idea that *policies* on intelligence gathering should be secret. The Germans clearly would not countenance the favored tools of the American lords of secrecy: simply ignoring laws when they inconvenience intelligence operations or having them read into oblivion with the intellectually dishonest opinions of government lawyers.

Thus the US-German relationship, a basic pillar of the Atlantic alliance, suffered its most serious crisis because of America's abusive and antidemocratic secrecy policies. Furthermore, Washington's passive reaction conveyed the message that for decision makers in Washington, NSA convenience was far more important than good relations with key allies. This muddled chapter with Germany demonstrated the stranglehold the lords of secrecy have over US policy when it affects them—and their instinctive hostility to the demands of democratic process coming from a sister democracy. It also demonstrated insanely distorted priorities on the subject of national security: costly surveillance operations with no track record of having yielded important actionable intelligence were viewed as more important than the military alliance that has been the bedrock of American security arrangements for two generations.

The NSA scandal unleashed by Edward Snowden's revelations also pointed to a new and fundamental fissure in the Atlantic alliance. Superficially, the crisis was seen as a German-American dispute, arguably the first really significant one since the founding of the Federal Republic in 1949. But this was only the state of play on the surface. Beneath it different cracks were revealed, reflecting the fact that this is an alliance of democracies in which governments show varying measures of responsiveness to the concerns of their populations. The instinctive initial posture of the Merkel government had indeed been to stress the importance of the security and intelligence relationship with America and to offer more effective defenses for Obama than he and his team did for themselves. The posture of the German intelligence community, led by the Bundesnachrichtendienst, or BND, was also defensive since there is no doubt that the BND was implicated in and that it benefited from much of the NSA's illegal surveillance activities. However, public opinion in the United States and Germany (as well as other nations of the Atlantic alliance) came quickly to adopt the same critical view of the NSA's overreach and to demand retrenchment.[42] The difference between the United States and Germany was fairly simple: the Merkel government moved, even if reluctantly at first, into the posture that public opinion demanded. But the lords of secrecy have bitterly resisted public opinion on surveillance issues, and most key decision makers inside the Washington Beltway have stood in solidarity with them.

One of the clearest manifestations of the intelligence community's concern about critical public opinion has been its rush to implement a gag rule. The gag rule points to a systematic refusal to come clean about harmful falsehoods and deceptions in the past. It also suggests arrogance and disrespect for democratic process, a hostile attitude toward both the public and the press. Against this must be considered the interest in protecting secrets, but when those secrets have already been revealed, that is at a low ebb.

Perhaps the worst single example comes in the conduct of National Intelligence Director Gen. James Clapper, the overlord of American secrecy. On March 12, 2013, he made a series of misleading statements to Congress about the scope of certain surveillance programs.[43] He was promptly called out. Republican congressman Justin Amash accused Clapper of perjury;[44] Republican sen. Rand Paul said that Clapper "directly lie[d] to Congress, which is against the law,"[45] and that he might need to do jail time. Former secretary of state George P. Shultz told the World Affairs Council he couldn't understand how Clapper kept his job because "he lied!"[46] The fact that Clapper retained his post in the face of these developments bears witness to the immunity enjoyed by the lords of secrecy.

Of course, Clapper never faced any real prospect of accountability for the crime of lying to Congress. Under the current system in Washington, the lawyers who would make that call at the National Security Division of the Justice Department effectively work for him.[47] Clapper responded with a cautiously hedged acknowledgment of his error and promised greater transparency.[48] Typically, however, he moved in the opposite direction, issuing rules that would make it easier for senior intelligence officials to make false public statements without being held to account.

Clapper's directive, issued on March 20, 2014,[49] but only disclosed to the public a month later, threatens criminal prosecution for employees of the intelligence community the instant they come into "contact with the media about intelligence-related information, including intelligence sources, methods, activities, and judgments."[50] The prohibition extends even to information that is *unclassified.* Under the new order even the most casual encounter between employees of the intelligence community and journalists may be viewed as a security violation and may be referred to the Justice Department for investigation and criminal prosecution.

The apparent object of the directive is to shut down all contact between journalists who report on the national security beat and members of the intelligence community, thereby ending all independent reporting on national security matters. Only the official statements of figures like Clapper and Gen. Keith Alexander would remain—statements that have a well-established record of inaccuracy blended with conscious deception. We know this precisely because of the actions of men and women in the intelligence community who took steps that would have violated the Clapper fatwa and are potentially prosecutable as a result. Coming at the end of a series of developments that demonstrate both the necessity of effective independent national security reporting and the unreliability of utterances of the lords of secrecy, this purportedly protective directive is, in reality, another impudent power grab.[51]

• • •

Notwithstanding these shortcomings, the basic rules the Obama administration has laid down on classification are sound and the criteria they set out are reasonable. If they were faithfully followed, they would mark a significant step forward in addressing the dilemma of overclassification. The problem is that these rules are not now and never have been fairly observed or enforced. Indeed, the key failing is that despite the actual text of the rules, the system in place tolerates or even encourages overclassification. Routinely classifying almost everything is the "safe" alternative for government servants, particularly those in the national security area.

As long as civil servants believe that they can use classification to hide documents that would be embarrassing to them or their agency if revealed, this sort of abuse will continue to flourish—as in fact it has since President Obama issued his own classification guidelines. This situation will only change when serious sanctions are applied to those who abuse the system. However, those who make and enforce these rules operate within the classification system itself, and most of them have engaged in rampant overclassification simply because that is what Washington's culture of secrecy commands.

The Brennan Center for Justice at New York University Law School, recognizing the significance of this problem, has offered six proposals to address it:

- Taking advantage of simple contemporary information systems, classifiers should prepare brief electronic forms devised with pull-down windows that force the sequential consideration of the major elements of the classification order and record the specific rationale for classification decisions and the person involved in the classification.

- The inspectors general of major agencies involved with classified information would be required to pursue periodic spot audits designed to identify personnel who abusively overclassify.

- Personnel identified repeatedly as abusers would face steadily more serious sanctions, starting with remedial training and ending with disciplinary action.

- Agencies would have to spend not less than 8 percent of their security classification budget on training, and their training materials would have to meet standards set by the central government office dealing with classification questions.

- There would be protections for persons who fail to classify information derived from others.

- Agencies dealing heavily with classified materials would allow holders of classified information to challenge classification decisions without revealing their names, and they would receive small cash rewards when they did so successfully.[52]

Each of these would likely contribute to changing the dynamics surrounding treatment of secrecy in a bureaucratic context, and that is most needed.

For the most part, Washington's culture of bureaucratic secrecy is neither sinister nor innocent. Rather, it is in the nature of bureaucrats and bureaucracies to use secrecy whenever they have access to it as a tool to expand their own power and influence at the expense of perceived rivals, including other agencies, parliamentary organs of accountability, and the fundamental institutions of democratic governance.

The American experience has amply borne out Weber's thesis, and indeed has shown that Weber's faith that parliamentary inquiry could hold these forces in check was too optimistic. It has also demonstrated that the pace of abuse and the problems associated with it are accelerating over time. The cache of secrets, and particularly the vast and unwieldy store of intercepted communications, is growing into a modern Tower of Babel, already essentially unmanageable and overshadowing all the institutions of American democracy. Like the Tower of Babel of yore, it is a monument to the unseemly thirst for power of those who built it[53] and to their indifference to the core values of their own society.

EPILOGUE

THE INTRUSION OF STATE SURVEILLANCE into the lives of citizens of democracies has grown at an astonishing pace, and may now be both more extensive and more subtle than anything Orwell envisioned. Since the conclusion of the cold war, the major reform proposed by Sen. Moynihan, and embraced to a significant extent by President Clinton and Congress, has been rendered meaningless by bureaucratic intrigue and practice. Although the existential conflict ended, replaced with less serious conflicts among weakly armed adversaries, the lords of secrecy expanded their realm, ballooning their budgets and dramatically enhancing their power within the Washington Beltway. This is a truly remarkable achievement, and for the most part it has escaped detection by mainstream media and the public.

For Max Weber, the answer to this problem was tight congressional oversight. Dedicated legislators can ask penetrating questions; unearth corruption, incompetence, and illegality; and keep secrecy within bounds. The post–cold war experience shows that committed legislators and dedicated staff do intend to perform that role. However, congressional oversight has failed in its fundamental charge of preventing large-scale infringement of the rights of citizens. On the rare occasions when Congress has taken this role seriously—as in the Senate committee's detailed probe of the use of torture and the establishment of black sites by the CIA—the blowback and intrigue from the agency in the crosshairs have been more than a match for Congress. The dramatic events detailed in March 2014 by Sen. Dianne Feinstein, showing how the CIA spied on and attempted repeatedly to obstruct the work of the Senate Select Committee on Intelligence, highlight that.

The fact that the torture report has been held in abeyance, unpublished now for so many years, reveals the CIA as a more skillful player within the Washington arena than the congressional investigators. Congressional inquiries play an important role in democracies when they are available to the public and provide a basis for well-informed public debate about the key policy issues they cover. But America's intelligence community has demonstrated true mastery when it comes to thwarting that process.

In an era of globalization and shrinking distances between major economic and financial centers, concerns about the destructive consequences of Washington's secrecy culture cannot be limited to the United States. The Snowden disclosures reveal vast and systematic violations of domestic law by American intelligence services on the soil of closely aligned democratic states, including key members of the NATO alliance. They also reveal a tight-knit network of sister intelligence services eager to break the bounds imposed by democratic governance through collaboration with one another. Foreign governments, such as Germany, have historically offered the United States vital support in its intelligence gathering—essentially allowing US agencies to maintain facilities on its soil and operate without limits. Yet when Germany made a simple request that US intelligence activities on its soil operate consistently with German law, this request was rebuffed as infeasible.[1] The recent disclosures have broadly shaken the confidence of many US allies, and they have led the publics in many aligned states to adopt an increasingly uneasy attitude toward America's intelligence agencies and the global technology and communications industries that serve them.

As Gen. Keith Alexander ended his record-setting eight-and-a-half-year term atop the NSA in the spring of 2014, he founded a private consulting firm that promised to help corporations shield themselves from hackers for as little as $1 million per month.[2] Apparently sensing the sudden benefits of public relations for the launch of his new business, Alexander became the subject of a number of profiles, a few of which dealt with their subject critically. The *Washington Post* revealed that Alexander was a man consumed by a passion to have his agency "collect everything."³ This passion had led him repeatedly to push through the limits that previously constrained the agency with new programs that afforded a glimpse into virtually everything that moved across the Internet and through most phone systems. Alexander had become the architect of a new Panopticon state.

For citizens of the new democracies of Central and Eastern Europe, however, the words "collect everything" would have a familiar ring. Erich Mielke, the leader of East Germany's dreaded Stasi and the dean of Soviet bloc intelligence agencies, had used the same words exhorting his colleagues at Stasi headquarters in Berlin-Lichtenberg in 1981: "Comrades, I must tell you again: we must collect everything! Nothing can be missed."⁴ When Chancellor Merkel expressed her outrage at NSA monitoring, saying it was "like the Stasi,"⁵ the East German native knew just what she was talking about—whereas US journalists who pushed back in the defense of the NSA quickly demonstrated the limits of their knowledge of the old Soviet-era intelligence services.⁶ There is nothing surprising about an intelligence agency striving to collect all possible data—this is the nature of the beast. What is truly alarming is that in the United States senior policy makers and the legislature failed to hold this instinct in check.

The recent chill in relations between the United States and Germany demonstrates how, over time, the excesses of the US intelligence community may come to threaten the Atlantic alliance itself—the most significant military alliance in human history. Moreover, these excesses are having increasingly damaging consequences for US businesses, as allies begin to turn away from American telecommunications, Internet service providers, and defense contractors⁷ who collaborate with the American intelligence community in legally and ethically dubious activities.

These developments, and the intelligence community's response to them, reflect disrespect for the basic democratic order and a denigration of alliances that were forged over generations at immense human cost and sacrifice. They serve the selfish interests of national security elites and their allied corporate service providers, not the interests of average Americans. And they have dramatically harmed the security of the United States.

The lords of secrecy are unlikely to be controlled in the absence of concerted efforts on numerous fronts. Legislative overseers must challenge representations and undertake serious investigations of the sort that the Senate undertook into the CIA use of torture. American allies need to intervene, preferably collectively, to insist that domestic law be upheld in democratic states. They must also be conscious of the collusion between intelligence services designed to evade domestic law restrictions.

Journalists and scholars need to keep an active and open brief on national security questions, carefully mindful of past evasions. Their reporting and writing should inform the public about developments in the arena of national security in order to enhance public discussion and democratic decision making.

The experiences of the new century challenge the country to be rigorous and skeptical when approaching a commitment to engage in a new conflict on foreign soil. The lords of secrecy have counseled the president to act covertly, avoid public deliberation, and avail himself of new technologies to avoid putting Americans in harm's way as essential props of a new way of warfare. These practices gradually exclude the public from the decision-making process and sideline Congress. They have enabled adventures undertaken without a proper regard for long-term consequences and a full appreciation of costs.

Finally, all of these developments point to the paramount role of conscientious whistleblowers. In view of the steady failure of other system safeguards, whistleblowers alone provide a meaningful safety brake on dangerously overextended secrecy claims. The case of Edward Snowden has demonstrated this beyond any serious doubt. If we track public opinion on issues surrounding the NSA, for instance, it is clear that the intelligence community was able to command broadly satisfactory levels of public support by misleading the public with the collusion or support of key political figures on both sides of the aisle. The Snowden disclosures have produced a clear about-face in public opinion, particularly within key demographics, the young and those who closely follow technology issues. Over time this should provide the impetus for meaningful legislative change and oversight.[8]

In the first months after the Snowden disclosures, nineteen bills were introduced to overhaul the NSA, some of which packed a real punch.[9] In June 2013, two Michigan congressmen, Democrat John Conyers and Republican Justin Amash, introduced a measure to defund the NSA's mass surveillance program affecting Americans and mandate publication of the secret opinions of the Foreign Intelligence Surveillance Court.[10] The two congressmen are often viewed as polar opposites on the American political spectrum—Conyers a liberal Democrat and Amash a Tea Party Republican—but they share a strong concern about the Snowden disclosures of NSA data trawling, and particularly its PRISM program.[11] When the measure came up for a vote, the administration, being informed that it did not appear that the votes could be mustered in the House to block it, went into panic mode. General Alexander was dispatched to Congress to harangue members for four hours with dire, and also factually unsubstantiated, claims that passage of the measure would have calamitous consequences for national security.[12] The measure prompted dramatic televised debate in which a long list of members, almost evenly divided between Democrats and Republicans, took to the floor to denounce the abuses of the NSA and demand retrenchment. On the final tally, the measure failed narrowly on a 205–217 vote, only after Republican leaders joined with the White House in an arm-twisting campaign pressing more than a dozen members who had indicated support for the measure to shift their votes. The incident pointed to an abrupt shift from prior votes on NSA appropriations that had consistently been uncontroversial. Tellingly, one fact linked the supporters of the NSA on both sides of the political aisle: heavy dependence on campaign contributions from the defense and intelligence industry.[13]

The incident was one of many in recent years that points to the final warning President Eisenhower delivered in his farewell speech.[14] Military and intelligence industry contractors, keen to ensure the continued flow of treasury cash in lucrative contracts, weighed in heavily in support of the beleaguered lords of secrecy. Nevertheless, even the Democratic and Republican leaders who successfully thwarted the Conyers-Amash initiative appear to realize that the press for reform of the NSA could not be entirely blocked. Their likely response will not be to block reform directly, but rather to gut the reforms and make them meaningless.

The Greeks believed that no system of government can be sustained forever. Democratic governments tended to decay into oligarchies or tyrannies, as happened in the Greek city-states of the fourth and fifth centuries before the common era. That same concern was a significant preoccupation of the American founding fathers, who struggled to find a formula with the necessary dynamics to sustain democratic governance.

Today American democracy is in a state of crisis. For much of the new century, attention has been focused on security threats from abroad—especially on the discrete actions of small, poorly armed, and weakly resourced terrorist groups. However, the more serious threats to American democracy are internal. They stem from a steady transfer of democratic decision making and authority away from the people and to unelected elites. This has occurred both with respect to the disproportionate securing of power by the one percent elite[15] and by the rise of national security elites who increasingly take the key decisions about national security matters without involving the people in any meaningfully democratic process. The result of these changes is clear: America is no longer what an Athenian would have recognized as a democracy. It is increasingly an oligarchy.

Our ultimate objective must not be to eliminate national security institutions or the institutional role of secrecy, for both can help ensure the strength, integrity, and independence of the state. Rather, it must lie in maintaining a healthy balance among needs for secrecy, privacy, and publicity—a balance that in the event of uncertainty must always be resolved in favor of the right of the people to know the risks they face and to participate meaningfully in decisions about how to cope with them. These are simultaneously rights and responsibilities inherent in citizenship. Without them democracy has little meaning.

ACKNOWLEDGMENTS

In extending thanks to the dozens of individuals whose comments and corrections over the past several years contributed to this book (the flaws and errors in which are nevertheless uniquely my own), I will inevitably forget important names that merit mention. Nevertheless, some names cannot go unmentioned. Much of the inspiration for this book came from discussions with two friends and mentors who served in earlier Republican administrations and who alerted me to some of the pernicious changes that had been introduced with respect to government secrecy since the time they served. First, Robert M. Pennoyer, who worked as a Department of Defense lawyer and then as a young assistant US attorney in the Eisenhower administration, handling some significant leak cases. Pennoyer's pragmatic insights and fervent devotion to the principles of democratic governance stimulated much of the thinking that led to this book. Second, the late Harold R. Tyler, Jr., who participated in the Church Committee hearings as counselor to then-CIA director George H. W. Bush, and whose observations about whistleblowers, leakers, and accountability helped me understand these issues from several different perspectives—including the institutional perspectives of the CIA and Justice Department.

Next, I would like to thank Sanford Levinson and his colleagues at the University of Texas School of Law, whose invitation to me to deliver the Harvey Weil Centennial lecture in February 2012 led to the first stab at this book; to my friends and colleagues at Columbia Law School; to my editors and friends at *Harper's* magazine; and to the University of Wisconsin at Madison and the University of Alabama at Tuscaloosa, whose speaking invitations allowed me to develop and expand my initial thoughts. Along the way I have benefited immensely from a continuing dialogue with participants on the Princeton University Listserv on the law of torture founded by Kim Lane Scheppele and Martin Lederman, and earlier drafts of the manuscript benefited from keen comments furnished by Andrew Q. Blane and Mark Shulman. My thoughts were also honed by attendance and participation at a number of conferences dealing with topics covered by this book, particularly at the University of Pennsylvania, New York University, Columbia University, and Fordham University. Even more impressive than the academic gatherings, however, was a public forum convened in Brewster County, Texas, in November 2013 to discuss questions surrounding a program for testing drones—where the sensible and highly critical remarks from an audience populated with ranchers and college students shored up my faith in the ability of ordinary citizens to tackle complex issues in the context of what best serves their own interests.

Finally, I am much indebted to support grants from the W. C. Bullitt Foundation and the Lannan Foundation, which facilitated research and timely retreats that enabled me to complete this book. If notwithstanding all this generous help there are mistakes in the text, they are, of course, entirely mine.

NOTES

PROLOGUE

1. Kappes ultimately had to settle for the number two position when Obama tapped Leon Panetta, a longtime California rival of Feinstein's, for the directorship. Kappes and his unusual relationship with Feinstein have been effectively portrayed by Jeff Stein, "Inside Man," *Washingtonian,* March 25, 2010.

2. Transcript of Remarks of Hon. Dianne Feinstein, March 11, 2014 (Feinstein Trans.), http://www.washingtonpost.com/world/national-security/transcript-sen-dianne-feinstein-says-cia-searched-intelligence-committee-computers/2014/03/11/200dc9ac-a928-11e3-8599-ce7295b6851c_story.html. The newspaper report to which she alludes is Mark Mazzetti, "C.I.A. Destroyed Tapes of Interrogations," *New York Times,* December 6, 2007.

3. Feinstein Trans.

4. In 1975–1976, Idaho sen. Frank Church chaired a predecessor of the Senate Intelligence Committee in a series of hearings and reports looking into CIA activities over the prior three decades, largely triggered by Seymour Hersh's disclosure of many of the agency's historically most sensitive operations, dubbed the "crown jewels," notably including agency-directed efforts to assassinate foreign leaders in Chile, the Congo, Cuba, the Dominican Republic, and Vietnam. Hersh, "Huge C.I.A. Operation Reported in U.S. Against Antiwar Forces, Other Dissidents in Nixon Years," *New York Times,* December 22, 1974.

5. John Rizzo, *Company Man: Thirty Years of Controversy and Crisis in the CIA,* pp. 1–30 (2014).

6. Jamie Doward and Ian Cobain, "Britain 'Attempts to Censor' US Report on Torture Sites," *Guardian,* August 2, 2014.

7. 18 U.S.C. § 2340A (1994). The statute was adopted as part of the United States' implementation of its obligations under the Convention Against Torture and Other Cruel, Inhuman or Degrading Treatment or Punishment, which was ratified the same year.

8. Feinstein Trans.

9. Mark Mazzetti, "Ex-Chief of C.I.A. Shapes Response to Detention Report," *New York Times*, July 25, 2014, describing the coordination of responses to the Senate investigation among a group of senior CIA officials involved in the black site and torture program, prominently involving former Director George J. Tenet and then-Director John O. Brennan.

10. Paul Lewis, "Obama: White House Won't Wade into CIA Torture Report Dispute at This Point," *Guardian*, March 12, 2014.

11. Feinstein Trans.

12. Stephen Braud, "CIA Lawyer at Center of Computer Snooping Clash," Associated Press, March 12, 2014, identifying Robert Eatinger as the CIA lawyer described by Dianne Feinstein in her speech and reviewing the stages of his career. The intimate role that CIA staff attorneys played in documenting, fixing the guidelines for, securing approval for, and supervising the implementation of the torture and black sites program is a central theme of John Rizzo's book, *Company Man*, especially pp. 181–230; Rizzo identified Eatinger as one of the legal staff members involved in these issues (pp. 13, 312).

13. The rulings emerged in Europe's highest court, the European Court for Human Rights, in Strasbourg, in three cases: *El-Masri v. Former Yugoslav Republic of Macedonia*, December 12, 2012, http://hudoc.echr.coe.int/sites /eng/pages/search.aspx?i=001-115621; *Al Nashiri v. Poland*, July 24, 2014, http://hudoc.echr.coe.int/sites/eng/pages/search.aspx?i=001-146044; and *Husayn (Abu Zubaydah) v. Poland*, July 24, 2014, http://hudoc.echr.coe.int /sites/eng/pages/search.aspx?i=001-123768.

14. Feinstein Trans. The speech and debate clause (U.S. Const. art. I, § 6, ¶ 8) grants immunity to members of Congress with respect to what they say and do in the discharge of their legislative duties. In *Gravel v. United States*, 408 U.S. 606 (1972), it was extended to congressional staffers dealing with classified materials under the supervision of a member of Congress.

15. Remarks of CIA Director John O. Brennan before the Council on Foreign Relations, March 11, 2014, http://www.cfr.org/intelligence/cia -director-brennan-denies-hacking-allegations/p32563.

16. Greg Miller, "CIA Director John Brennan Apologizes for Search of Senate Committee's Computers," *Washington Post*, July 31, 2014.

17. Ali Watkins, "New sparks fly between CIA, Senate Intelligence Committee," McClatchy, September 12, 2014.

18. Burgess Everett, "2 Dems: CIA Director John Brennan Should Resign," Politico, July 31, 2014, http://www.politico.com/story/2014/07 /mark-udall-cia-john-brennan-resign-109610.html; Burgess Everett, "Rand

Paul: Fire Brennan," Politico, August 1, 2014, http://www.politico.com
/story/2014/08/rand-paul-fire-john-brennan-cia-109661.html.

19. Carl Hulse and Mark Mazzetti, "Obama Expresses Confidence in
C.I.A. Director," *New York Times*, August 2, 2014.

20. Rachel Maddow on MSNBC's *Rachel Maddow Show*, March 5, 2014,
http://www.msnbc.com/rachel-maddow-show/watch/cia-being-investigated
-for-spying-on-congress-183787075611.

21. Hannah Arendt, *Crises of the Republic* (1972), especially the essay
"Lying in Politics."

CHAPTER 1: BATTLING FOR DEMOCRACY

1. Albert Camus, "Chroniques algériennes," (1958), reproduced in *Essais*
(1965), p. 898.

2. Two wars were in Iraq and Afghanistan, and a third covert war was
run by the CIA and JSOC in Pakistan, Yemen, and Somalia.

3. The war powers resolution requires that the president notify Congress
within forty-eight hours of committing armed forces to military action. It
then prohibits the armed forces from remaining for more than sixty days in
the absence of explicit congressional authorization, while providing a further
thirty-day withdrawal period. War Powers Resolution of 1973, codified at
50 U.S.C. §§ 1541–1548.

4. Jon Cohen, "Poll: Conditional Support for Libya No-Fly Zone,"
Washington Post, March 14, 2011; Michael Memoli, "70% of Americans
Back No-Fly Operation in Libya, CNN Poll Finds," *Los Angeles Times*,
March 22, 2011; Emily Swanson, "Libya Poll: Plurality of U.S. Public
Supports Airstrikes, but Majority Unsure of Goal," Huffington Post, March
28, 2011.

5. Typical was a letter that Speaker Thomas Foley hand-delivered to
President Bush at the outset of a meeting on October 30, 1990: "Recent
reports and briefings indicate that the United States has shifted from a
defensive to an offensive posture and that war may be imminent. We believe
that the consequences could be catastrophic—resulting in the massive loss of
lives, including 10,000 to 50,000 Americans. This could only be described as
war. Under the U.S. Constitution, only the Congress can declare war. . . . We
demand that the Administration not undertake any offensive military action
without the full deliberation and declaration declared by the Constitution."

Quoted in George H.W. Bush and Brent Scowcroft, *A World Transformed* (1998), p. 389.

6. "I do not believe the president requires any additional authorization from the Congress before committing U.S. forces to achieve our objectives in the Gulf," Cheney testily told Sen. Edward M. Kennedy at a Senate Armed Services Committee hearing. Garry Wills, *Bomb Power: The Modern Presidency and the National Security State* (2011), p. 193.

7. Remarks of Sen. Jim Webb on the floor of the Senate, *Richmond Times-Dispatch*, May 9, 2012, http://politics.blogs.timesdispatch .com/2012/05/09/webb-seeks-congressional-approval-for-military/.

8. *Presidential Power to Use the Armed Forces Abroad Without Statutory Authorization*, 4A Op. O.L.C. 185 (1980); *Presidential Authority to Use United States Military Forces in Somalia*, 16 Op. O.L.C. 6 (1992); *Deployment of United States Armed Forces into Haiti*, 18 Op. O.L.C. 173 (1994); *Proposed Deployment of United States Armed Forces into Bosnia*, 19 Op. O.L.C. 327 (1995); *Authorization for Continuing Hostilities in Kosovo*, 24 Op. O.L.C. 327 (2000); *Re: Deployment of United States Armed Forces to Haiti* at 3–4 (Mar. 17, 2004); *Authority to Use Military Force in Libya*, 35 Op. O.L.C. 10 (Apr. 1, 2011).

9. Justin Elliott, "How Many Private Contractors Are There in Afghanistan? Military Gives Us a Number," talking points memo, December 2, 2009, http://talkingpointsmemo.com/muckraker/how-many-private -contractors-are-there-in-afghanistan-military-gives-us-a-number.

10. Scott Horton, Kevin Lanigan, and Michael McClintock, *Private Security Contractors at War* (2007); Catherine Holmqvist, *Private Security Companies: The Case for Regulation* (2005).

CHAPTER 2: KNOWLEDGE-BASED DEMOCRACY

1. This perspective is increasingly reflected in studies by American social scientists. See, for instance, Martin Gilens, *Affluence and Influence: Economic Inequality and Political Power in America* (2014), concluding that given the control over political decision making by social and economic elites in America, claims that the nation is a democracy by any reasonable definition are hard to support.

2. Josiah Ober, *Mass and Elite in Democratic Athens* (1989), pp. 80–81.

3. See, for example, Josiah Ober, *The Athenian Revolution* (1996), pp. 18–31; Ober, *Mass and Elite in Democratic Athens*, pp. 50–52.

4. Consider, for instance, these passages from one of the preeminent German historians of the era, Eduard Meyer, all referencing the struggle between the oligarchic and democratic parties in Athens at the time of the Peloponnesian War in a fashion that reveals sympathy for the oligarchic party and distrust of the democrats: "The wonderful freedom of democracy, and of her leaders, had manifestly been proven inefficient" (*Geschichte des Altertums* 5:65 [1884–1902]); "some of these leaders [of the democratic party] were perhaps honest fanatics . . . so utterly deprived of sound judgment that they really believed" (ibid., 4/2:359); "now when it had become too late, they turned to the political form [i.e., rule by an emperor] which made possible Rome's greatness" (ibid.).

5. Gregory L. White and Philip Zimbardo, *The Chilling Effects of Surveillance: Deindividuation and Reactance* (1975), conclude that "threat or actuality of government surveillance may psychologically inhibit freedom of speech," and that, where surveillance is widespread, "the boundaries between paranoid delusions and justified cautions indeed become tenuous."

6. See, for example, Randall G. Bowdish, "Cry Terror and Let Slip the Media Dogs," in *Countering Terrorism and Insurgency in the 21st Century*, vol. 2, ed. James J. F. Forest (2007).

7. Thucydides, *History of the Peloponnesian War* 2.38.

8. Patrick J. Deneen, *Democratic Faith* (2005), pp. 121–122.

9. Plato, *Protagoras* 320c–328d.

10. Ibid., 322d.

11. This aspect of the relationship between Protagoras and Socrates is well developed by I. F. Stone in *The Trial of Socrates* (1988).

12. *Mass and Elite in Democratic Athens* (1989); *The Athenian Revolution* (1996); and *Democracy and Knowledge* (2008), pp. 454–466.

13. *Democracy and Knowledge*, p. 268.

14. Joel Mokyr, *The Gifts of Athena: The Historical Origins of the Knowledge Economy* (2002).

15. Immanuel Kant, *Anthropologie in pragmatischer Hinsicht (Vorrede)* (1798).

16. Jeremy Bentham, "Essay on Political Tactics" in *Of Publicity, Works* (1821), 2:310ff.

17. Denis Diderot, *Œuvres complètes* 11:69, translation in J. H. Mason, *The Irresistible Diderot* (1982), p. 5.

18. Bernard Bailyn, *The Ideological Origins of the American Revolution* (1968).

19. François Furet, *Penser la révolution française* (1978).

20. John Adams, *A Dissertation on the Canon and Feudal Law* (1765).

21. Ibid.

22. See Hugh Bowden, *Mystery Cults of the Ancient World* (2010).

23. Euripides, *The Suppliants*, 430.

24. Friedrich August von Hayek, "The Use of Knowledge in Society," *American Economic Review* 35 (1945): 543–544.

25. Joseph Schumpeter, *Capitalism, Socialism, and Democracy* (1942), p. 175.

26. von Hayek, "The Use of Knowledge in Society," p. 548.

27. "Thus when we say that our Western civilization derives from the Greeks, we ought to realize what it means. It means that the Greeks started for us that great revolution which, it seems, is still in its beginning—the transition from the closed to the open society." Karl R. Popper, *The Open Society and Its Enemies* (1962), 1:175.

28. Andrei Dmitrievich Sakharov, Speech before the General Assembly of the USSR Academy of Sciences, June 1964.

29. Andrei Dmitrievich Sakharov, Nobel Prize lecture, December 11, 1975.

30. Andrei D. Sakharov, "Tomorrow: The View from Red Square," *Saturday Review*, August 24, 1974, p. 12.

31. Mill, who describes his "intoxication" with Greek philosophers in his youth, must nevertheless be reckoned something of an elitist critic of Athenian democracy, perhaps as one who saw the institution through Plato's eyes. He felt that successful democratic dialogue would always involve a measure of deference to those with expertise—"not the blind submission of dunces to men of knowledge, but the intelligent deference of those who know much to those who know still more." While his typically precise formulation still strikes the balance in favor of democracy, a concern about a possible tyranny of the uninformed masses comes through. John Stuart Mill, *Auguste Comte and Positivism, Collected Works*, 10:313–314; and John Stuart Mill, "Review of Grote's *The History of Greece*," *Collected Works*, 11:271–272.

32. "The strongest point to be made in behalf of even such rudimentary political forms as democracy has attained, popular voting, majority rule and so on, is that to some extent they involve a consultation and discussion which concerns social needs and troubles." John Dewey, "The Public and Its Problems," *Later Works*, 2:364.

33. Jürgen Habermas, *Strukturwandel der Öffentlichkeit: Untersuchungen zu einer Kategorie der bürgerlichen Gesellschaft* (1962).

34. Winston Churchill, speech in the House of Commons, Hansard, November 11, 1947, vol. 444, cc. 206–207.

CHAPTER 3: BUREAUCRACY AND SECRETS

1. Daniel Patrick Moynihan, *Secrecy: The American Experience* (1988), p. 227.

2. Phillip Knightley, *The Second Oldest Profession: Spies and Spying in the Twentieth Century* (1986), p. 262.

3. John Henry Wigmore, *Evidence* ¶ 2378.

4. Georg Simmel, *Soziologie: Untersuchungen über die Formen der Vergesellschaftung* (1908), translated in Kurt H. Wolff, *The Sociology of Georg Simmel* (1950), p. 376.

5. Max Weber, "Politik als Beruf," in *Gesammelte politische Schriften* (1988), p. 505.

6. Max Weber, *Wirtschaft und Gesellschaft* (1918), pp. 730–731.

7. Adam Goldman and Matt Apuzzo, "CIA Officers Make Grave Mistakes, Get Promoted," Associated Press, February 9, 2011.

8. *El Masri v. Former Yugoslav Republic of Macedonia*, European Court of Human Rights, Judgment of December 13, 2012.

9. John Cook, "Chief of CIA's Global Jihad Unit Revealed on Line," *Gawker*, September 22, 2011.

10. Dana Priest, "Wrongful Imprisonment: Anatomy of a CIA Mistake," *Washington Post*, December 4, 2005.

11. Frances's appointment as a US consular officer in connection with this position was reported to Congress and published in the *Congressional Record*, http://thomas.loc.gov/cgi-bin/query/R?r110:FLD001:S54850. The British government's statement of concern concerning her appointment was confirmed to me when I interviewed an official of the Foreign and Commonwealth Office and an officer of the CIA's Clandestine Service, each of whom has requested anonymity.

12. Ali Soufan, *The Black Banners: The Inside Story of 9/11 and the War Against al-Qaeda* (2011).

13. Ray Nowosielski and John Duffy, "Who Is Richard Blee?" documentary podcast, May 27, 2013, https://www.youtube.com/watch?v=9ue2n XcMDLs.

14. Jane Mayer, *The Dark Side,* pp. 273, 282.

15. Ibid.

16. Marcus Stern, "Disgraced Senior CIA Official Heads to Prison Still Claiming He's a Patriot," ProPublica, February 27, 2009, http://www.pro publica.org/article/disgraced-senior-cia-official-heads-to-prison-still -claiming-hes-a-patriot.

17. David Johnston and Mark Mazzetti, "Interrogation Inc.: A Window into C.I.A.'s Embrace of Secret Jails," *New York Times,* August 12, 2009.

18. R. Jeffrey Smith, "Files Unsealed Before Sentencing Detail Rule-Breaker's Rise at CIA," *Washington Post,* February 26, 2009.

19. Onell R. Soto, "Randy 'Duke' Cunningham: 'Overwhelming Case' Forced Cunningham to Accept Deal," *San Diego Union-Tribune,* November 30, 2005, reporting on Rep. Cunningham's acceptance of a plea bargain with federal prosecutors.

20. This account rests on the stellar exposé work of Aram Roston, particularly as reported in "The Man Who Conned the Pentagon," *Playboy,* January–February 2010.

21. Paul Vale, "Donald Rumsfeld Tells Al Jazeera 'I Am Delighted You Are Doing What You Are Doing,'" Huffington Post, September 30, 2011, http://www.huffingtonpost.co.uk/2011/09/29/donald-rumsfeld-tells-al-_n _986856.html.

22. Ron Suskind, *The One Percent Doctrine: Deep Inside America's Pursuit of Its Enemies* (2006), p. 142.

23. Ibid., p. 160.

24. Scott Horton, "Unredacting 'The Interrogator,'" *Harper's,* July 5, 2011.

25. Edward A. Shils, *The Torment of Secrecy: The Background and Consequences of American Security Policies* (1956), pp. 21–35.

26. Ibid., pp. 37–44.

27. Ibid. While remarking on the extreme role of publicity in American society, de Tocqueville criticized its ability to lead to a potential "tyranny of the majority" and intrude into the privacy space of citizens. "Whenever social conditions are equal, public opinion presses with enormous weight upon the minds of each individual; it surrounds, directs, and oppresses him; and this arises from the very constitution of society much more than from its political laws. As men grow more alike, each man feels himself weaker in re-gard to all the rest; as he discerns nothing by which he is considerably raised above them or distinguished from them, he mistrusts himself as soon as they

assail him. Not only does he mistrust his strength, but he even doubts of his right; and he is very near acknowledging that he is in the wrong, when the greater number of his countrymen assert that he is so. The majority do not need to force him; they convince him. In whatever way the powers of a democratic community may be organized and balanced, then, it will always be extremely difficult to believe what the bulk of the people reject or to profess what they condemn." Alexis de Tocqueville, *Democracy in America* (1840), trans. Henry Reeve (1899), chap. 31.

28. "The very word 'secrecy' is repugnant in a free and open society; and we are as a people inherently and historically opposed to secret societies, to secret oaths and to secret proceedings. We decided long ago that the dangers of excessive and unwarranted concealment of pertinent facts far outweighed the dangers which are cited to justify it. Even today, there is little value in opposing the threat of a closed society by imitating its arbitrary restrictions. Even today, there is little value in insuring the survival of our nation if our traditions do not survive with it. And there is very grave danger that an announced need for increased security will be seized upon by those anxious to expand its meaning to the very limits of official censorship and concealment. That I do not intend to permit to the extent that it is in my control." John F. Kennedy, speech to the American Newspaper Association, April 27, 1961.

29. Shils, *Torment of Secrecy*, p. 47.

30. Ibid., pp. 44–47.

31. Ibid., p. 47.

32. Arthur Lawrence and Alfred Charles Harmsworth, *Journalism as a Profession* (1903), pp. 184–185.

33. Shils, *Torment of Secrecy*, p. 51.

34. Ibid., p. 57.

35. Francis E. Rourke, "Secrecy in American Bureaucracy," *Political Science Quarterly* 72 (1957): 540.

36. *United States v. Andolschek*, 142 F.2d 503 (2d Cir. 1944) (holding that when the government chose to prosecute an individual for a crime, it was not free to deny him the right to meet the case made against him by introducing relevant documents, including those that have been classified as secret).

37. Rourke, "Secrecy in American Bureaucracy," p. 81.

38. Daniel Patrick Moynihan, *Secrecy: The American Experience* (1998), p. 59.

39. Ibid., p. 73.

40. Ibid., p. 73.

41. This led Truman to direct the preparation of what ultimately became the president's daily briefing, the principal vehicle for intelligence community briefings of the president. John L. Helgerson, *CIA Briefings of Presidential Candidates* (1996), chap. 2, http://www2.gwu.edu/~nsarchiv /NSAEBB/NSAEBB116/cia/Chapter%202%20-%20Truman%20and%20 Eisenhower%20Launching%20the%20Process.htm.

42. *Final Report of the National Commission on Terrorist Attacks Upon the United States*, 2004, recommendation 13.3, pp. 416–419.

43. Kenneth R. Mayer, *With the Stroke of a Pen: Executive Orders and Presidential Power* (2001), p. 145.

44. House of Representatives, Committee on Government Operations, *Availability of Information from Federal Departments and Agencies*, 86th Cong., 2d sess., July 2, 1960, House Report 86-2084, p. 36.

45. Moynihan, *Secrecy*, p. 154.

46. Daniel Patrick Moynihan, "How America Blew It," *Newsweek*, December 10, 1990, p. 10.

47. How dairy farmers met their unattainable quotas was the subject of a popular "Radio Erevan" joke. It envisioned a call-in program, with the announcer answering a series of questions: "Can Soviet Armenia increase its milk production by 10 percent next year?" Answer: "Yes!" Question: "Can Soviet Armenia increase its milk production by 20 percent next year?" Answer: "With difficulty, but yes, comrades." Question: "Can Soviet Armenia increase its milk production by 30 percent next year?" Answer: "Yes, but it would be awfully watery."

48. Moynihan quoted Secretary of State George P. Schultz: "In Washington, and especially from the CIA and its lead Soviet expert, Bob Gates, I heard that the Soviets wouldn't change and couldn't change, that Gorbachev was simply putting a new face on the same old Soviet approach to the world and to their own people. 'The Soviet Union is a despotism that works,' Gates said." This was roughly four years before the final collapse of the Soviet Union, by which time Gates was director of the CIA. "Somehow it came to be that that is how a career officer rose to the top," Moynihan added. *Secrecy*, p. 200. Moynihan was also convinced that the CIA director doled out contracts and grants in order to buy votes to support its programs. In a memorandum of a meeting with President Clinton, Moynihan noted that he had seen Gates attempt to "corrupt" Sen. David L. Boren by offering a $150

million grant for the Boren scholarships. *Daniel Patrick Moynihan: A Portrait in Letters of an American Visionary,* ed. Steven R. Weisman (2010), p. 607.

49. This point was made most effectively by President Harry S. Truman in an op-ed he published shortly after the Bay of Pigs fiasco: "I decided to set up a special organization charged with the collection of all intelligence reports from every available source," wrote Truman. "I never had any thought when I set up the CIA that it would be injected into peacetime cloak and dagger operations." Harry S. Truman, "Limit CIA Role to Intelligence," *Washington Post,* December 22, 1963. The Truman column is a trenchant exposure of the CIA's mission creep, and of the harmful consequences that flowed for the agency's prime mission.

50. Moynihan, *Secrecy,* p. 195.

51. "In a culture of secrecy, that which is not secret is easily disregarded or dismissed." *Secrecy,* pp. 222–223.

52. Moynihan, *Secrecy,* p. 75, quoting Information Security Oversight Office, *1996 Report to the President* (1996), p. ii.

53. Information Security Office, *2006 Report to the President* (2006), p. 13. Many of the secrecy claims are preposterous and frivolous, though without access to the classified documents, such judgments are difficult for outsiders to make. For instance, Mayer found that an Army War College manual quoting the Constitution and providing basic information concerning the organization of the executive branch and its war powers, issued publicly at one point, was later removed and classified. Mayer, p. 145.

CHAPTER 4: THE RISE OF THE NATIONAL SECURITY STATE

1. James Madison, *Universal and Perpetual Peace* (1792).

2. John Maynard Keynes, *Burke's Timidity on Embarking on War* (1904), in Robert Skidelsky, *John Maynard Keynes: Economist, Philosopher, Statesman* (2003), p. 97.

3. These events were recorded in Xenophon's *Hellenica,* bk. 1, chaps. 5–7, and in Diodorus Siculus, *Bibliotheca historica,* bk. 13. A good modern account is contained in Donald Kagan, *The Peloponnesian War* (2003).

4. See, for instance, the work of the Army's Center for Army Lessons Learned in Fort Leavenworth, much of which is made available to the public: http://usacac.army.mil/cac2/call/mission.asp.

5. A striking exception is the MSNBC documentary *Hubris*, narrated by Rachel Maddow, based on the book *Hubris: The Inside Story of Spin, Scandal, and the Selling of the Iraq War*, by Michael Isikoff and David Corn.

6. *Hubris* deals with this issue by showing footage of a speech Vice President Cheney gave to a convention of the Veterans of Foreign Wars in August 2002. "There is no doubt that Saddam Hussein now has weapons of mass destruction. There is no doubt he is amassing them to use against our friends, against our allies, and against us," Cheney states. It then cuts to an interview with Gen. Anthony Zinni, who had recently served as US commander in chief for the Central Command, who had shared the stage at this event with Cheney. Zinni states, "It was a shock. It was a total shock. I couldn't believe the vice president was saying this, you know? In doing work with the CIA on Iraq WMD, through all the briefings I heard at Langley, I never saw one piece of credible evidence that there was an on-going program. And that's when I began to believe they're getting serious about this. They wanna go into Iraq." The documentary can be viewed at https://www.youtube.com/watch?v=B5FaMbnINwc.

7. *Report of the Commission on the Intelligence Capabilities of the United States Regarding Weapons of Mass Destruction,* unclassified version, March 31, 2005, http://www.gpo.gov/fdsys/search/pagedetails.action ?granuleId=&packageId=GPO-WMD&fromBrowse=true.

8. Greg Miller and Bob Drogin, "Intelligence Analysts Whiffed on a 'Curveball,'" *Los Angeles Times,* April 1, 2005, reporting on how CIA analysts who correctly questioned a key false source were driven out of the agency; Scott Shane, "C.I.A. Answers Criticism with Pledge to Do Better," *New York Times,* April 2, 2005.

9. Joe Murphy, "Whitewash (Part Two); Blair Was Unscathed by Hutton and Now He Survives Again," *Evening Standard,* July 14, 2004.

10. In his charge to the commission on June 15, 2009, Prime Minister Gordon Brown wrote that "no British document and no British witness will be beyond the scope of the inquiry. I have asked the members of the committee to ensure that the final report will be able to disclose all but the most sensitive information—that is, all information except that which is essential to our national security." Hansard, June 15, 2009, http://www.publications .parliament.uk/pa/cm200809/cmhansard/cm090615/debtext/90615-0004. htm. Note the limitation to *"British* document" and *"British* witness." It was understood from the outset that much of the information would be American, and that this, in deference to Washington, would be off-limits.

11. "Deal Reached on Release of 'Gist' of Blair-Bush Iraq Talks," BBC News, May 29, 2014, http://www.bbc.com/news/uk-politics-27625117.

12. Secret cable of September 22, 2009, concerning a meeting between Undersecretary of State Ellen Tauscher and Foreign Minister David Miliband, http://www.theguardian.com/world/us-embassy-cables -documents/226331.

13. *Private Security Contractors at War: Ending the Culture of Impunity* (2007).

14. *Federalist 55.*

15. Robert Michels, *Zur Soziologie des Parteiwesens in der modernen Demokratie: Untersuchungen über die oligarchischen Tendenzen des Gruppenlebens* (1911).

16. Ken Prewitt and Alan Stone, *The Ruling Elites: Elite Theory, Power, and American Democracy* (1973), p. 20.

17. Garry Wills, *Bomb Power: The Modern Presidency and the National Security* (2010), p. 137.

18. Sallie Pisani, *The CIA and the Marshall Plan* (1991), p. 58.

19. NSA sec. 503(e).

20. NSA sec. 503(a).

21. NSA sec. 503(a)(5). This provision gave rise to a whole species of secret internal government opinions holding that the Constitution and certain statutes had no applicability outside of the territory of the United States so as to allow certain covert actions.

22. NSA sec. 503(b)(1).

23. NSA sec. 501(2)(e).

24. David Halberstam, *The Best and the Brightest* (1972), p. 578.

25. The report, prepared by the National Security Agency, can be examined at http://www.nsa.gov/public_info/declass/gulf_of_tonkin/.

26. Both McNamara and Bundy were later remarkably candid in acknowledging their failings in the critical period entering into the war and in lamenting the fact that these steps occurred without more substantial contemporaneous public discussion and debate. See Gordon Goldstein, *Lessons in Disaster: McGeorge Bundy and the Path to War in Vietnam* (2008).

27. See, for example, Jeffrey A. Jacobs, *The Future of the Citizen-Soldier Force* (1994), p. 47; Library of Congress Federal Research Division, *Historical Attempts to Reorganize the Reserve Components* (2007), pp. 15–16.

28. Among the significant contemporary writings on the subject, the following merit mention: Steven Kelman, *Push Comes to Shove: The Escalation of Student Protest* (1970); John E. Mueller, *War, Presidents, and Public Opinion* (1973); Thomas Powers, *The War at Home: Vietnam and the American People, 1964–1968* (1973); Herbert Schandler, *The Unmaking of a President: Lyndon Johnson and Vietnam* (1977); and James Webb, *A Sense of Honor* (1981).

29. *The Writings of Thomas Jefferson*, memorial ed. (1903–1904), 14:184.

30. Ober, *Athenian Legacies*, p. 85; Ober, *Athenian Revolution*, pp. 64–66.

31. Aristotle, *Politics* 1304a, 1321e. "Athenian democracy was strengthened by the masses who served in the navy and who won the victory at Salamis, because the leadership that Athens then gained rested on sea power."

32. Aristotle, *Nicomachean Ethics* 3.8.

33. A good history of this consultative process can be found in Laura A. Dickinson, *Outsourcing War and Peace: Preserving Public Values in a World of Privatized Foreign Affairs* (2010), pp. 31ff.

34. Allison Stanger, *One Nation Under Contract: The Outsourcing of American Power and the Future of Foreign Policy* (2009); see also Laura Dickinson, *Outsourcing War and Peace*.

CHAPTER 5: DRONES AND THE ART OF STEALTH WARFARE

1. See Elisabeth Sköns, "US Military Expenditure," http://www.sipri.org /yearbook/2013/files/sipri-yearbook-2013-chapter-3-section-2; for a comparative chart reflecting the major shares of global defense spending, see SPIRI Military Expenditures Database 2013, http://milexdata.sipri.org.

2. David Zucchino, "Drone Pilots Have a Front-Row Seat on War, from Half a World Away," *Los Angeles Times*, February 21, 2010.

3. National Security Adviser Richard Clarke put it more colorfully in an interview by Mark Mazzetti: "If the predator gets shot down, the pilot goes home and fucks his wife. It's OK. There's no POW issue here." *The Way of the Knife* (2013), p. 92.

4. Stimson Center, *Recommendations and Report of the Task Force on U.S. Drone Policy,* June 2014, p. 11, http://www.stimson.org/spotlight

/recommendations-and-report-of-the-stimson-task-force-on-us-drone
-policy/.

5. Gary D. Solis, *The Law of Armed Conflict* (2010), pp. 272–285.

6. A noteworthy example is the remark of John O. Brennan, then President Obama's senior counterterrorism adviser, that "there hasn't been a single collateral death because of the exceptional proficiency, precision of the capabilities we've been able to develop"—a claim he soon had to withdraw. Scott Shane, "C.I.A. Is Disputed on Civilian Toll in Drone Strikes," *New York Times,* August 11, 2011.

7. The total casualties resulting from drone strikes on Pakistani soil number between 2,000 and 4,000. While the US government has provided little data to support its claims of minimal, or even no, innocent civilian deaths, three independent observers, using varying methodologies and definitions, have undertaken tallies: the Bureau of Investigative Journalism (BIJ), the New America Foundation (NAF), and the *Long War Journal* (LWJ). Of these three, BIJ has consistently been the most independent and objective —for instance, using the term "alleged militants" to describe situations in which the United States or Pakistani authorities have linked the dead to known terrorist organizations. Similarly, BIJ has drawn heavily on a compilation of independent press reports, including significant input from observers on the ground in Pakistan. By comparison, LWJ and NAF also refer to press accounts, though with more limited reach (and notably including fewer on-the-ground accounts out of Pakistan), and tend to accept US government characterizations concerning targeting without independent verification and to build substantially off US government-sourced information. See Bureau of Investigative Journalism, "Get the Data: Drone Wars," August 11, 2011, http://www.thebureauinvestigates.com/2011/08/10/pakistan-drone -strikes-the-methodology2/; New America Foundation, "Drone Wars Methodology," http://natsec.newamerica.net/drones/methodology; the *Long War Journal,* "Charting the Data for US Air Strikes in Pakistan, 2004–2014," October 10, 2013, with periodic updates, http://www.longwar journal.org/pakistan-strikes.php. A good summary of the effective critique these studies present for CIA claims can be found in Scott Shane, "C.I.A. Is Disputed on Civilian Toll in Drone Strikes," *New York Times,* August 11, 2011. A useful side-by-side comparison of the three studies is offered by the Stimson Center's "Data Comparison of Casualties from Pakistan UAV

Strikes in 2011," October 2013, http://www.stimson.org/images/uploads
/reporting_on_civilian_casualties_from_targeted_strikes_in_pakistan.pdf.

8. A good discussion of the limited public information available about
"signature strikes" can be found in Cora Currier and Justin Elliott,
"The Drone War Doctrine We Still Know Nothing About," ProPublica,
February 26, 2013, http://www.propublica.org/article/drone-war-doctrine
-we-know-nothing-about.

9. Charlie Savage, "Top U.S. Security Official Says 'Rigorous Standards'
Are Used for Drone Strikes," *New York Times,* April 30, 2012, quoting
remarks by then–counterterrorism adviser John O. Brennan; Micah Zenko,
"How the Obama Administration Justifies Targeted Killings," CFR blog,
July 5, 2012, collecting statements of various Obama and Bush administration officials, http://blogs.cfr.org/zenko/2012/07/05/how-the
-obama-administration-justifies-targeted-killings/.

10. Samuel J. Brannan, "Sustaining the U.S. Lead in Unmanned Systems,"
2014, http://csis.org/files/publication/140227_Brannen_UnmannedSystems
_Web.pdf. "The barriers to entry for basic unmanned systems capability are
already low and will continue to drop, raising the real potential that lesser
powers and nonstate actors will also field systems in growing numbers."

11. Martha Raddatz, Nasser Atta, and Brian Ross, "Al Qaeda's Anwar
al-Awlaki Killed in CIA Drone Strike," ABC News, September 30, 2011,
http://abcnews.go.com/Blotter/anwar-al-awlaki-killed-officials-yemen
-confirm-al/story?id=14638303; Mark Mazzetti, Scott Shane, and Charlie
Savage, "How a U.S. Citizen Came to Be in America's Cross Hairs," *New
York Times,* March 9, 2013.

12. Memorandum for the Attorney General re: Applicability of Federal
Criminal Laws and the Constitution to Contemplated Lethal Operations
Against Shaykh Anwar al-Aulaqi, July 16, 2010, accessible as attached
to the Second Circuit opinion in *The New York Times Co. et al. v. U.S.
Department of Justice, et al.,* June 23, 2014, http://www.nytimes.com
/interactive/2014/06/23/us/23awlaki-memo.html?_r=0.

13. Eric Holder, speech at Northwestern University, March 5, 2012,
http://www.justice.gov/iso/opa/ag/speeches/2012/ag-speech-1203051
.html. I offer analysis and commentary in "Holder Dances the Assassination
Tango," *Harper's,* March 8, 2012.

14. Secret cable of December 21, 2009, from US Embassy Sana'a, http://
www.theguardian.com/world/us-embassy-cables-documents/240955.

15. Secret cable of January 4, 2010, from US Embassy Sana'a, http://
www.theguardian.com/world/us-embassy-cables-documents/242380.

16. Amy Davidson, "An American Teenager in Yemen," *New Yorker*, October 18, 2011; Conor Friedersdorf, "How Team Obama Justifies the Killing of a 16-Year-Old American," *Atlantic,* October 24, 2012.

17. Karen DeYoung and Peter Finn, "U.S. Acknowledges Killing of Four U.S. Citizens in Counterterrorism Operations," *Washington Post,* May 22, 2013, http://www.washingtonpost.com/world/national-security/us -acknowledges-killing-of-four-us-citizens-in-counterterrorism-operations /2013/05/22/7a21cf84-c31d-11e2-8c3b-0b5e9247e8ca_story.html.

18. Scahill, *Dirty Wars,* pp. 48–60, 270–284.

19. The National Security Act authorizes the CIA to conduct "covert action" whenever a presidential finding authorizes this. National Security Act of 1947, § 503, codified at 50 U.S.C. § 413b. "Covert action" has historically included paramilitary operations, but Congress stipulated that "traditional military activities" could *not* constitute "covert action." American government lawyers have nevertheless concluded that the CIA's decade-long drone war, heavily conducted on the Pakistan-Afghanistan frontier and closely coordinated with military operations on the frontier, does not constitute a "traditional military activity" and thus passes muster under the NSA. This conclusion renders the prohibition under the law meaningless.

20. Military commanders have viewed Afghanistan and immediately adjacent areas of Pakistan, particularly the Federally Administered Tribal Areas, as a single theater of combat, but they have been very cautious about saying so in public statements because of the legal consequences flowing from this label. See, for example, Jennifer C. Daskal, "The Geography of the Battlefield: A Framework for Detention and Targeting Outside the 'Hot' Conflict Zone," *University of Pennsylvania Law Review* 161 (2012): 1165; and Ryan Goodman and Thomas Earnest, "10 Years of Drone Strikes in Pakistan: But Do You Know Whether It's an 'Area of Active Hostilities'?" *Just Security,* June 18, 2014, http://justsecurity.org/11828/drone-strikes -pakistan-fata-area-active-hostilities/.

21. Bureau of Investigative Journalism, "Get the Data: Drone Wars," August 11, 2011, http://www.thebureauinvestigates.com/2011/08/10 /pakistan-drone-strikes-the-methodology2/.

22. David Alexander, "Retired General Cautions Against Overuse of 'Hated' Drones," Reuters, January 7, 2013, http://www.reuters.com/article /2013/01/07/us-usa-afghanistan-mcchrystal-idUSBRE906080201301o7.

23. Akbar Ahmed, *The Thistle and the Drone: How America's War on Terror Became a Global War on Tribal Islam* (2013), pp. 332–333.

24. James Walsh, "The Effectiveness of Drone Strikes in Counter-insurgency and Counterterrorism Campaigns," U.S. Army War College Strategic Studies Institute, September 2013, http://www.strategicstudies institute.army.mil/pubs/display.cfm?pubID=1167.

25. A good roundup of the conflicting accounts of the strike is furnished by Christine Hauser, "The Aftermath of Drone Strikes on a Wedding Convoy in Yemen," *New York Times,* December 19, 2013.

26. "Bush Names Pakistan 'Major Ally,'" BBC News, June 17, 2004, http://news.bbc.co.uk/2/hi/south_asia/3814013.stm.

27. United Nations Human Rights Council, *Report of the Special Rapporteur on Extrajudicial Summary or Arbitrary Executions,* May 28, 2010, http://www2.ohchr.org/english/bodies/hrcouncil/docs/14session /A.HRC.14.24.Add6.pdf.

28. Greg Miller, "Former Intelligence Chief Dennis Blair: U.S. Should Suspend Unilateral Drone Strikes in Pakistan," *Washington Post,* July 29, 2011; Josh Gerstein, "Ex-DNI Dennis Blair: Get CIA Out of Long-Term Drone Campaigns," *Politico,* November 30, 2011; Scott Horton, "Blair Addresses the CIA, Drones, and Pakistan," *Harper's,* December 1, 2011.

29. Ahmed Rashid, *Pakistan on the Brink: The Future of America, Pakistan, and Afghanistan* (2012); and Akbar Ahmed, *The Thistle and the Drone,* p.275.

30. Pew Research Global Attitudes Project, "Pakistani Public Opinion Ever More Critical of U.S.: 74% Call America an Enemy," January 27, 2012, http://www.pewglobal.org/2012/06/27/pakistani-public-opinion-ever -more-critical-of-u-s/. The Pew poll showed net public support for America's drone war in only two nations: the United States, where people knew relatively little about it, and India, where schadenfreude over the damage to Pakistan was plainly a determinative factor.

31. Remarks by the President at the National Defense University, May 23, 2013, http://www.whitehouse.gov/the-press-office/2013/05/23 /remarks-president-national-defense-university.

32. See Walsh, "The Effectiveness of Drone Strikes in Counterinsurgency and Counterterrorism Campaigns." Walsh argues that drone strikes "in Pakistan are associated with increases in subsequent insurgent violence in the country."

33. Far from zealously guarding its oversight role with respect to drones, Congress satisfied itself with occasional polite inquiries, abdicating responsibility for meaningful oversight and accountability. A key demonstration

came with respect to proposed legislation that would have required the director of national intelligence to publicly disclose more information about drone strikes, including data about resulting loss of life and casualties. At the request of the Obama administration, senators removed the reporting requirement from proposed legislation before bringing it to a vote. Spencer Ackerman, "U.S. Senators Remove Requirement for Disclosure over Drone Strike Victims," *Guardian,* April 28, 2014.

CHAPTER 6: THE WAR ON WHISTLEBLOWERS

1. This maxim has been a newsroom staple for most of the last century, attributed variously to the British press baron Lord Northcliffe, William Randolph Hearst, and Katherine Graham.

2. In November 2010 Secretary of Defense Robert Gates described government claims that the leaks of cables would put American lives at risk as "overwrought." Elisabeth Bumiller, "Gates on Leaks, Wiki and Otherwise," *New York Times,* November 30, 2010.

3. These materials are powerfully summarized and reviewed by Glenn Greenwald in his book *No Place to Hide: Edward Snowden, the NSA, and the U.S. Surveillance State* (2014), pp. 148–268.

4. *Federalist* 51 (James Madison): each branch "should have a will of its own;" each must possess "the necessary constitutional means and personal motives to resist encroachments of the others."

5. A strong example comes with the discovery of detailed information about a Bush-era NSA surveillance program, often referred to as "the president's program," which included information trawling that affected tens of millions of Americans. James Risen and Eric Lichtblau secured this information from a senior government source and prepared a detailed story on it in fall 2004, well before the presidential elections. Apparently fearing retaliation from the Bush administration, the *New York Times* declined to publish the story until it was slated to appear in Risen's book *State of War.* This is a case of the paper erring in favor of secrecy on a matter that, particularly after the Snowden leaks, spawned not only considerable public debate but also a decisive shift in public opinion against the NSA. A second example also relates to the *Times.* Before the CIA's Bay of Pigs operation, the *Times* gained information about the plans but held them secret, considering national security concerns. President Kennedy subsequently told *Times* editor Turner

Catledge, "If you had printed more about the operation, you would have saved us from a colossal mistake." "The Nation and the New York Times: Bay of Pigs Déjà Vu," *The Nation,* July 6, 2006.

6. See, for example, Gerard Sinzdak, "An Analysis of Current Whistleblower Laws: Defending a More Flexible Approach to Reporting Requirements," *California Law Review* 96 (2008): 1633, 1638–1640.

7. Obama-Biden 2008 Campaign, "The Changes We Need in Washington," http://obama.3cdn.net/oo8occ578614b42284_2aomvyxpz.pdf.

8. Erwin Griswold, "Secrets Not Worth Keeping: The Courts and Classified Information," *Washington Post,* February 15, 1989.

9. Anthony Lewis, "Abroad at Home: The Pardons in Perspective," *New York Times,* March 3, 2001.

10. Official Secrets Act (1989).

11. "Letting Go of the AIPAC Case," *Los Angeles Times,* May 7, 2009.

12. Michael Isikoff, "'Double Standard' in White House Leak Inquiries?" MSNBC, October 18, 2010, http://www.nbcnews.com/id/39693850/ns/us _news-security/#.U7ynVhYvogY; Josh Gerstein, "Alleged State Department Leaker Fights Charges," *Politico,* February 3, 2011.

13. Anne E. Marimow, "A Rare Peek into a Justice Department Leak Probe," *Washington Post,* May 19, 2013.

14. Anne E. Marimow, "Ex–State Department Adviser Stephen J. Kim Sentenced to 13 Months in Leak Case," *Washington Post,* April 2, 2014.

15. James Risen, "George Bush insists that Iran must not be allowed to develop nuclear weapons. So why, six years ago, did the CIA give the Iranians blueprints to build a bomb?," *Guardian,* January 5, 2006, reproduc- ing passages of Risen's book *State of War: The Secret History of the CIA and the Bush Administration* (2006).

16. Emily Bazelon, "Will Eric Holder Back Off?," Slate, June 2, 2014, http://www.slate.com/articles/news_and_politics/jurisprudence/2014/06 /supreme_court_turns_down_james_risen_s_appeal_now_it_s_up_to_eric _holder.html; Charlie Savage, "Holder Hints Reporter May Be Spared Jail in Leak," *New York Times,* May 27, 2014, reporting that Attorney General Eric Holder "hinted" that prosecutors may not seek to jail Risen if he refuses to give evidence in the Sterling trial.

17. Siobhan Gorman, "Little-Known Contractor Has Close Ties with Staff of NSA," *Baltimore Sun,* January 29, 2006; Gorman, "NSA Killed System That Sifted Phone Data Legally," *Baltimore Sun,* May 18, 2006.

18. 18 U.S.C. § 1030; Josh Gerstein, "Ex–NSA Official Thomas Drake Takes Plea Deal," *Politico*, June 9, 2011.

19. *United States v. Drake*, United States District Court for the District of Maryland, transcript, July 15, 2011, pp. 12–22, 40–43.

20. Debra J. Saunders, "Edward Snowden: Moscow's Accidental Tourist," *San Francisco Chronicle*, May 31, 2014, quoting Feinstein's comments to the *Chronicle*'s editorial board.

21. The numerous statements made by American political figures prejudging Snowden and accusing him of treason and other conspicuously political crimes, demanding the death penalty, and suggesting that it might be appropriate to kidnap him, coupled with the Obama administration's bizarre and illegal conduct in pressuring allies to ground the plane of Bolivian president Eva Morales, all furnish useful ammunition that Snowden could use to secure political asylum in any rule-of-law state. The grant of asylum usually involves a discretionary element, however, and the fact that many nations denied Snowden's asylum request can best be explained by their unwillingness to offend the world's sole superpower, the United States.

22. Jane Mayer, "The Secret Sharer: Is Thomas Drake an Enemy of the State?," *New Yorker*, May 23, 2011.

23. In what may be the most significant piece of scholarship on the subject since Shils and Moynihan, David Pozen offers a comprehensive and very convincing dissection of the official narrative and includes alternative justifications. Pozen, "The Leaky Leviathan," *Harvard Law Review* 127 (2013): 512.

24. Elias Canetti, in *Masse und Macht* [Crowds and Power] (1960), views the process of holding and disseminating secrets as the very essence of modern political power. He observes that by entrusting a secret to a confidant and enforcing duties with respect to it, the person imparting the secret gains power and leverage over the recipient. The more widespread this process is, and the more tightly guarded the secrets, the more inherently authoritarian the state. But the use of secrecy as a relationship lever accurately reflects both the way a bureaucracy deals with persons with security clearances and the way some leakers attempt to deal with the media. *Masse und Macht*, p. 146.

25. Jimmy Orr, "Ooops! Congressman Leaks Secret Iraq Trip on Twitter," *Christian Science Monitor*, February 8, 2009; Nate Reens, "Pete Hoekstra: Intelligence Leak Watchdog or Serial Secret Sharer?" MLive.com,

June 26, 2012, http://www.mlive.com/news/grand-rapids/index.ssf/2012/06/pete_hoekstra_intelligence_lea.html.

26. Michael D. Shear, "White House Orders Review After Spy's Name Is Revealed," *New York Times,* May 27, 2014.

27. Pozen, "The Leaky Leviathan."

28. Statement of National Security Adviser Gen. James Jones on WikiLeaks, July 25, 2010, http://www.whitehouse.gov/the-press-office/statement-national-security-advisor-general-james-jones-wikileaks.

29. Jake Tapper and Kirit Radia, "Comments on Prisoner Treatment Cause State Department Spokesman to Lose His Job," ABC News, March 13, 2011, http://abcnews.go.com/blogs/politics/2011/03/state-department-spokesman-pj-crowley-resigned-bradley-manning/; Bruce Ackerman and Yochai Benkler, "Private Manning's Humiliation," *New York Review of Books,* April 28, 2011.

30. Ed Pilkington, "Bradley Manning's Treatment Was Cruel and Inhuman, UN Torture Chief Rules," *Guardian*, March 12, 2012.

31. Scott Horton, "Inhumanity at Quantico," *Harper's*, March 7, 2011, reporting on Johnson's remarks about Manning's detention at a meeting of the Association of the Bar of the City of New York.

32. "Quantico Brig Gets New Commander," *St. Louis Post-Dispatch,* January 28, 2011.

33. Ed Pilkington, "Bradley Manning's Jail Conditions Improve Dramatically After Protest Campaign," *Guardian*, May 4, 2011.

34. On the other hand, Manning's Internet communications with Adrian Lamo provide a rationale linked to broad concerns of criminality or wrongdoing, as was developed in the evidence submitted by the defense in Manning's court-martial. Ed Pilkington, "Adrian Lamo Tells Manning Trial About Six Days of Chats with Accused Leaker," *Guardian*, June 4, 2013.

35. US Department of Defense, Army Counterintelligence Center, "Wikileaks.org—An Online Reference to Foreign Intelligence Services, Insurgents, or Terrorist Groups?" March 18, 2008, http://file.wikileaks.org/file/us-intel-wikileaks.pdf.

36. Mayer, *The Dark Side*, pp. 289–294.

37. No doubt because of the high risk of a federal judge striking down the program, extreme efforts were taken to insure that no one who could challenge it would know about it and that no case would ever come before a court. Nevertheless, one federal judge has already pronounced the program unconstitutional under Fourth Amendment

analysis, *Klagman v. Obama*, 457 F. Supp.2d 1 (D.D.C. 2013). A review board appointed by President Obama also concluded that the program was "likely unconstitutional." Privacy and Civil Liberties Oversight Board, Report on Telephone Records Program Conducted under Section 215 of the USA PATRIOT Act and on the Operations of the Foreign Intelligence Surveillance Court, January 23, 2013, http:// www.pclob.gov/ meetings-and-events/2014meetingsevents/23-january-2014-public-meeting.

38. Dana Priest and William M. Arkin, "Top Secret America: A Hidden World, Growing Beyond Control," *Washington Post,* September 10, 2010, http://projects.washingtonpost.com/top-secret-america/articles/a-hidden -world-growing-beyond-control/.

39. Thucydides, *History of the Peloponnesian War* 6.72.

40. Benjamin Franklin, *Poor Richard's Almanack* (1732) ¶ 559. It perhaps bears noting that Franklin published the work pseudonymously, using the name Richard Saunders.

41. Laura Smart and Daniel M. Wegner, "The Hidden Costs of Hidden Stigma," in *The Social Psychology of Stigma* (2003). Smart and Wegner collect psychological literature on the human inability to maintain secrets and the psychological costs of doing so over time.

42. Pozen, "The Leaky Leviathan," 582: "more vigorous enforcement of the laws against leaking would lead to a greater amount of unlawful disclosures, or at least a greater amount of destructive disclosures."

43. The simple solution is for the Justice Department to revert to its historical and prudent approach, which Judge Tyler described. An alternative would be to introduce a public accountability defense such as that recently proposed by Yochai Benkler, "A Public Accountability Defense for National Security Leakers and Whistleblowers," *Harvard Law & Policy Review* 8 (2014): 231.

CHAPTER 7: THE PATH TO QUASI-WAR: LIBYA AND SYRIA

1. Thucydides, *History of the Peloponnesian War* 2.39–41.

2. James Madison, *Debates in the Federal Convention of 1787,* proceedings of Friday, August 17.

3. "In time of actual war, great discretionary powers are constantly given to the Executive Magistrate. Constant apprehension of War, has the same tendency to render the head too large for the body. A standing

military force, with an overgrown Executive will not long be safe com-
panions to liberty. The means of defence against foreign danger have
been always the instruments of tyranny at home. Among the Romans
it was a standing maxim to excite a war, whenever a revolt was appre-
hended. Throughout all Europe, the armies kept up under the pretext of
defending, have enslaved the people." James Madison, speech before the
Constitutional Convention, June 29, 1787. Max Farrand, *Records of the
Federal Convention of 1787* (1911), 1:465.

4. "The constitution supposes, what the History of all Governments
demonstrates, that the Executive is the branch of power most interested
in war, & most prone to it. It has accordingly with studied care, vested the
question of war in the Legislature. But the Doctrines lately advanced strike
at the root of all these provisions, and will deposit the peace of the Country
in that Department which the Constitution distrusts as most ready without cause to renounce it. For if the opinion of the President not the facts
& proofs themselves are to sway the judgment of Congress, in declaring
war, and if the President in the recess of Congress create a foreign mission,
appoint the minister, & negociate a War Treaty, without the possibility of a
check even from the Senate, untill the measures present alternatives over-
ruling the freedom of its judgment; if again a Treaty when made obliges the
Legislature to declare war contrary to its judgment, and in pursuance of
the same doctrine, a law declaring war, imposes a like moral obligation, to
grant the requisite supplies until it be formally repealed with the consent of
the President & Senate, it is evident that the people are cheated out of the
best ingredients in their Government, the safeguards of peace which is the
greatest of their blessings." James Madison, letter to Thomas Jefferson, April
2, 1798, in *The Writings of James Madison* (1906), 6:312–314.

5. Charlie Savage, "Barack Obama's Q&A," *Boston Globe*, December 20,
2007.

6. Elliott Abrams, "Egypt Protests Show George W. Bush Was Right
About Freedom in the Arab World," *Washington Post*, January 29, 2011;
Peter Wehner, "Vindication for Bush's Freedom Agenda," *Commentary*,
January 28, 2011.

7. Shadi Mokhtari, "George Bush and the Turn to Human Rights in the
Arab World," Open Democracy, February 25, 2011, http://www.open
democracy.net/shadi-mokhtari/george-bush-and-turn-to-human-rights-in
-arab-world.

8. Notwithstanding a recommendation by the 9/11 Commission that information concerning the overall magnitude of the national intelligence budget be made public, the intelligence community's obsession with secrecy has stretched into the budgetary arena. Nevertheless, in fiscal year 2010, the National Intelligence Program budget was $53.1 billion, while the Military Intelligence Program was $27 billion, for a total in excess of $80 billion. Ken Dilanian, "Overall U.S. Intelligence Budget Tops $80 Billion," *Los Angeles Times*, October 28, 2010.

9. The nonaligned movement was launched in 1961 as a project largely led by Indian prime minister Jawaharlal Nehru. It sought to unite developing world states in opposition to the cold war. It counts 120 members, including every African state other than South Sudan, http://www.nam.gov.za.

10. Joan Rohlfing, "Libya: Nuclear Programme Overview," Nuclear Threat Initiative, February 2013, http://www.nti.org/country-profiles/libya/nuclear/.

11. Scott MacLeod, "Behind Gaddafi's Diplomatic Turnaround," *Time*, May 18, 2006.

12. The concept of "responsibility to protect" was defined by the United Nations in a statement issued in 2005 (Outcome Document of the 2005 United Nations World Summit [A/RES/60/1, 138–140]) and was restated by the secretary-general as follows:

(1) The State carries the primary responsibility for protecting populations from genocide, war crimes, crimes against humanity and ethnic cleansing, and their incitement;

(2) The international community has a responsibility to encourage and assist States in fulfilling this responsibility; and

(3) The international community has a responsibility to use appropriate diplomatic, humanitarian and other means to protect populations from these crimes. If a State is manifestly failing to protect its populations, the international community must be prepared to take collective action to protect populations, in accordance with the Charter of the United Nations.

See *Secretary-General's 2009 Report (A/63/677) on Implementing the Responsibility to Protect*, http://www.un.org/en/preventgenocide/adviser/responsibility.shtml.

13. United Nations Security Council Resolution 1973 (March 17, 2011) authorized the creation of a no-fly zone in Libya and the use of all necessary means (short of military occupation) to protect civilian lives.

14. U.S. Department of Justice, Office of Legal Counsel, Authority to Use Force in Libya, April 1, 2011, http://www.justice.gov/olc/opiniondocs /authority-military-use-in-libya.pdf.

15. David E. Sanger and Tom Shanker, "Gates Warns of Risks of a No-Flight Zone," *New York Times,* March 2, 2011; David Lerman, "No-Fly Zone over Libya Urged by McCain, Kerry as Gates, Mullen Have Doubts," Bloomberg News, March 7, 2011, http://www.bloomberg.com/news /2011-03-06/no-fly-zone-over-libya-urged-as-mccain-kerry-downplay -risks.html.

16. Austria, Prussia, and Russia sent troops onto the territory of the Polish-Lithuanian Commonwealth three times in the late eighteenth century (in 1772, 1793, and 1795), each time carving off specific provinces; with the last partition, Poland's king was forced to abdicate and the country disappeared from the map. Contemporaneous English-language reporting referred to these events as "war." These developments, which were widely criticized as cynical and illegitimate by Enlightenment writers, helped drive the intellectual dialogue about "universal peace" during this time, including contributions by James Madison (*Universal Peace,* 1792), Immanuel Kant (*Zum ewigen Frieden,* 1795), and Jeremy Bentham (*Plan for a Universal and Perpetual Peace,* 1789).

17. The House of Commons deliberated and approved action on March 21, 2011. The full Hansard record of the debates and vote can be found at http://www.parliament.uk/business/news/2011/march/debate-on-military -action-in-libya/.

18. The Assemblée nationale conducted initial debates on March 22, 2011, http://www.assemblee-nationale.fr/13/cri/2010-2011/20110144.asp, and concluded their debate with a vote authorizing prolongation of a military mission in Libya on July 12, 2011, http://www.assemblee-nationale .fr/13/cri/2010-2011-extra/20111012.asp.

19. U.S. Congress, House of Representatives, 112th Cong., 1st sess., H.R. Res. 292 (adopted June 3, 2011), https://beta.congress.gov/bill/112th -congress/house-resolution/292.

20. U.S. Department of State/U.S. Department of Defense, United States Activities in Libya, June 15, 2011, http://s3.documentcloud.org/documents /204673/united-states-activities-in-libya-6-15-11.pdf.

21. Charlie Savage and Mark Landler, "White House Defends Continuing U.S. Role in Libya Operation," *New York Times,* June 15, 2011.

22. Charlie Savage, "Two Top Lawyers Lost to Obama in Libya War Policy Debate," *New York Times,* June 17, 2011.

23. James Rowley, "Senators Question Obama Assertion Libya Mission Not Hostilities," Bloomberg News, June 28, 2011, http://www.bloomberg .com/news/2011-06-28/senators-question-obama-assertion-libya-mission -not-hostilities.html; Paul Starobin, "A Moral Flip-Flop? Defining a War," *New York Times,* August 6, 2011.

24. Mark Hosenball, "Obama Secret Syria Order Authorized Support for Rebels," Reuters, August 2, 2012.

25. C. J. Chivers and Eric Schmitt, "Arms Airlift to Syria Rebels Expands, with Aid from C.I.A.," *New York Times,* March 24, 2013.

26. Jackie Calmes, Michael R. Gordon, and Eric Schmitt, "President Gains McCain's Backing on Syria Attack," *New York Times*, September 2, 2013.

27. Ann Gearan and Karen DeYoung, "Obama's 'Red Line' Warning to Syria on Chemical Arms Draws Criticism," *Washington Post,* August 21, 2012.

28. Peter Finn and Ann Gearan, "Obama Warns Syria amid Rising Concern over Chemical Weapons," *Washington Post,* December 3, 2012.

29. Colum Lynch and Karen DeYoung, "Britain, France Claim Syria Used Chemical Weapons," *Washington Post,* April 18, 2013; Ann Gearan and William Booth, "U.S. Still Evaluating Claims That Syrian Government Used Chemical Weapons," *Washington Post,* April 23, 2013.

30. In a letter to Sen. Carl Levin, chair of the Senate Armed Services Committee, on April 25, 2013, White House director of legislative affairs Miguel E. Rodriguez stated that "our intelligence community does assess with varying degrees of confidence that the Syrian regime has used chemical weapons on a small scale in Syria, specifically the chemical agent sarin." But it noted, "our standard of evidence must build on these intelligence assessments, as we seek to establish credible and corroborated facts." The letter was published by the *Washington Post,* http://apps.washingtonpost.com /g/page/national/white-house-letter-to-sen-carl-levin-on-allegations-of -syrias-use-of-chemical-weapons/118/?hpid=z1.

31. "White House: Syria Chemical Weapons Kill up to 150," Associated Press, June 13, 2013.

32. In two articles published in the *London Review of Books,* Seymour Hersh mustered the evidence, drawing heavily on an unidentified American military intelligence source, for the proposition that Syrian rebel groups had staged the use of sarin in an effort to draw the United States more deeply into the conflict on their side. Hersh's perspective has not gained a wide following within the US foreign policy community. But his writing has very persuasively demonstrated the depth to which the Syrian war has been a covert war involving many different intelligence services, imperfectly aligned interests, and a great deal of duplicity and intrigue, almost all of which had passed under the radar of major western media. Seymour M. Hersh, "Whose Sarin?" *London Review of Books,* December 19, 2013; Hersh, "The Red Line and the Rat Line," *London Review of Books,* April 17, 2014.

33. Michael R. Gordon, "U.S. and Russia Reach Deal to Destroy Syria's Chemical Arms," *New York Times,* September 14, 2013.

34. "Tony Blair: Iraq War Made UK 'Hesitant' over Syria Intervention," BBC News, September 6, 2013, http://www.bbc.com/news/uk-23983036, quoting remarks of Prime Minister Cameron.

35. Anthony Faiola, "British Prime Minister David Cameron Loses Parliamentary Vote on Syrian Military Strike," *Washington Post,* August 29, 2013.

36. "Syrie: Un vote du Parlement, pas 'tabou' pour Hollande, dit Vidalies," *Le Point,* September 3, 2013, http://www.lepoint.fr/societe /syrie-un-vote-du-parlement-pas-tabou-pour-hollande-dit-vidalies-03 -09-2013-1720498_23.php.

37. Slate's John Dickerson noted that after Obama called for a vote, eighteen separate lines of argument were advanced, for the most part by Republican critics of Obama, against authorizing bombing Syria over the use of sarin gas. John Dickerson, "Hawks, Doves, and Fence-Sitters," Slate, September 3, 2013, http://www.slate.com/articles/news_and_politics/politics /2013/09/obama_congress_and_syria_arguments_for_and_against_the _bombing_resolution.html.

38. Camus, *Chroniques algériennes,* in *Essais* (1965), p. 898.

CHAPTER 8: DROWNING IN SECRETS

1. The thesis is now downloadable as an ebook (with all redactions), http://netlibrary.ws/Results.aspx?PageIndex=10041&SearchAcademic Collection=Agriculture%5EAgriculture%5ENaval%20Science%5E

Literature%5ECriminology%5EChemistry%5ETime%20Series%5E
Social%20Sciences&LanguageDropDownValue=eng&DisplayMode=List.

2. Elizabeth Goitein and David M. Shapiro, *Reducing Overclassification Through Accountability* (2011), p. 5.

3. Department of Homeland Security Office of Inspector General, *The Removal of a Canadian Citizen to Syria*, March 2008, http://www.oig.dhs .gov/assets/Mgmt/OIGr_08–18_Jun08.pdf.

4. Commission of Inquiry into the Actions of Canadian Officials in Relation to Maher Arar, *Report on the Events Relating to Maher Arar: Analysis and Recommendations* (2006), http://www.pch.gc.ca/cs-kc/arar /Arar_e.pdf.

5. Scott Horton, "More on Maher Arar," *Harper's*, June 5, 2008; Horton, "The Missing IG Report on Maher Arar," *Harper's*, November 16, 2007.

6. The redacted document can be viewed at http://www2.gwu.edu/~ns archiv/nukevault/ebb457/.

7. For instance, mandatory declassification review conducted in 2010 established that 92 percent of reviewed documents did not need to be classified. US National Archives and Records Administration, Information Security Oversight Office, *2010 Report to the President* 20 (2011), http:// www.archives.gov/isoo/reports/2010-annual-report.pdf.

8. Steve Watkins, "Price Tag for Security Classifications Jumps to $11.6B," *Federal Times*, July 7, 2014.

9. Robert Norton Smith, *The Colonel: The Life and Legend of Robert R. McCormick* (1997), p. 417.

10. Sen. Moynihan had a different take on the *Tribune* incident from the summer of 1942. He concludes that the leaks were more likely information planted by the Roosevelt administration to serve other strategic purposes, and that this explains Roosevelt's unwillingness to entertain an Espionage Act prosecution. Moynihan, *Secrecy*, pp. 133–134.

11. The Intelligence Identities Protection Act of 1982, codified at 50 U.S.C. §§ 421–426. The act was put in place following the murder of CIA Athens station chief Richard Welch in 1975, after his identity had been revealed in *CounterSpy* magazine. Greek newspapers had published the information after calling *CounterSpy* to confirm.

12. US Department of Justice Office of the Inspector General, *A Review of the FBI's Performance in Uncovering the Espionage Activities of Aldrich Hazen Ames*, April 21, 1997.

13. Peter Finn, "Lawyers Showed Photos of Covert CIA Officers to Guantánamo Bay Detainees," *Washington Post*, August 21, 2009; Scott Horton, "CIA Attacks the John Adams Project," *Harper's*, March 25, 2010.

14. Steve Coll, "The Spy Who Said Too Much: Why the Administration Targeted a CIA Officer," *New Yorker*, April 1, 2013; Scott Horton, "The CIA's Torturer-Protection Program," *Harper's*, January 11, 2013.

15. The principal opinions in question are: (1) Memorandum for Alberto R. Gonzales re: Standards of Conduct for Interrogation under 18 U.S.C. §§ 2340–2340A, Aug. 1, 2002; (2) Memorandum for John Rizzo re: Interrogation of al Qaeda Operative, Aug. 1, 2002; (3) Memorandum for James B. Comey re: Legal Standards Applicable under 18 U.S.C. §§ 2340–2340A, Dec. 30, 2004; (4) Memorandum for John A. Rizzo re: Application of 18 U.S.C. §§ 2340–2340A to Certain Techniques That May Be Used in the Interrogation of a High-Value al Qaeda Detainee, May 10, 2005; (5) Memorandum for John A. Rizzo re: Application of 18 U.S.C. §§ 2340–2340A to the Combined Use of Certain Techniques in the Interrogation of High Value al Qaeda Detainees, May 10, 2005; (6) Memorandum for John A. Rizzo re: Application of United States Obligations Under Article 16 of the Convention Against Torture to Certain Techniques That May Be Used in the Interrogation of High Value al Qaeda Detainees, May 30, 2005. They have been collected and published with commentary in David Cole, ed., *The Torture Memos: Rationalizing the Unthinkable* (2009).

16. Jane Mayer, *Dark Side*, p. 65 (attributing this to former OLC assistant attorney general Jack Goldsmith).

17. Ewen McAskill, "Obama: 'I Believe Waterboarding Was Torture, and It Was a Mistake.'" *Guardian*, April 29, 2009.

18. Ewen McAskill, "Obama Releases Bush Torture Memos: Insects, Sleep Deprivation, and Waterboarding Among Approved Techniques by the Bush Administration," *Guardian*, April 16, 2009.

19. *New York Times Co. et al. v. U.S. Department of Justice et al.*, http://www.nytimes.com/interactive/2014/06/23/us/23awlaki-memo.html?_r=0.

20. The first report was James Gordon Meek, "Experts: Al Qaeda in Yemen May Send American Jihadis, Recruited by Anwar al-Awlaki, to Attack U.S.," *New York Daily News*, February 4, 2010.

21. House Committee on Government Reform, Subcommittee on National Security, Emerging Threats, and International Relations, "Drowning in a Sea of Faux Secrets: Policies on Handling of Classified and

Sensitive Information," March 14, 2006, http://fas.org/sgp/congress/2006
/faux.html.

22. Jonathan Abel, "Do You Have to Keep the Government's Secrets?
Retroactively Classified Documents, the First Amendment, and the Power
to Make Secrets out of the Public Record," *University of Pennsylvania Law
Review* 163 (2015): XXX, http://papers.ssrn.com/sol3/papers.cfm?abstract
_id=2399547. Abel identifies the case studies cited here.

23. James Bamford, "How I Got the N.S.A. Files . . . How Reagan Tried
to Get Them Back," *The Nation*, November 6, 1982; Bamford, *The Puzzle
Palace: A Report on America's Most Secret Agency* (1982). The book was
released in an expanded edition with a slightly changed title in 2001.

24. Letter of Representatives Henry Waxman and John Tierney to
Secretary of Defense Donald Rumsfeld, March 25, 2004, http://oversight
-archive.waxman.house.gov/documents/20040629071638-64384.pdf.

25. The document can be examined at http://www2.gwu.edu/~nsarchiv
/NSAEBB/NSAEBB179/Aid-7.pdf. The most sensitive portion of the memorandum is apparently the CIA's strategic conclusion that climate conditions
in Eastern Europe would not be conducive to the use of hot-air balloons.

26. The key source of rules for classification process is Executive Order
13526, issued by President Obama at the end of his first year in office, on
December 29, 2009, published in the *Code of Federal Regulations*, 75:707.

27. Ibid., § 1.2(a)(1)–(3).

28. Ibid., § 1.1(a)(4).

29. Ibid., § 1.1.

30. "If there is a significant doubt about the need to classify information,
it shall not be classified." Ibid., § 1.1(b).

31. As has often been the case, however, the government decision
to make documents public followed discoveries made by an academic,
Wellesley professor Susan M. Reverby, which in turn were highlighted in
the media. Stephen Smith, "Wellesley Professor Unearths a Horror: Syphilis
Experiments in Guatemala," *Boston Globe*, October 2, 2010. The Guatemala
program parallels a similar program run about the same time in Tuskegee,
Alabama, focusing on black sharecroppers.

32. Executive Order 12958, April 17, 1995, published in the *Code of
Federal Regulations*, 60:19, 285.

33. Kyl-Lott Amendment to the Strom Thurmond National Defense
Authorization Act of 1999, codified at 50 U.S.C. § 2672(b)(1) and 42 U.S.C.
§§ 2014(y) and 2163.

34. The closest Obama's executive order comes to this issue is non-operative language contained in the order's preamble: "Our democratic principles require that the American people be informed of the activities of their Government. Also, our Nation's progress depends on the free flow of information both within the Government and to the American people. Nevertheless, throughout our history, the national defense has required that certain information be maintained in confidence in order to protect our citizens, our democratic institutions, our homeland security, and our inter-actions with foreign nations. Protecting information critical to our Nation's security and demonstrating our commitment to open Government through accurate and accountable application of classification standards and routine, secure, and effective declassification are equally important priorities."

35. A recent example came in response to the June 2013 order from President Obama to "declassify and make public as much information as possible about certain sensitive U.S. Government surveillance programs while protecting sensitive classified intelligence and national security infor-mation." This order recognized the need for declassification to inform the intense policy debate that the WikiLeaks disclosures unleashed, a debate that captures the essence of democratic process. DNI Clapper then reviewed and released a large cache of documents the secrecy of which had up to that point been fiercely guarded. See Office of the Director of National Intelligence, DNI Clapper Declassifies and Releases Telephone Metadata Collection Documents, July 31, 2013, http://fas.org/irp/news/2013/07/dni-metadata .pdf; DNI Clapper Declassifies Additional Documents Regarding Collection Under Section 501 of the Foreign Intelligence Surveillance Act, January 13, 2014, accessible at http://icontherecord.tumblr.com/post/73652799309 /dni-clapper-declassifies-additional-documents; ODNI Releases Statistical Transparency Report Regarding Use of National Security Authorities, June 27, 2014, accessible at http://www.dni.gov/index.php/newsroom/reports -and-publications/204-reports-publications-2014/1084-odni-releases -statistical-transparency-report-regarding-use-of-national-security -authorities.

36. For instance, foreign service officer Peter Van Buren was threatened with sacking by the State Department for including a link to the WikiLeaks website in a blog post he wrote, creating the new crime of *linking* as opposed to *leaking*. Lisa Rein, "State Dept. Moves to Fire Peter Van Buren, Author of Book Critical of Iraq Reconstruction Effort," *Washington Post*, March 14, 2012.

37. Hubert Gude, Jörg Schindler, and Fidelius Schmid, "Merkel's Mobile: Germany Launches Investigation into NSA Spying," *Der Spiegel*, June 4, 2014, http://www.spiegel.de/international/germany/germany-expected-to -open-investigation-into-nsa-spying-on-merkel-a-973326.html; Hans Leyendecker and Georg Mascolo, "Folgenlose Massenausspähung der NSA," *Süddeutsche Zeitung*, June 4, 2014.

38. "The NSA's Secret Spy Hub in Berlin," *Der Spiegel*, October 27, 2013, http://www.spiegel.de/international/germany/cover-story-how-nsa -spied-on-merkel-cell-phone-from-berlin-embassy-a-930205.html; Mark Mazzetti and David E. Sanger, "Tap on Merkel Provides Peek at Vast Spy Net," *New York Times*, October 30, 2013.

39. The term "five eyes" (or "FVEY") refers to a series of secret signals intelligence–sharing agreements among Australia, Canada, New Zealand, the United Kingdom, and the United States. The pact reportedly offers protections against illegal surveillance intrusions to the citizens of the five states not available to the citizens of other nations, but documents released by Snowden reflected information-sharing arrangements that appeared to be aimed at dodging the civil liberties restrictions of individual states by having other intelligence services do the probing. Nicholas Watt, "NSA 'Offers Intelligence to British Counterparts to Skirt UK law,'" *Guardian*, June 10, 2013.

40. Mark Landler, "Merkel Signals That Tension Persists over U.S. Spying," *New York Times*, May 2, 2014.

41. "Kuriose Verbindung zwischen Spionagefällen," *Süddeutsche Zeitung*, July 11, 2014; "Mutmaßlicher Spion stand bereits 2010 unter Verdacht," *Süddeutsche Zeitung*, July 11, 2014; "Bundesregierung wirft obersten US-Geheimdienstler raus," *Süddeutsche Zeitung*, July 10, 2014; "BND-Mitarbeiter unter Spionage Verdacht," *Süddeutsche Zeitung*, July 4, 2014.

42. "Umfrage: NSA-Affäre verunsichert die Deutschen," Heise-Online, July 29, 2014; "Umfrage zu US-Spionage Deutsche lässt NSA-Affäre kalt," *Stern*, November 2, 2013; Philipp Wittrock, "Reaktion auf NSA-Affäre: Merkel schützt ihre Umfragedaten," *Der Spiegel*, July 14, 2013.

43. In the course of a Senate hearing, Sen. Ron Wyden asked Clapper to comment on remarks made by NSA director Gen. Keith Alexander, deriding as "absolute nonsense" claims that the NSA had "millions or hundreds of millions" of files on people. Wyden asked him to clarify this: "Does the NSA collect any type of data at all on millions or hundreds of millions of

Americans?" Clapper responded, "No sir." Wyden, obviously surprised by
the denial, followed up: "It does not?" and Clapper said, "Not wittingly.
There are cases where they could inadvertently, perhaps, collect, but not
wittingly." Video footage available at Andy Greenberg, "Watch Top U.S.
Intelligence Officials Repeatedly Deny NSA Spying on Americans over the
Last Year,"*Forbes*, June 6, 2013, http://www.forbes.com/sites/andygreenberg
/2013/06/06/watch-top-u-s-intelligence-officials-repeatedly-deny-nsa
-spying-on-americans-over-the-last-year-videos/. In an interview with
NDR journalist Hubert Seipel on January 27, 2014, Edward Snowden recalls
watching this public deception by Clapper and deciding to leak materials
that demonstrated the full scope of Clapper's deception. The interview can
be viewed at http://www.ardmediathek.de/tv/ARD-Sondersendung/Edward
-Snowden-interview-in-english/Das-Erste/Video?documentId=19295624
&bcastId=3304234.

44. Carlo Muñoz, "GOP's Amash: Clapper Should Resign," *The Hill*,
June 12, 2013.

45. Spencer Ackerman, "Rand Paul Accuses James Clapper of Lying to
Congress over NSA Surveillance," *Guardian*, June 18, 2013.

46. Secretary Shultz's remarks can be viewed at https://www.youtube
.com/watch?v=8NtH2pbmstQ.

47. But see Ryan Reilly, "Eric Holder: DOJ Reviewing Materials on
Whether James Clapper Lied to Congress," Huffington Post, April 8, 2014,
showing the Justice Department going through the motions following numerous congressional requests.

48. Eli Lake, "Spy Chief: We Should've Told You We Track Your Calls,"
Daily Beast, February 17, 2014.

49. Intelligence Community Directive 119, March 20, 2014, http://www
.dni.gov/files/documents/ICD/ICD%20119.pdf.

50. Ibid., C(2).

51. The editors of the *Washington Post*, perhaps the most reliable ally the
intelligence community has in the print media world, described the Clapper
directive: "Mr. Clapper wants the American people to know only what he or
other chiefs approve, when they approve it. Mr. Clapper's own performance
—his untruthful answer to a question in an open congressional hearing
about government surveillance programs—should give everyone pause about
his commitment to transparency." "The U.S. Intelligence Chief's Gag Order
Does Not Stir Trust," *Washington Post*, April 23, 2014.

52. Elizabeth Goitein and David M. Shapiro, *Reducing Overclassification Through Accountability* (2011), pp. 3, 33–49.

53. Flavius Josephus, *Antiquities of the Jews,* bk. 1, chap. 4 (c. 93). "Nimrod excited them to such an affront. . . . He also gradually changed the government into tyranny, seeing no other way of turning men from the fear of God, but to bring them into a constant dependence on his power."

EPILOGUE

1. Mark Landler, "Merkel Signals Tension Persists over U.S. Spying," *New York Times,* May 2, 2014.

2. Shane Harris, "The NSA's Cyber King Goes Corporate," *Foreign Policy,* July 29, 2014.

3. Ellen Nakashima and Joby Warrick, "For NSA Chief, Terrorist Threat Drives Passion to 'Collect It All'," *Washington Post,* July 14, 2013.

4. Jens Gieseke, *Der Mielke-Konzern: Die Geschichte der Stasi, 1945– 1990* (2006).

5. Ian Traynor and Paul Lewis, "Merkel Compared NSA to Stasi in Heated Encounter with Obama," *Guardian,* December 17, 2013.

6. Scott Horton, "Back in the GDR," *Harper's,* July 18, 2013.

7. See, for example, Mark Scott, "Irked by N.S.A., Germany Cancels Deal with Verizon," *New York Times,* June 26, 2014; and Alonso Soto and Brian Winter, "Saab Wins Brazil Jet Deal After NSA Spying Sours Boeing Bid," Reuters, December 18, 2013.

8. Daniel DeSilver, "Most Young Americans Say Snowden Has Served the Public Interest," Pew Research Center, January 24, 2014, http://www .pewresearch.org/fact-tank/2014/01/22/most-young-americans-say -snowden-has-served-the-public-interest/; 57 percent of eighteen- to twenty-nine-year-olds say that Snowden leaks *served* rather than *harmed* the public interest; Jonathan D. Salant, "Snowden Seen as Whistle-Blower by Majority in New Poll," Bloomberg News, July 10, 2013, http://www .bloomberg.com/news/2013-07-10/snowden-seen-as-whistleblower-by -majority-in-new-poll.html; "U.S. Voters Say Snowden Is Whistle-Blower, Not Traitor, Quinnipiac University National Poll Finds; Big Shift on Civil Liberties vs. Counter-Terrorism," Quinnipiac University, July 10, 2013, http://www.quinnipiac.edu/news-and-events/quinnipiac-university-poll /national/release-detail?ReleaseID=1919; Emily Swanson, "Americans Might Not Support Edward Snowden, but They Support Disclosing

Programs," *Huffington Post*, April 1, 2014, http://www.huffingtonpost
.com/2014/04/01/edward-snowden-support_n_5071938.html.

9. Michelle Richardson and Robyn Green, "NSA Legislation Since the
Leaks Began," ACLU Blog, August 15, 2013, http://www.aclu.org/blog
/national-security/nsa-legislation-leaks-began.

10. Ginger Gibson, "Justin Amash, John Conyers Introduce NSA Bill,"
Politico, June 18, 2013, http://www.politico.com/story/2013/06/justin
-amash-john-conyers-nsa-bill-92982.html.

11. The PRISM program, launched by the NSA in 2007 and joined by
the British intelligence unit GCHQ somewhat later, was pursued with the
apparent collaboration of Internet service providers such as Apple, AOL,
Facebook, Google, Microsoft, Skype, Yahoo, and YouTube. It allowed the
NSA unfiltered, direct, and free rein to collect all private communications
traveling through the collaborating service providers. Curiously, the ma-
jor Internet service providers involved issued denials, apparently assuming
that the government would back them in their public misdirection. Barton
Gellman and Laura Poitras, "U.S., British Intelligence Mining Data from
Nine U.S. Internet Companies in Broad Secret Program," *Washington Post*,
June 7, 2013; Glenn Greenwald and Ewen MacAskill, "NSA Prism Program
Taps in to User Data of Apple, Google and Others," *Guardian*, June 6, 2013.

12. Spencer Ackerman, "NSA Surveillance: Narrow Defeat for
Amendment to Restrict Data Collection," *Guardian*, July 24, 2013.

13. David Kravets, "Lawmakers Who Upheld NSA Phone Spying
Received Double the Defense Industry Cash," *Wired*, July 26, 2013.

14. David D. Eisenhower, Farewell Address, January 17, 1961, "Now this
conjunction of an immense military establishment and a large arms industry
is new in the American experience. The total influence—economic, political, even spiritual—is felt in every city, every Statehouse, every office of the
federal government. We recognize the imperative need for this development.
Yet, we must not fail to comprehend its grave implications. Our toil, resources, and livelihood are all involved. So is the very structure of our society. In the councils of government, we must guard against the acquisition of
unwarranted influence, whether sought or unsought, by the military-indus-
trial complex. The potential for the disastrous rise of misplaced power exists
and will persist. We must never let the weight of this combination endanger
our liberties or democratic processes. We should take nothing for granted.
Only an alert and knowledgeable citizenry can compel the proper meshing

of the huge industrial and military machinery of defense with our peaceful methods and goals, so that security and liberty may prosper together."

15. The sharply disproportionate influence of a one-percent oligarchic elite in the United States on the formation of economic policy is now a broadly accepted fact among economists. See, for instance, Simon Johnson, "The Quiet Coup," *Atlantic*, May 2009; Joseph E. Stiglitz, "Of the 1%, by the 1%, for the 1%," *Vanity Fair*, May 2011.

INDEX

Photo by David Barreda

Scott Horton is a contributing editor at *Harper's Magazine* and a recipient of the National Magazine Award for reporting for his writing on law and national security issues. Horton lectures at Columbia Law School and continues to practice law in the emerging markets area. A lifelong human rights advocate, Horton served as counsel to Andrei Sakharov and Elena Bonner, among other activists in the former Soviet Union.

The Nation Institute
Nation.

Founded in 2000, **Nation Books** has become a leading voice in American independent publishing. The inspiration for the imprint came from the *Nation* magazine, the oldest independent and continuously published weekly magazine of politics and culture in the United States.

The imprint's mission is to produce authoritative books that break new ground and shed light on current social and political issues. We publish established authors who are leaders in their area of expertise, and endeavor to cultivate a new generation of emerging and talented writers. With each of our books we aim to positively affect cultural and political discourse.

Nation Books is a project of The Nation Institute, a nonprofit media center established to extend the reach of democratic ideals and strengthen the independent press. The Nation Institute is home to a dynamic range of programs: our award-winning Investigative Fund, which supports groundbreaking investigative journalism; the widely read and syndicated website TomDispatch; our internship program in conjunction with the *Nation* magazine; and Journalism Fellowships that fund up to 20 high-profile reporters every year.

For more information on Nation Books, the *Nation* magazine, and The Nation Institute, please visit:

www.nationbooks.org
www.nationinstitute.org
www.thenation.com
www.facebook.com/nationbooks.ny
Twitter: @nationbooks